Contents

Introduction 5

Chapter 1 – Canva Overview and Pricing Plans 7

Creating an Account 7

Plans and Pricing 10

The Canva Interface 11

Chapter 2 – Preparing for Your First Project 15

Play with Canva Tutorial 15

The Projects Area 17

Creating Folders 19

Uploading Files From Your Computer 23

Uploading Files From a Cloud Storage Account 28

Chapter 3 – Creating & Editing Projects 31

Templates 31

Starting From a Blank Project 35

The Canva Toolbar 38

Adding and Editing Elements 46

Editing an Existing Design or Template 57

Creating Animated Designs 61

Creating a Presentation 67

Copying, Moving and Downloading Your Projects 72

Chapter 4 - Sharing and Social Media 78

Sharing 78

Social Media Templates 88

Connecting Social Media Accounts for Posting 91

Canva Whiteboard 100

Using Comments 104

Chapter 5 – Photo, Video and PDF Editors..109

Using the Photo Editor 109

Editing Videos...112

Editing PDF Files 121

Chapter 6 – Extra Features 125

Magic Design Templates...125

Canva Desktop App 130

Canva Assistant 132

Canva Print 136

Canva Apps..142

Photos 147

Icons 151

Mockups...154

Docs 157

Chapter 7 – Canva Settings and Getting Help................................162

Canva Settings 162

Insights..169

Education Resources 171

Help and Training 172

What's Next? 178

About the Author 181

CANVA
MADE EASY

Bringing Your Ideas to Life

By James Bernstein

Bernstein, James
Canva Made Easy
Part of the Digital Design Made Easy series

For more information on reproducing sections of this book or sales of this book,
go to **www.madeeasybookseries.com**

Introduction

With all the advances in technology over the past ten years or so, it is much easier for people to perform many tasks on their own that they previously needed to have others do for them. And of course, this meant spending money to have others do this work for you!

Thanks to modern computers, smartphones and tablets, we can now do things such as create our own websites, collaborate with others on shared documents, backup our files to the cloud, edit photos and videos, and attend meetings while in our pajamas at home!

One popular thing that many of us like to do is design our own graphics for things such as flyers, business cards, social media posts, websites, birthday cards and so on. There are many online tools you can use to accomplish this and of course you can also use software installed on your computer such as Photoshop, Illustrator, Publisher just to name a few.

But if you are the type who prefers an easy-to-use application that can handle all these design tasks in one place, then you need to check out Canva. This online app provides the tools you need to design just about anything for just about any occasion without needing to install expensive software on your computer. And since everything is done online, you can work on your creations from any device with an internet connection.

The Canva website is broken down into categories making it easy to find what you are looking for. Plus, the search feature does a great job of helping you when can't find what you are looking for. In fact, you might find yourself creating a project that you weren't expecting to create because you saw a suggestion on the Canva website and realized how easy and fun it would be to do so.

Once you start working with Canva, you will easily get the hang of how the online app works and how you can create projects and store them within the app and even share them with others. And since it is so easy to use, it actually makes the design process fun rather than feel like work.

The goal of this book is to get you up and running with Canva and show you how to navigate the interface, create different types of projects, edit photos and videos, collaborate with others, download your work and more. Since you can do so much with Canva, it will be impossible to show you everything without having a 1000 page book that costs $100 but once you learn how to create and edit projects, the skills you will learn will apply to all the other areas of the Canva website. I will be

Introduction

working with the free Canva account but will be pointing out many of the features that you can use with the Pro or Teams account. So on that note, let's get to designing!

Chapter 1 – Canva Overview and Pricing Plans

As you read in the introduction, Canva can be used for just about any design task you can think of. Plus, it can also be used to edit existing designs, photos and videos. The interface might be a little intimidating at first since there is a lot going on but once you play around a bit, you will find that everything is well organized and easy to find.

Creating an Account
Before you can start using Canva, you will need to create an account that you will use to log in with. This way, all your saved designs and other work will be kept within this account and if you log in to another device with this account, you will have all your work waiting for you.

When you first go to the Canva website at **https://www.canva.com/,** you will have the opportunity to log in with an existing account or you can click the *Sign up* button to create a new account.

When you click the Sign up button, you will have the option of connecting your Google or Facebook account to your new Canva account, or signing up using your email address.

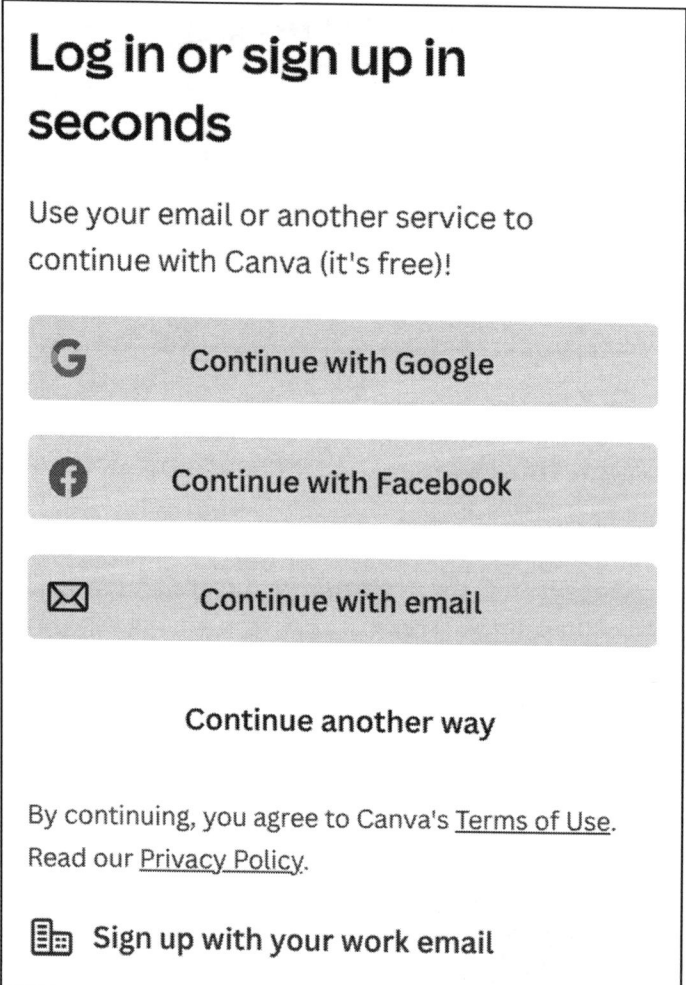

Figure 1.1

Many people are ok with connecting their Google or Facebook accounts and using that to sign in, but I prefer not to have too many online services "connected" to each other, so I prefer to sign up using my email address.

Once you enter your email address and name and then you will be emailed a verification code that you need to type into the next box within 10 minutes. Then after you enter the code, you might see a screen asking you what you will be using Canva for. This is used for recommendations when using the app so it's not critical that you choose a particular answer.

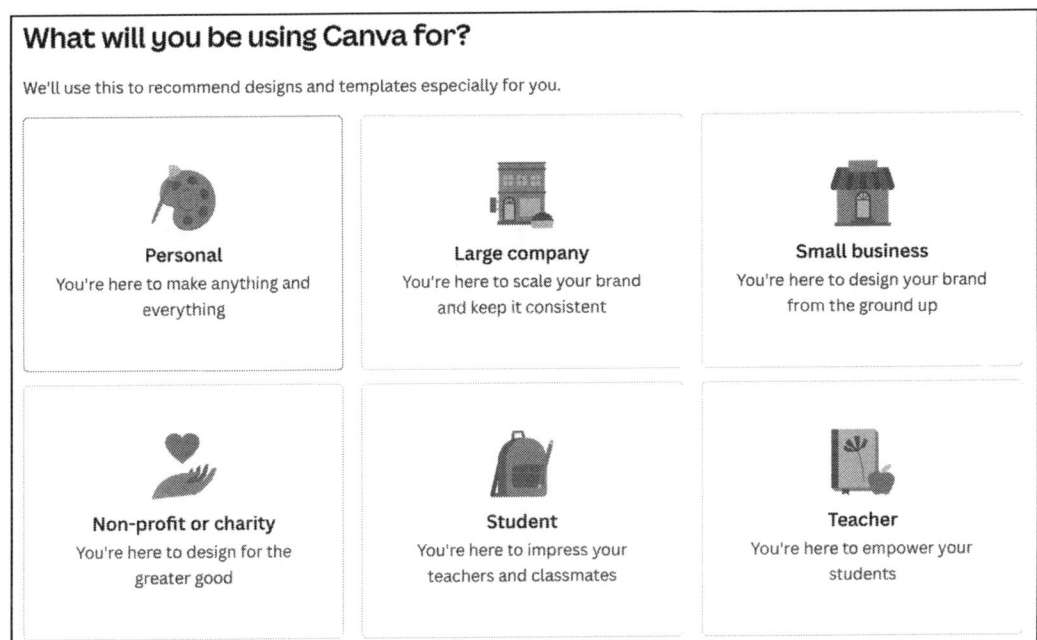

Figure 1.2

You might then get an offer to try Canva Pro for free for 30 days which you can do now or later after you get used to how Canva works. I recommend waiting so you will get a feel as to what parts of the app you need the professional version for, especially since you will have to give them your credit card number to do the trail.

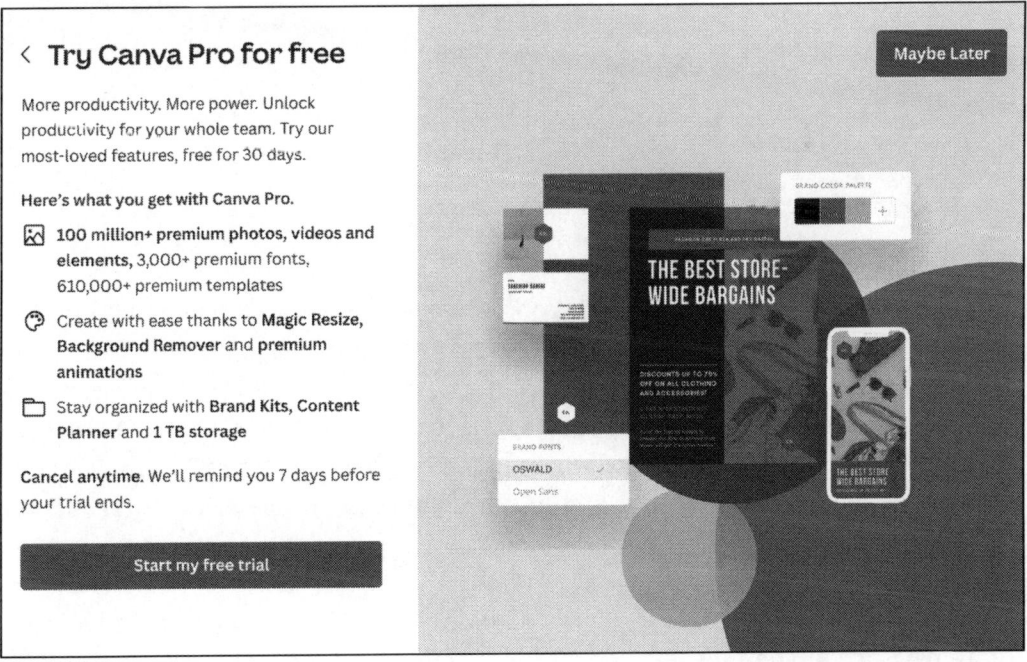

Figure 1.3

Plans and Pricing

If you go to the Canva website, you can see the available subscription plans and how much they will cost to use. You can also see a breakdown of what features are included in each plan.

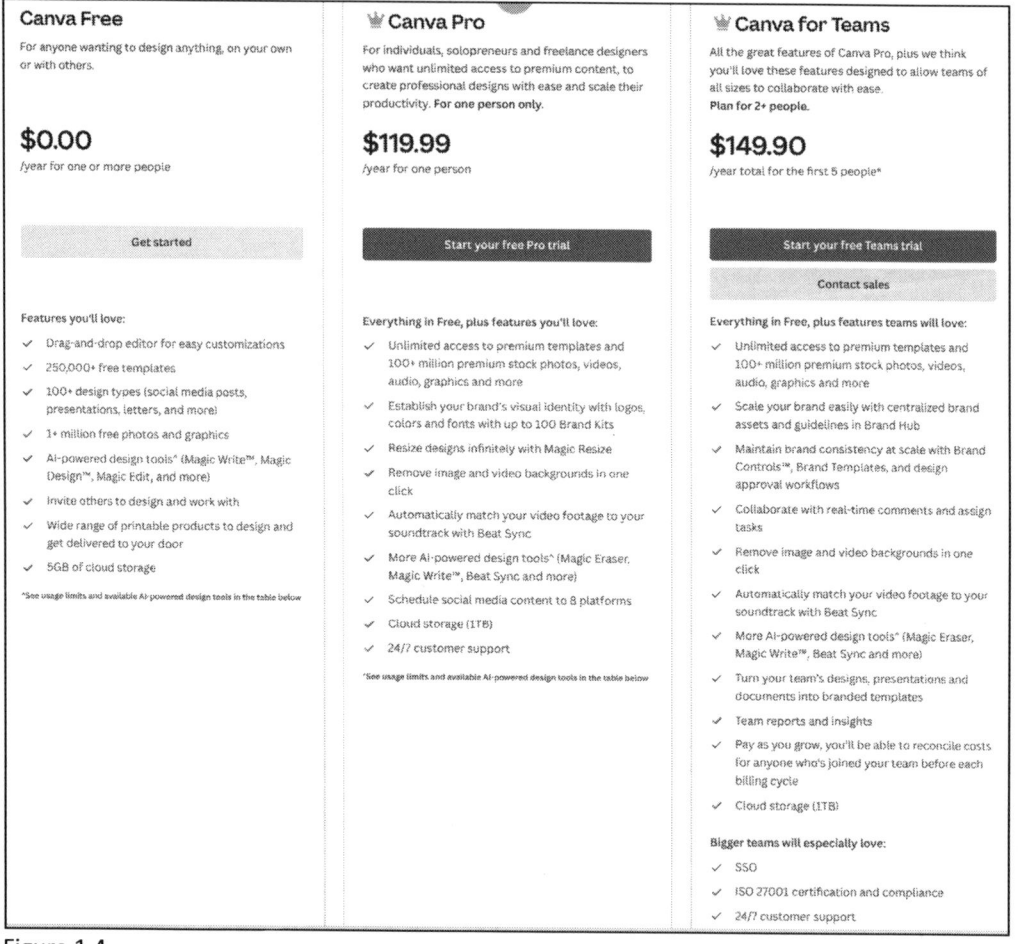

Figure 1.4

For most people, the Free plan will work just fine but if you find yourself needing some of the extra features and plan on using Canva on a regular basis, you might want to try the Pro plan. The main reason to use the Pro plan for many people is that you get access to all of the graphics, photos, templates etc. that you don't get with the Free plan and you might find yourself not being able to find what you are looking for because a lot of the higher end elements are only available with the Pro and Teams plan.

The Teams version is useful if you are collaborating with other people and need to do things such as share designs and folders and use workflows. It also features real-time collaboration and comments, so your team is always up to date when it comes to any changes that are made to your projects.

If you are a teacher or a student, you can request a free Canva account with many of the advanced features enabled. You will need to provide verification of your teacher or student status to take advantage of this type of account.

Teachers	Schools and Districts
100% free for primary and secondary teachers and their students. Create engaging, personalized lesson plans, projects, videos, and more. Help your students learn with ease and express themselves.	100% free for K-12 students and teachers. All-in-one creation and communication tool for your entire district, with enterprise-level deployment.
Get verified	Contact us
✓ 100+ million images, videos, animations, audio, and more	✓ 100+ million images, videos, animations, audio, and more
✓ Thousands of high-quality, educational templates for every subject, grade, and ability	✓ Thousands of high-quality, educational templates for every subject, grade, and ability
✓ Remove background images with Background Remover	✓ Remove background images with Background Remover
✓ Resize designs with Magic Resize	✓ Resize designs with Magic Resize
✓ 100GB cloud storage	✓ 100GB cloud storage
✓ Certified as FERPA, COPPA, and GDPR compliant by iKeepsafe, and has safe-for-school content	✓ Certified as FERPA, COPPA, and GDPR compliant by iKeepsafe, and has safe-for-school content
✓ LMS integrations - Canvas, Schoology, D2L, Google Classroom, and more	✓ LMS integrations - Canvas, Schoology, D2L, Google Classroom, and more
✓ Invite students and other teachers to a class space via code, email invite, or Google Classroom	✓ Deploy Canva for Education across the entire district and connect via SSO
✓ Send assignments for students to complete in Canva or via LMS	✓ Manage accounts and access options in one place
	✓ Provision and manage all teacher, student and staff accounts via Roster Sync
	✓ Upload school or district logos, colors, and fonts, for consistent communication
	✓ Free PD resources and trainings for teachers and staff
Canva for Education isn't available yet for colleges or universities. See our other plans.	✓ Ongoing support from the Canva team

Figure 1.5

The Canva Interface
The first time you log into your Canva account, you might be a bit overwhelmed with all the menus and options you have to choose from. This is completely

understandable because there is a lot going on within the Canva interface. But once you figure out how everything is organized, you will realize that it's very easy to find what you are looking for. That doesn't mean there still isn't a lot going on!

The Canva website is broken down into four main areas. At the left side of the screen, you will have your navigation section where you can view your projects, templates, brand info and apps. At the very top, you will see some of the main categories that contain several subcategories.

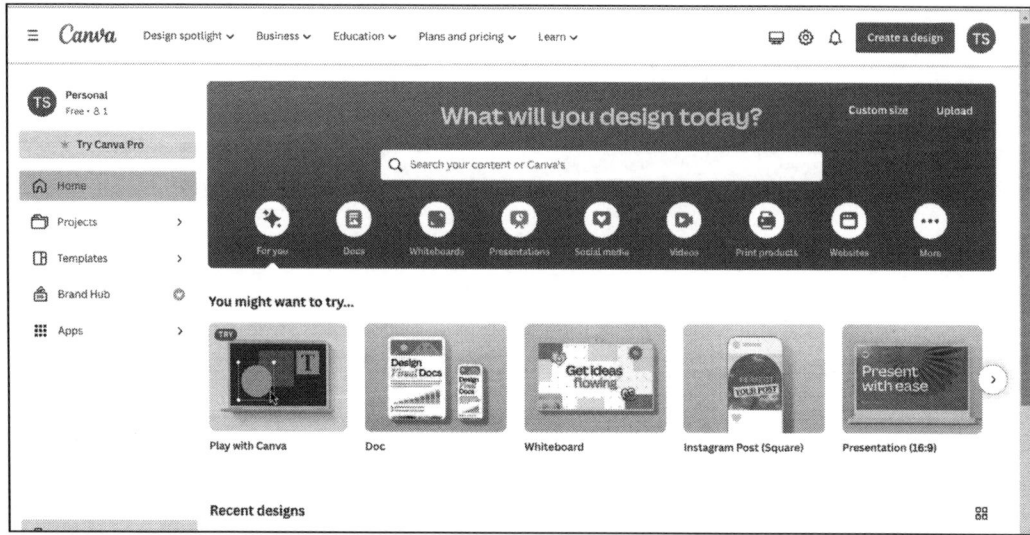

Figure 1.6

For example, if you were to click on the *Business* dropdown menu item at the top, you would be shown additional resources that can be used for creating designs and publications for your business (Figure 1.7).

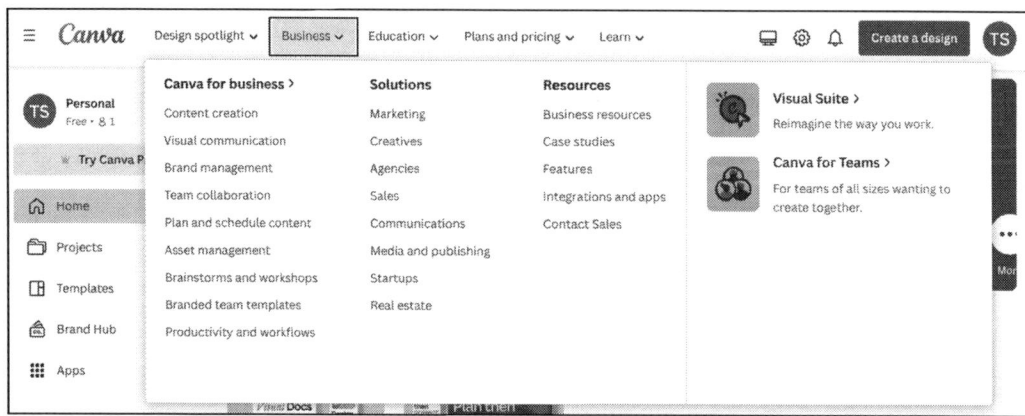

Figure 1.7

The area below this is where you can search for ideas or view designs from the various categories such as Docs, Whiteboards, Presentations, Social media, Videos, Print products, Websites and more. When you click on one of these categories such as Docs for example, you will be shown design ideas and templates related to that category (Figure 1.8).

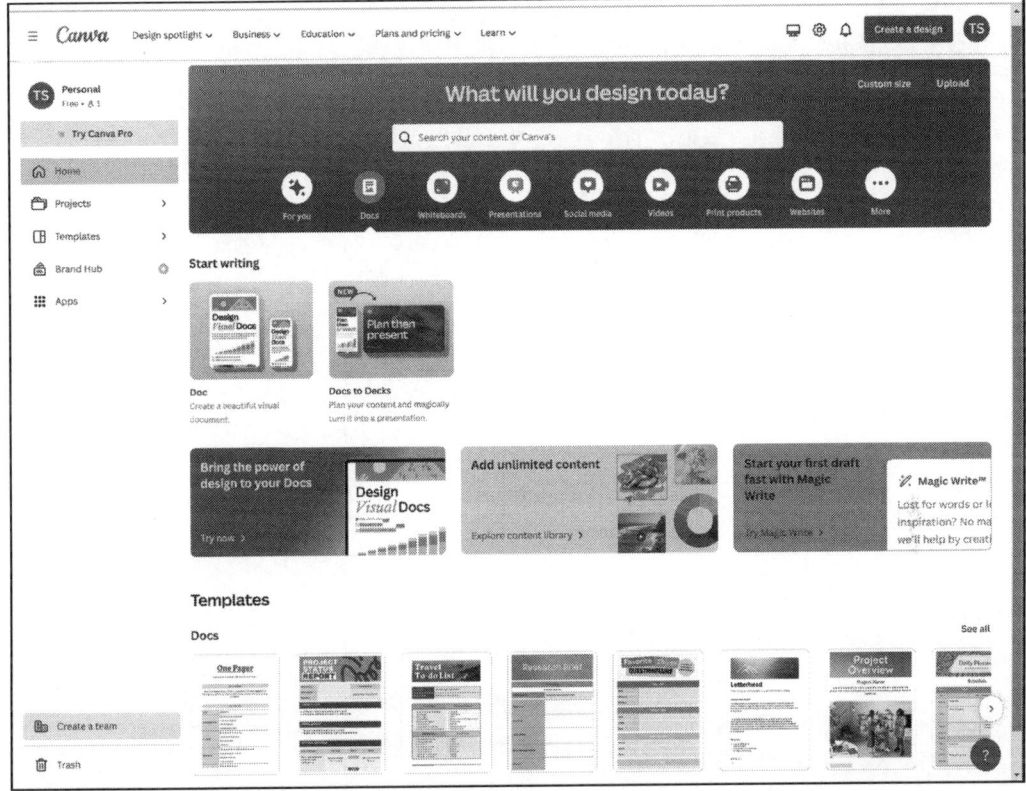

Figure 1.8

If you were to click on the first icon labeled *For you*, this area would then show your recent designs, giving you a quick way to continue working on them.

Finally, the *Create a design* button at the upper right corner of the screen can be used to start a quick design from one of the suggested ideas and also includes a search box to help you find what you are looking for if it's not listed below (Figure 1.9). You can also create a custom sized design from here or import a file to be used with your design or other saved work.

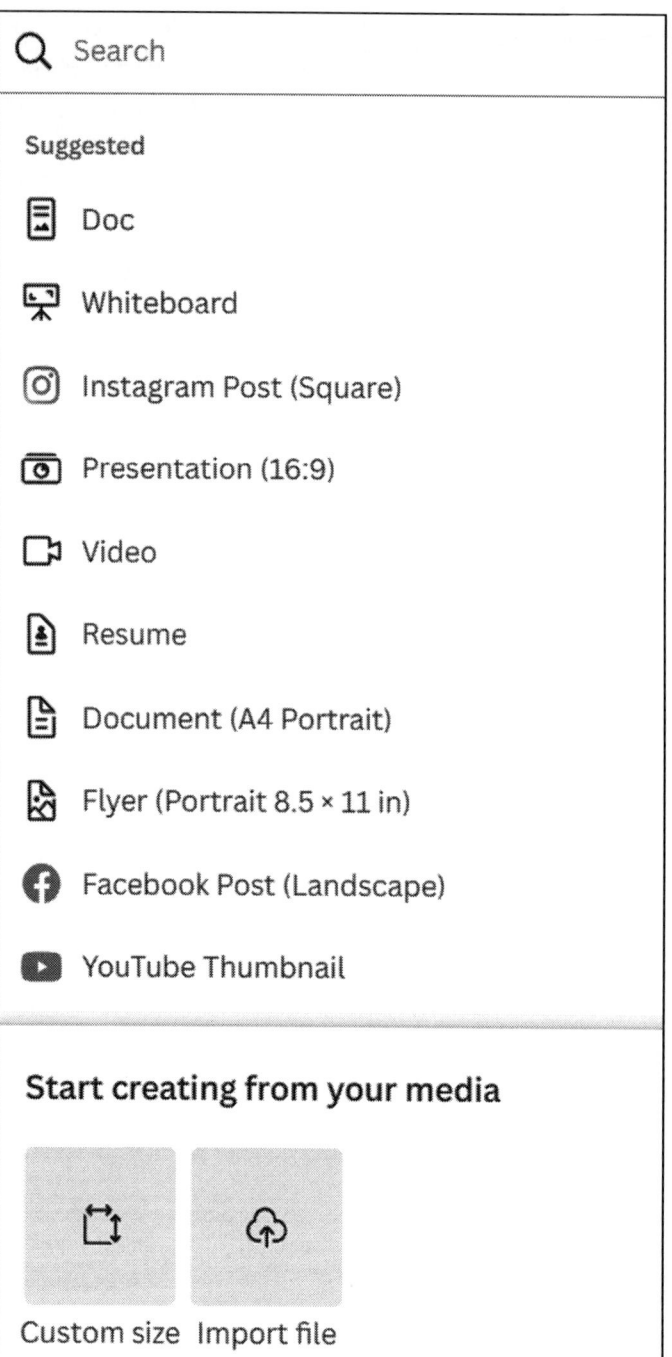

Figure 1.9

Chapter 2 – Preparing for Your First Project

Before you jump into your first project, I recommend taking some time to browse around the Canva interface and look at all the sections and options so you will have an idea of where you will need to go within the app to find the tools you need for your design.

I would definitely check out all the design categories because they are very helpful when it comes to setting up your project because they give you a solid foundation to build from. If you are feeling like a design expert, you can start with a blank project, but you might want to start with a design category or even a template just to get the hang of things.

Play with Canva Tutorial
One tool that you can use in Canva to help you get used to how the app works is the *Play with Canva* design. If you click on the *For you* icon, you should have this listed under the available selections.

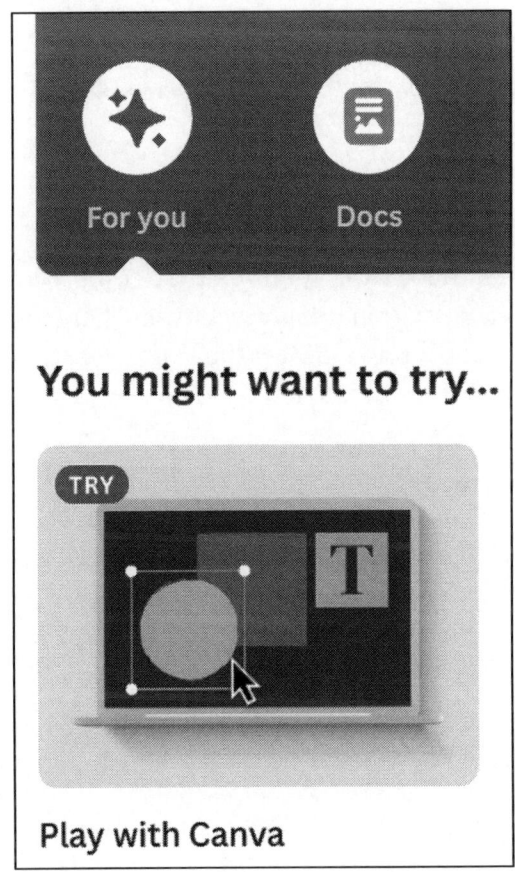

Figure 2.1

When you click on it, you will then have a presentation style project opened that you can then use to learn how Canva works while being able to edit the design at the same time.

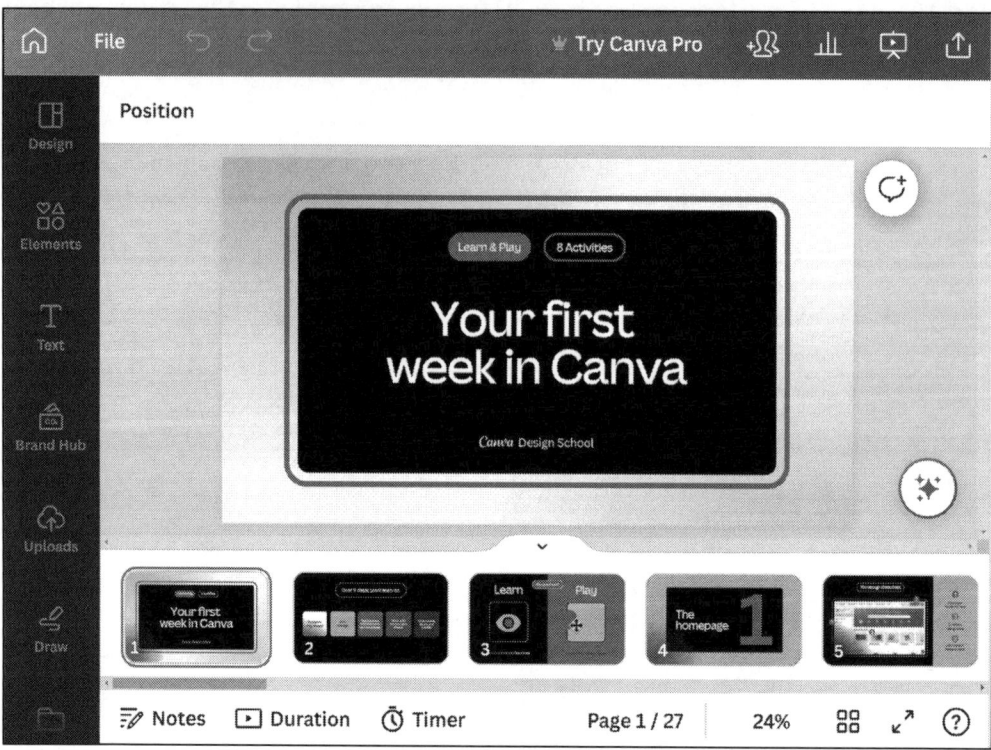

Figure 2.2

As you go through the slides, you can read about the features that come with Canva and then practice what you have learned within the project itself. There are also interactive videos you can watch as you go along that will show you the steps to complete the task. Then you can try it out for yourself and customize it to your liking (Figures 2.3 & 2.4).

Figure 2.3

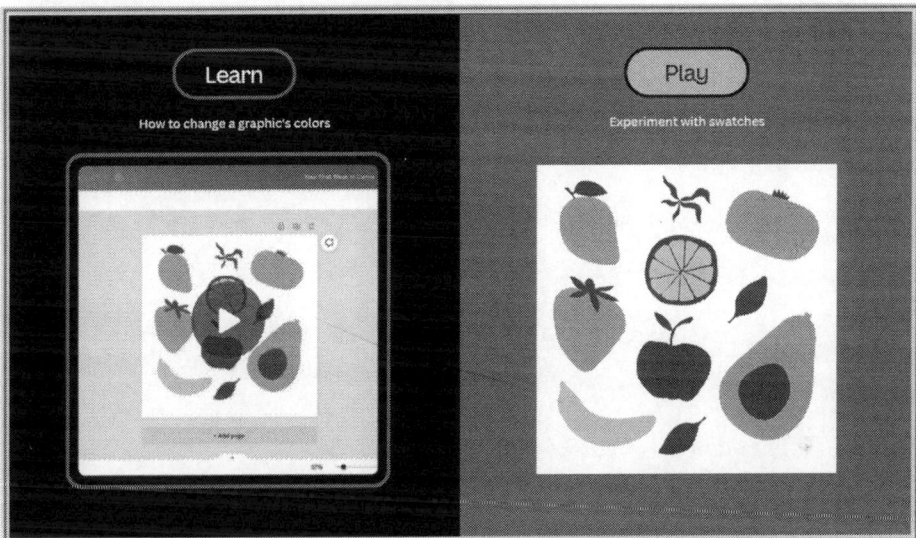

Figure 2.4

The Projects Area

One area you will most likely be spending a bit of time in is the Projects area which can be accessed from the navigation section on the left side of the page. If you don't see this option, click on the three vertical lines next to the Canva logo to expand the navigation section. The Projects area is where you can see all your projects in one place and manage them as needed. This section is broken down into three parts which are *All*, *Folders* and *Designs*. The All section is shown by default but if you only want to view your folders or your designs, you can simply click on the appropriate section at the top of the page.

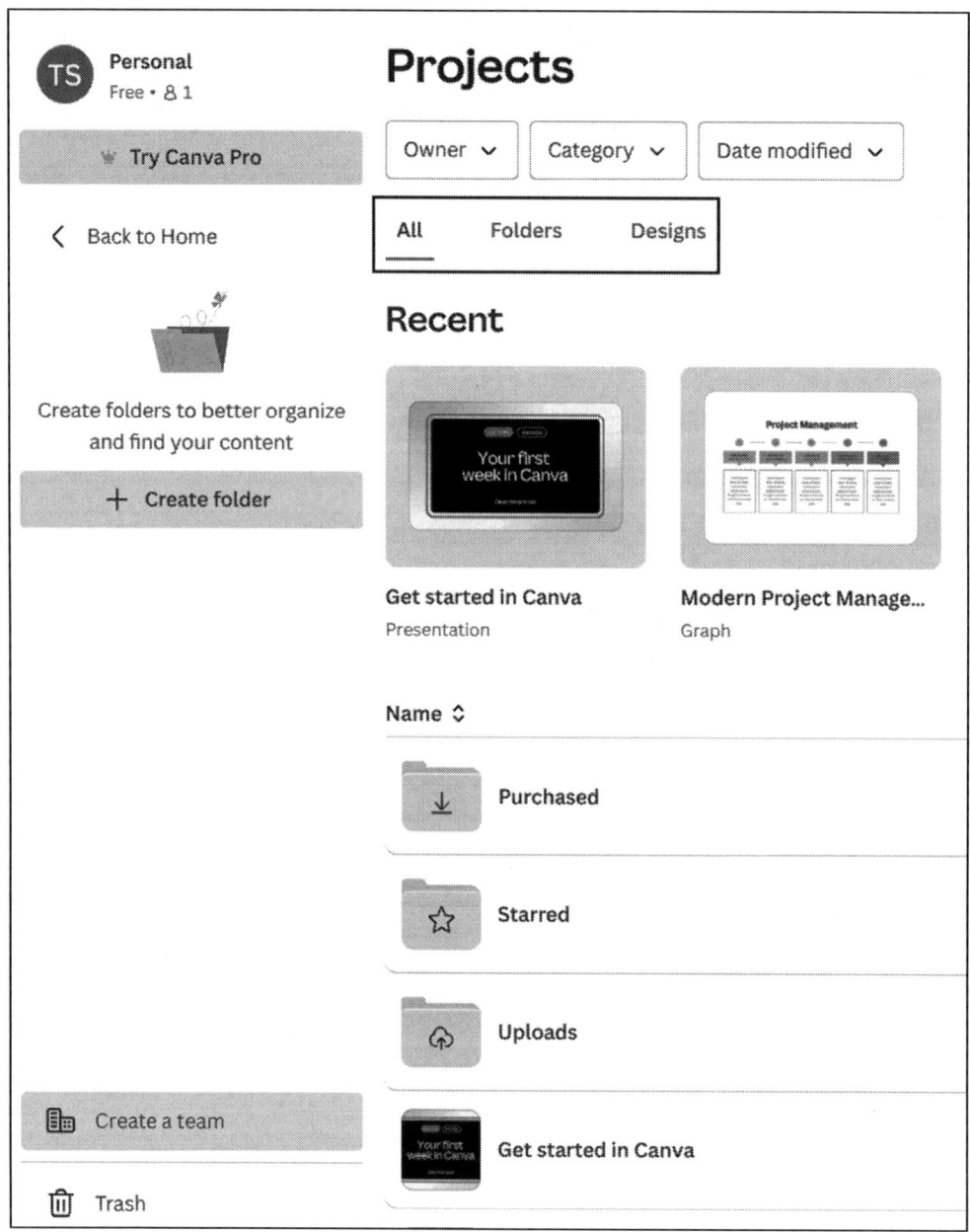

Figure 2.5

If you want to filter which folders or projects you see on the screen, you can use the *Owner*, *Category* and *Date* modified drop down lists to choose what information is shown here.

The *Recent* section will display your most recently edited projects, making it easy to quickly open them again to continue where you left off. Under that you will see your folders and then your projects listed below that. You can sort items in the Projects area by name or by last edited date by clicking on the column header name for the one you wish to sort by.

Creating Folders

If you plan on creating several projects that are not necessarily related to each other, you might want to consider making folders for them so it's easy to keep things organized.

Canva has some default folders that come with the app called *Purchased*, *Starred* and *Upload*. When you buy something like a piece of clipart or other graphic, it will be stored in your Purchased folder. The *Starred* folder is where you can keep items that you mark as starred (favorites). Finally, the Upload folder is where you can go to see files you have uploaded to your account (discussed next).

To create your own custom folder, you can either click on the *Create folder* button off to the left while in the Projects section or you can click on the *Add new* button at the upper right and then click *Folder*.

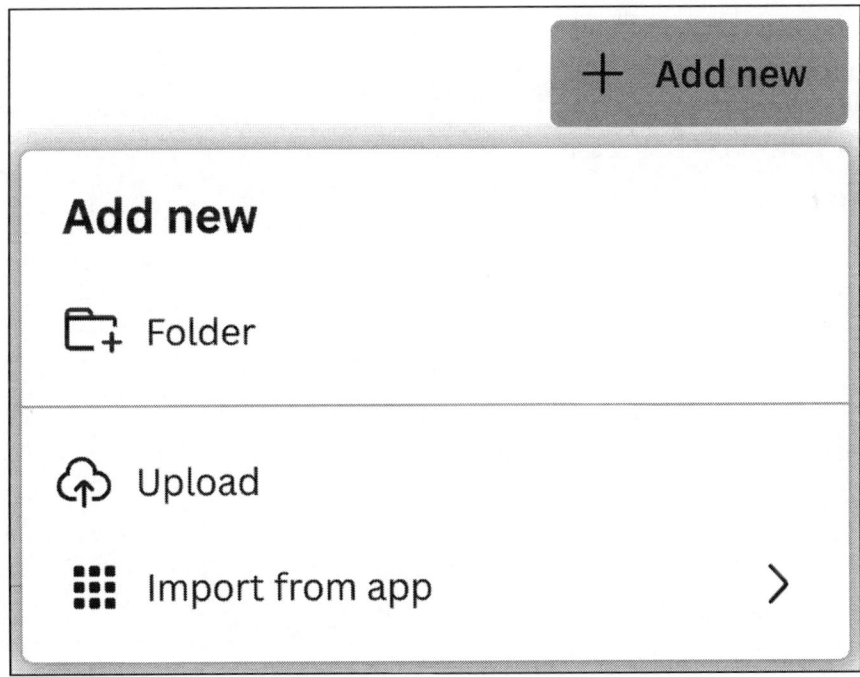

Figure 2.6

Then all you need to do is give your new folder a name and if you want to share its contents with any team members you have configured, you can do so during the folder creation process. You can always add team members later if you do not have any to add when creating the folder.

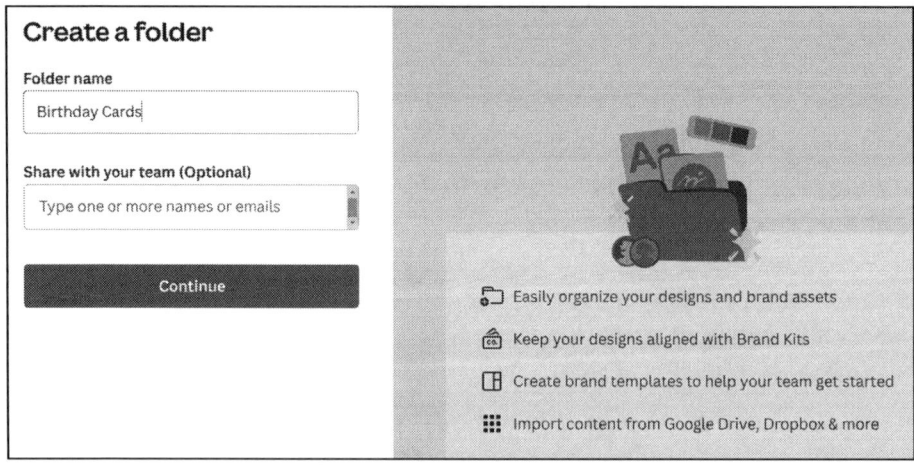

Figure 2.7

Now your new folder will be shown with the existing folders as seen in figure 2.8.

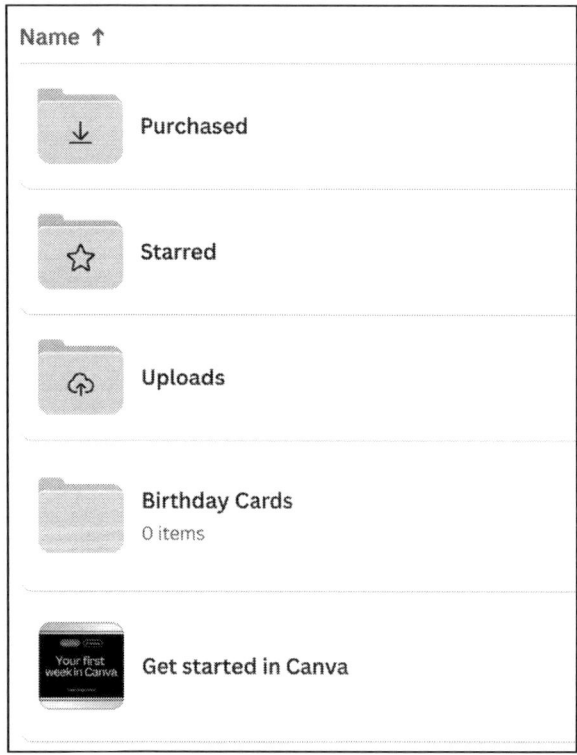

Figure 2.8

If you want to make a folder within a folder (subfolder), you can click on the main folder to go into it and then repeat the folder creation process. Once you go into that subfolder, you will see the path at the top of the screen telling you what location you are in at the moment.

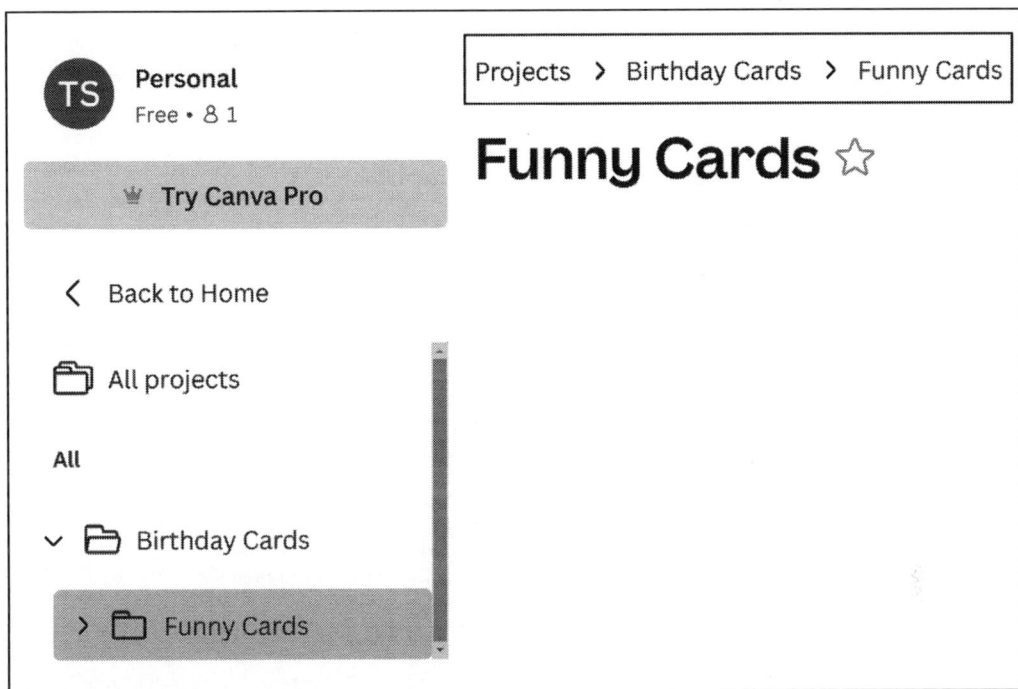

Figure 2.9

If you would like to edit or remove a folder, you can click on the ellipsis (...) next to the folder name and then choose from one of the options as seen in Figure 2.10.

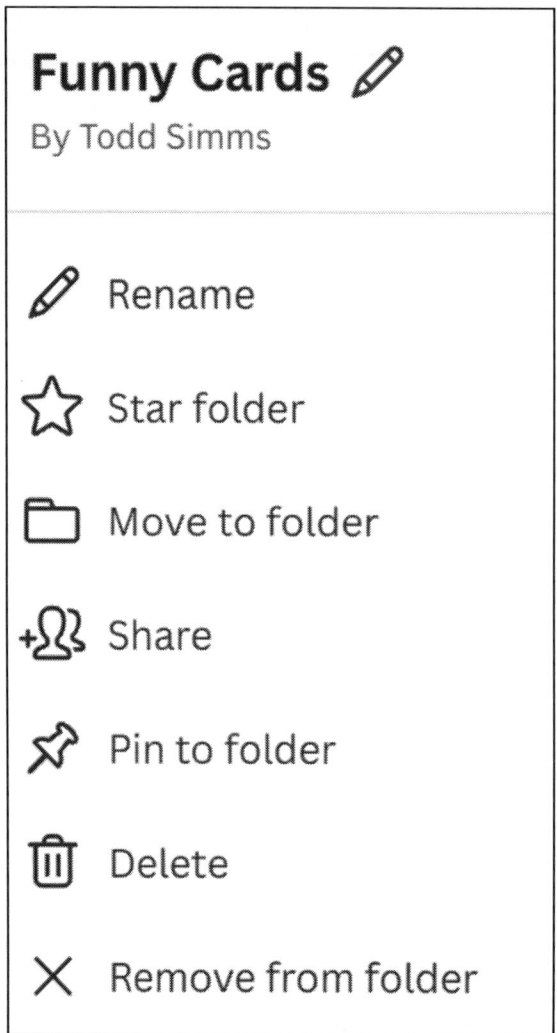

Funny Cards 🖉

By Todd Simms

🖉   Rename

☆   Star folder

🗀   Move to folder

+👥   Share

📌   Pin to folder

🗑   Delete

✕   Remove from folder

Figure 2.10

Most of these choices should be obvious but there might be a couple that are not. The *Move to folder* option will let you move this folder and its contents to a different folder. The *Pin to folder* option will pin the folder to the top for easy access. You might be wondering what the difference is between *Delete* and *Remove from folder* is. Delete will move the folder and its contents to the trash. While Remove from folder will take the folder and its contents out of the root folder and place it in your main folder area (All Projects) with any other uncategorized files and folders. When you move a folder or file to the trash, it is recoverable for 30 days until it is permanently deleted.

Uploading Files From Your Computer

Canva has a huge number of images, videos, clipart, and other graphics that you can use with your designs, but you might find that you want to use unique images of your own for your projects.

If you have images, documents or video files that you want to use with your project, you can click on the *Add new* button and then choose *Upload* to have these files transferred to your Canva account.

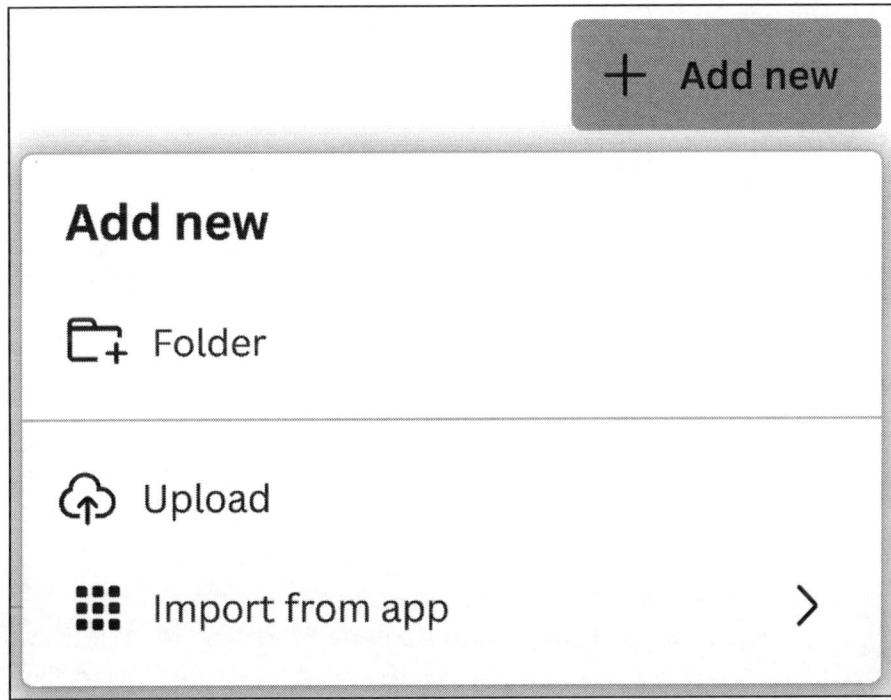

Figure 2.11

All you need to do is browse to the folder on your hard drive that contains the files you want to upload and then select one or more and click the *Open* button.

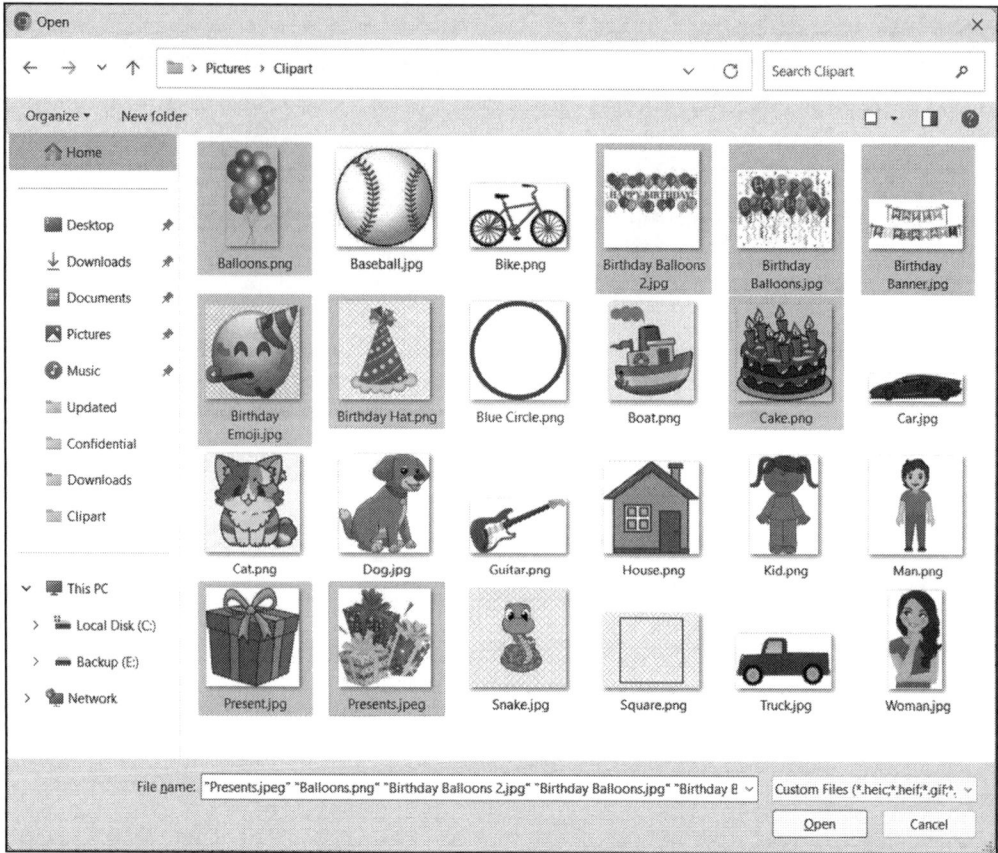

Figure 2.12

Once the file upload is complete, you will see your files in the main project area even though they are technically kept in your *Uploads* folder. Figure 2.13 shows the main Projects area, and you can see some of the newly uploaded clipart files. Figure 2.14 shows these same files in the Uploads folder which is where they actually reside.

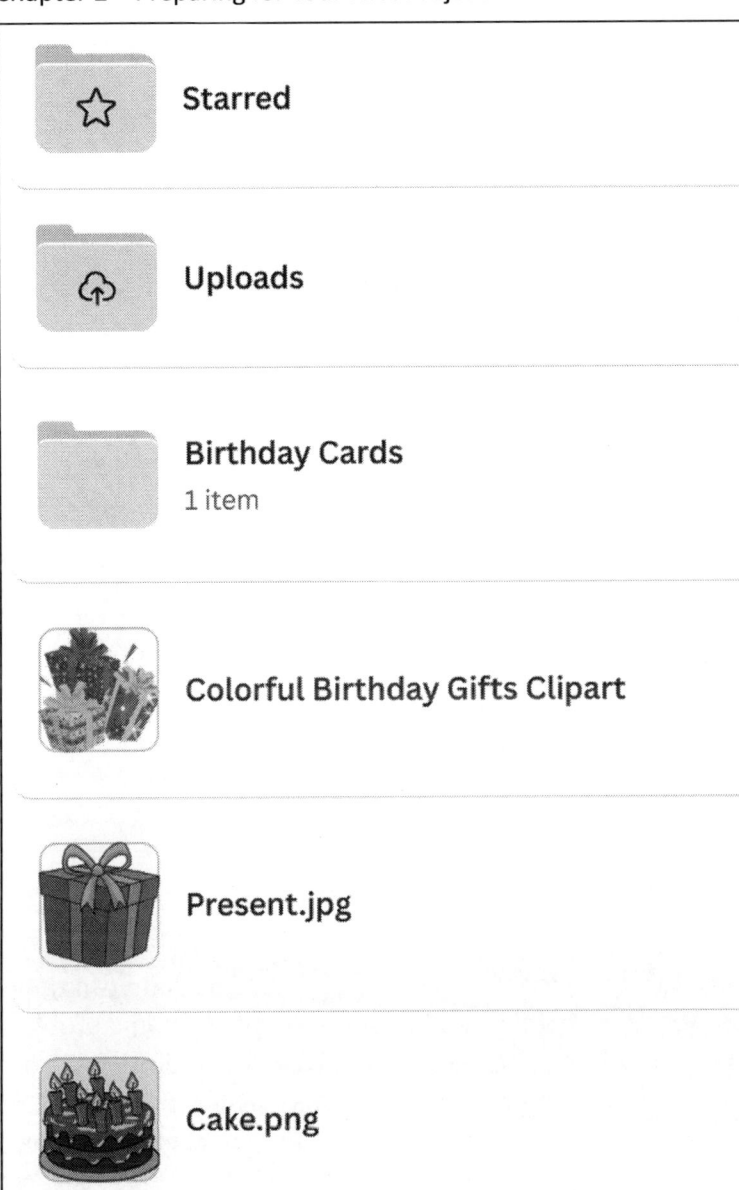

Figure 2.13

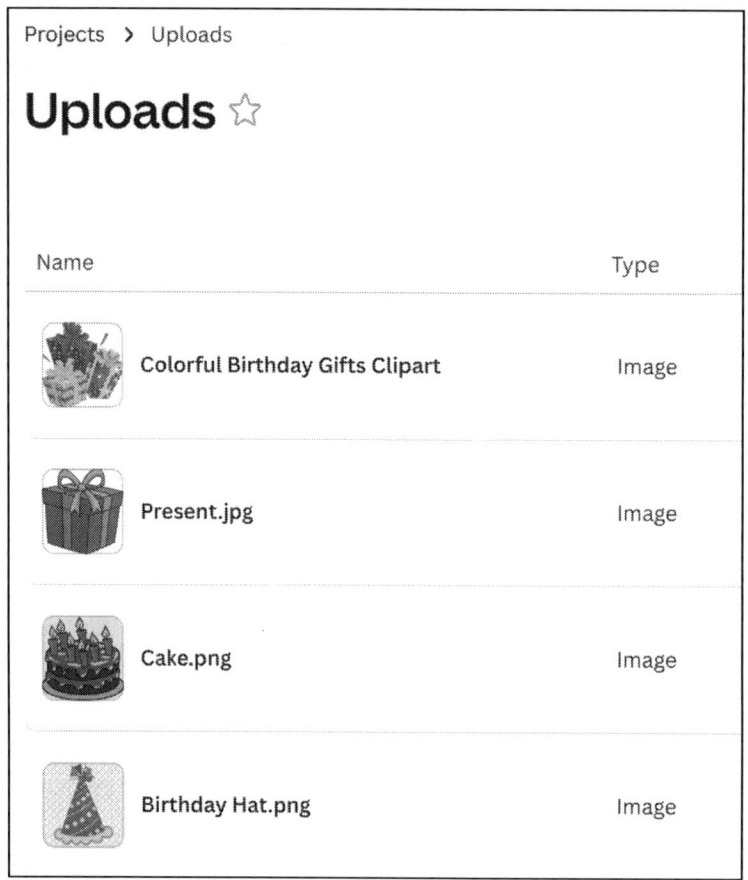

Figure 2.14

You do not have to keep your uploaded files in the Uploads folder and can move them to any other folder you have configured in your account. The only problem with this is when you are in a project and click on the Uploads option, it will not show your files if you have moved them out of the Uploads folder. Figure 2.15 shows my newly uploaded files when I click the Uploads section while in a project.

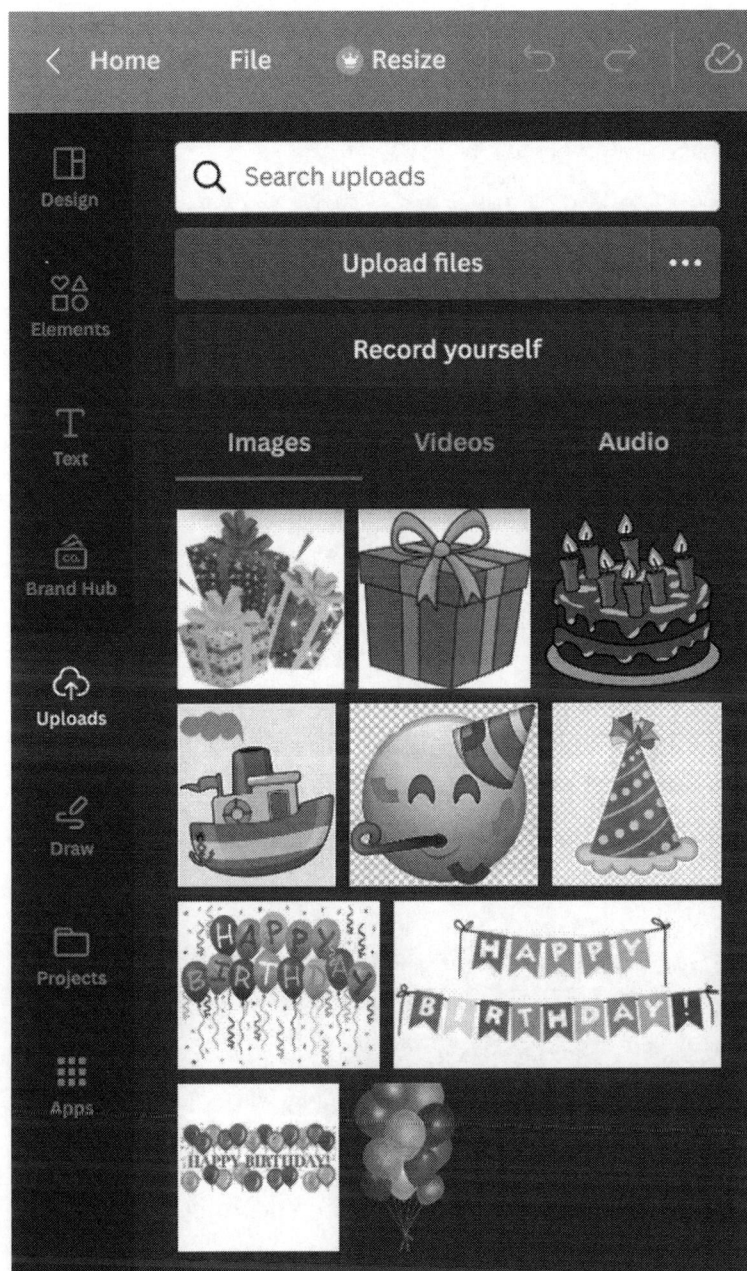

Figure 2.15

To make sure your files go to your Upload folder, you should make sure you are in that folder before choosing the upload option.

If you want to keep your files in a different folder yet still be able to access them, you can go to the *Projects* section while working on a design and browse to the folder that contains your files and add them that way.

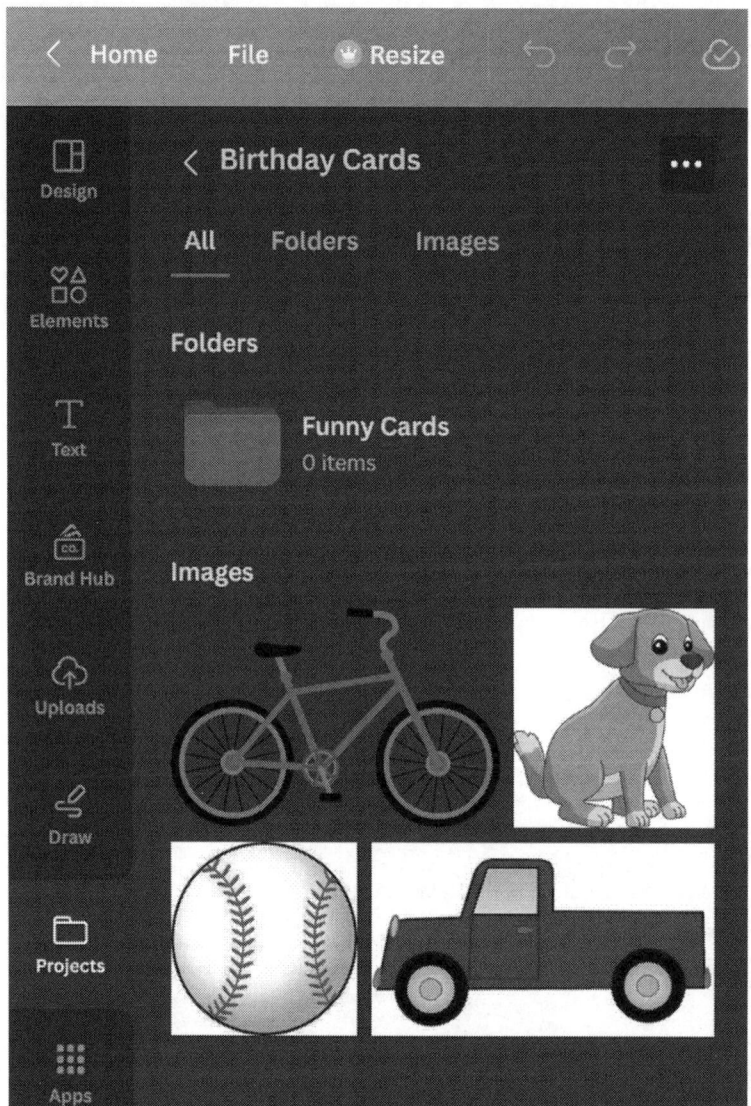

Figure 2.16

I will be getting into how to use your uploaded files in your projects in the next chapter.

Uploading Files From a Cloud Storage Account

Another option you have for adding files to Canva is to connect to your online cloud storage accounts and import them into Canva. If you choose the *Import from app* option, you can add files from Google Drive, Microsoft OneDrive and Dropbox assuming you have one or more of these accounts.

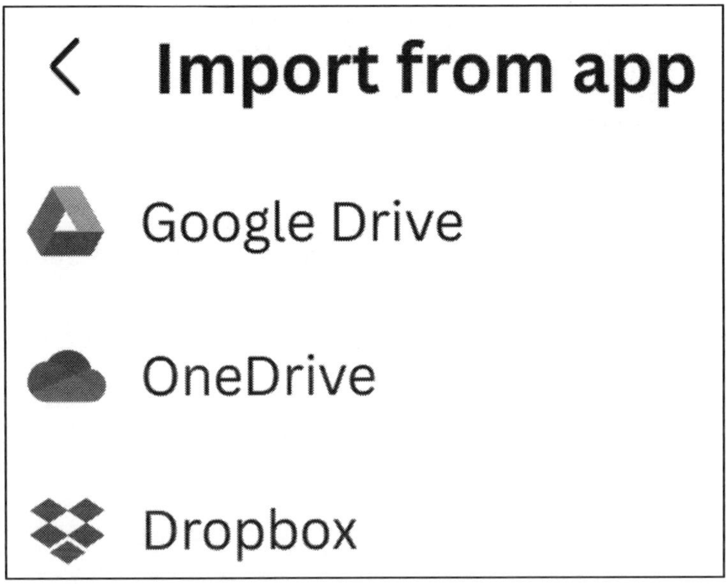

< Import from app

Google Drive

OneDrive

Dropbox

Figure 2.17

Once you choose the cloud storage service you want to use, you will need to connect your Canva account to that cloud storage account by giving Canva permission to access your files and folders. If you are not logged into your cloud storage account already, you will be prompted to do so and then agree on the permissions that Canva needs in order to transfer files to your Canva account.

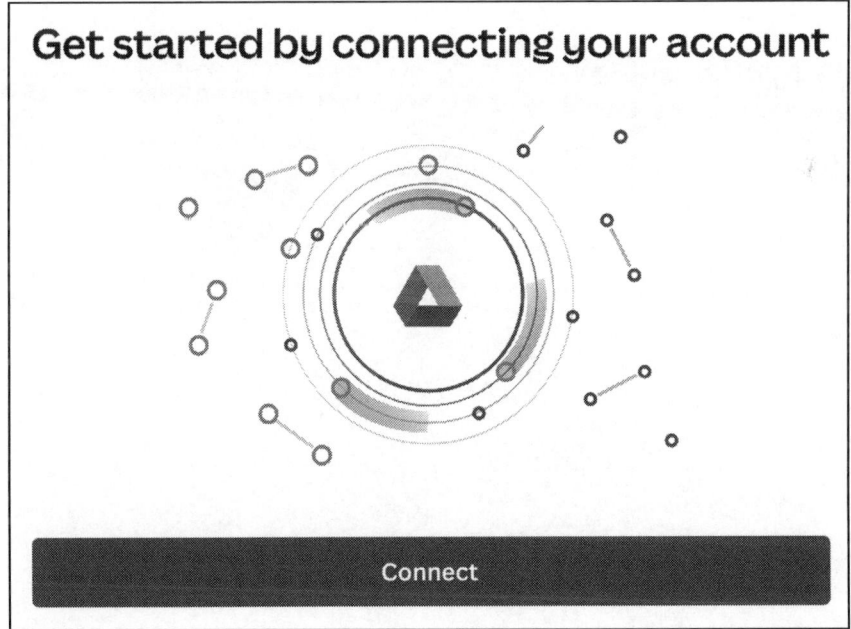

Figure 2.18

Once you have your account connected, you will then see your online files and can choose which ones you want to upload to your Canva account.

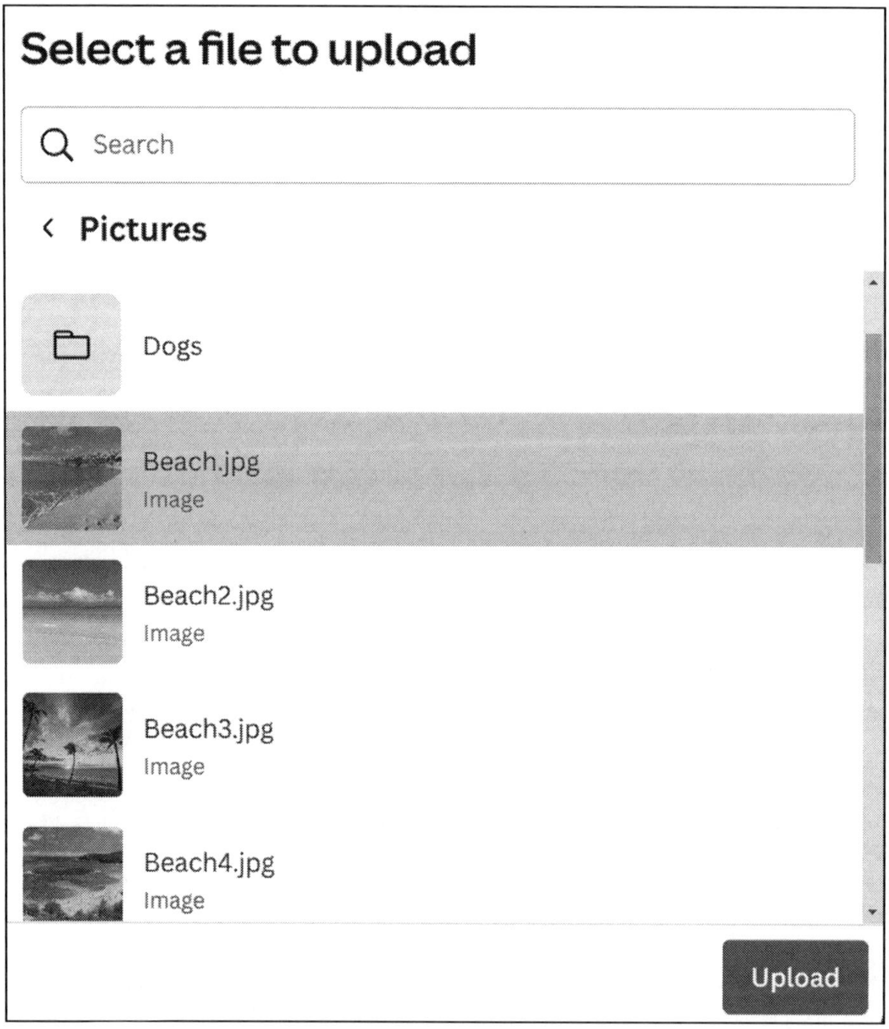

Select a file to upload

Q Search

< **Pictures**

Dogs

Beach.jpg
Image

Beach2.jpg
Image

Beach3.jpg
Image

Beach4.jpg
Image

Upload

Figure 2.19

Chapter 3 – Creating & Editing Projects

Now that you have a general idea of how the Canva interface looks and how to get started with creating folders and uploading files, it's time to start designing some works of art. As I mentioned before, you can start from scratch or use one of the many included design ideas that come with Canva and edit it to make it your own.

Templates

Templates are preconfigured projects that you can load into your app and then customize to make them your own. Since Canva has so many templates for just about any topic, you might find yourself using them more than creating designs from scratch.

When you click on the Templates section in the navigation area on the left side of the app, you will see several categories shown underneath the Templates section, at the top of the page, and also in the middle area of the page.

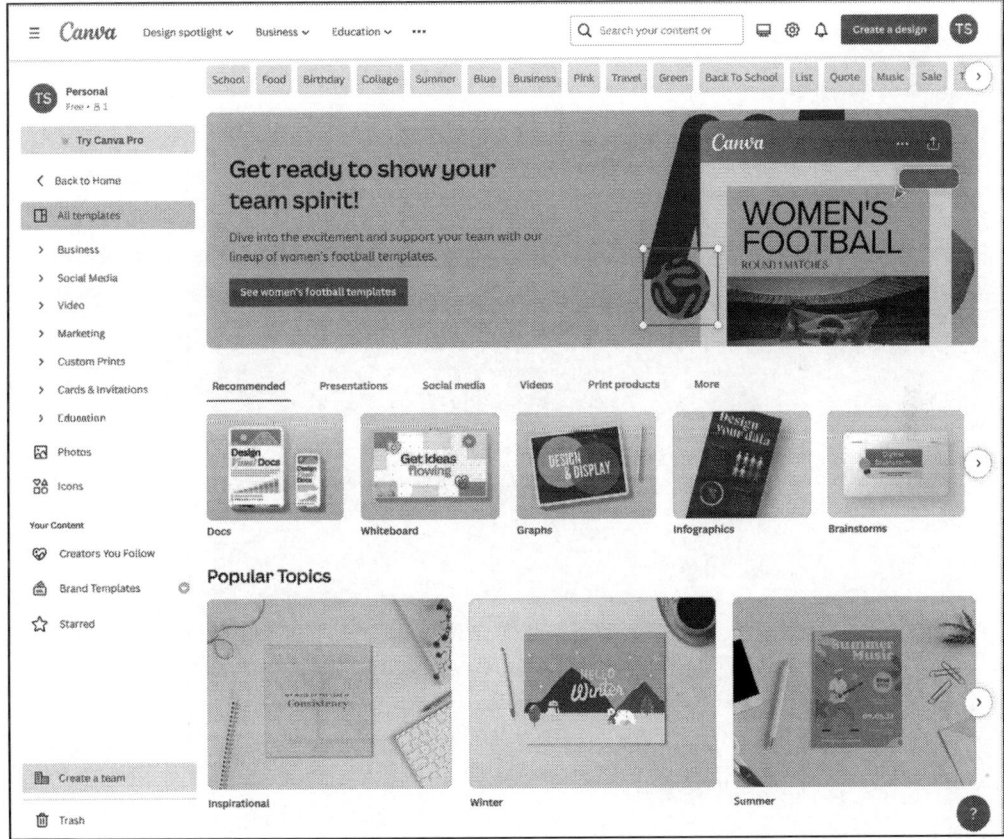

Figure 3.1

You can also use the search box to find designs that might not fit into one of the categories you see on the main templates page.

As you scroll down the page, you will see other sections such as popular topics, featured collections, inspired by your last design, trending, new in Canva and so on. If you know exactly what you are looking for, your best bet is to just use the search box.

I am going to create a birthday card so I will click on the birthday category that was at the top of the page. Figure 3.2 shows the various templates that are related to birthdays but notice how it includes things such as Instagram posts and frames so to narrow it down, I will type birthday cards in the search box and the results are shown in figure 3.3. At the upper left corner, you can also see that it found 4,093 templates!

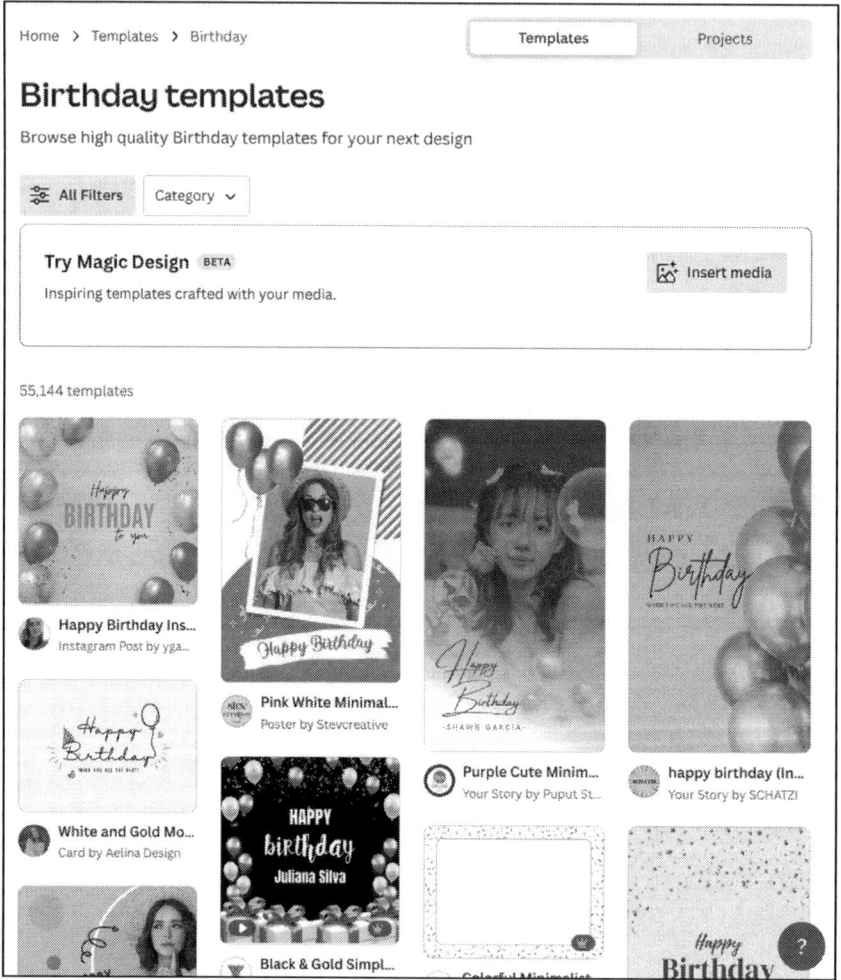

Figure 3.2

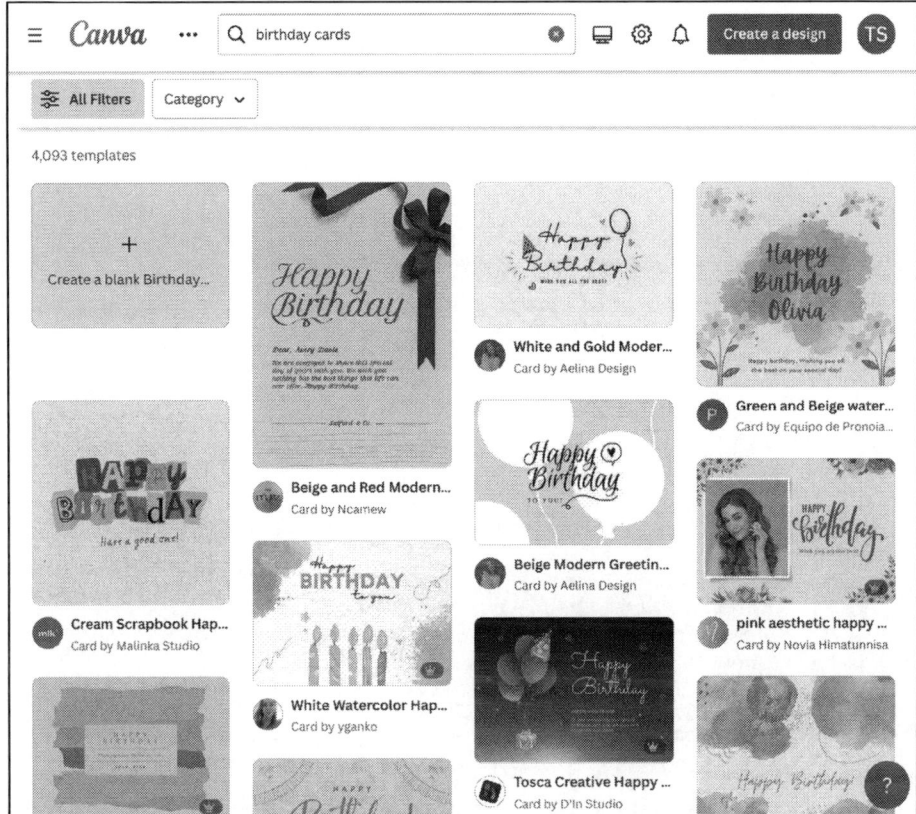

Figure 3.3

I can also click the *All Filters* button to narrow down my search results by attributes such as category, style, format and theme etc. If I scroll down to the bottom of the filters list, I can even have it display only free templates or templates that contain a certain color.

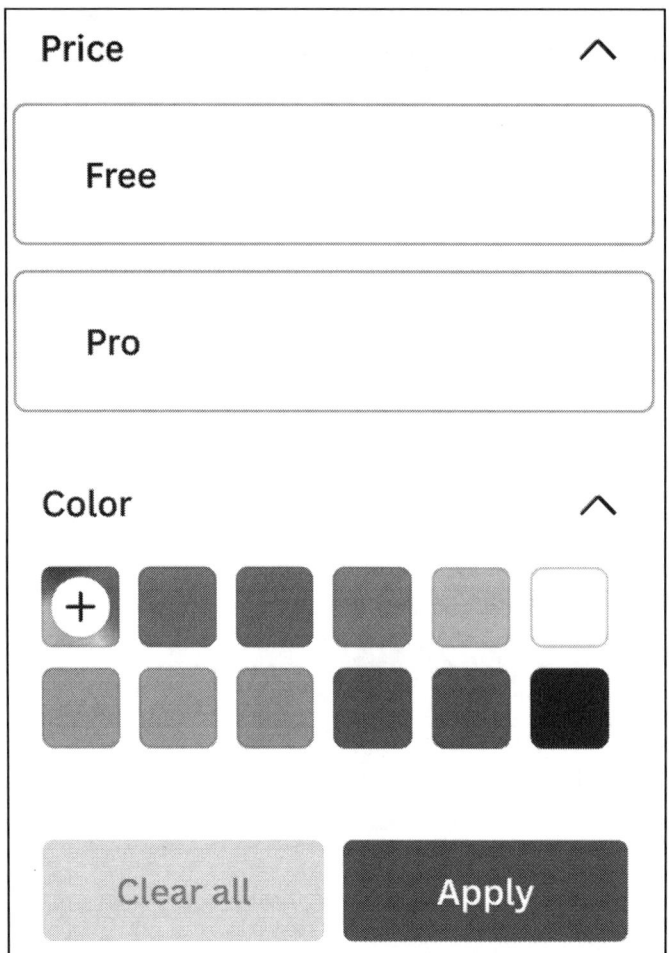

Figure 3.4

One thing to take note of when choosing a design or template to work with is that not all of them are free. If you see a gold crown logo and the word PRO next to one, that means you cannot use it with the free account (Figure 3.5).

Figure 3.5

Starting From a Blank Project

Just because there are more than enough templates to help you design just about anything you can think of, that doesn't mean you have to use one of them. If you have your project already planned out in your mind or just want to make a totally unique design, you can start from a blank canvas.

If you click the *Create a Design* button, you can then choose the *Custom size* or *Import file* option to start your new blank project.

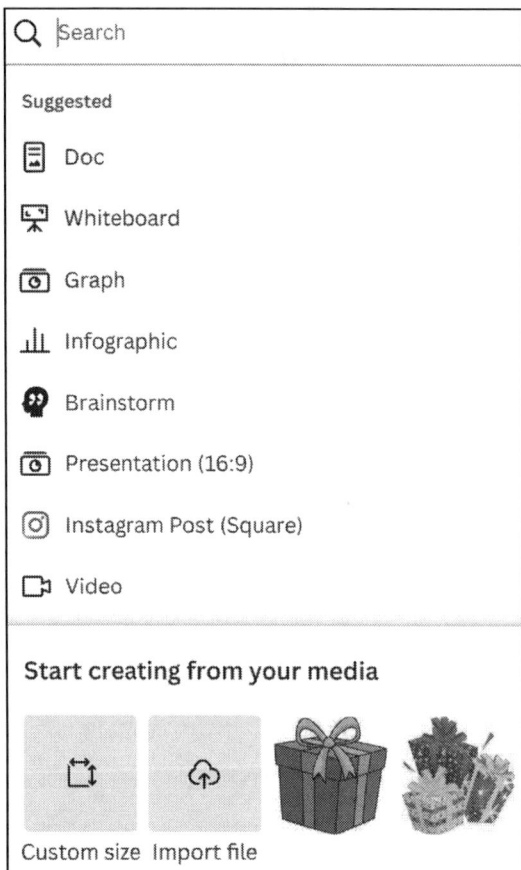

Figure 3.6

If you choose the Import file option, you can then select one of your uploaded files and then use it in a new blank design or add it to an existing template. There is even an option to edit the photo using Canva's photo editor tool.

Figure 3.7

If you choose the Custom size option, you can then type in the dimensions you want to use in pixels, inches, millimeters or centimeters. I will create a 4x6 inch design for the birthday card I want to design. When you type in specific dimensions, Canva will suggest designs based on that size such as a recipe card.

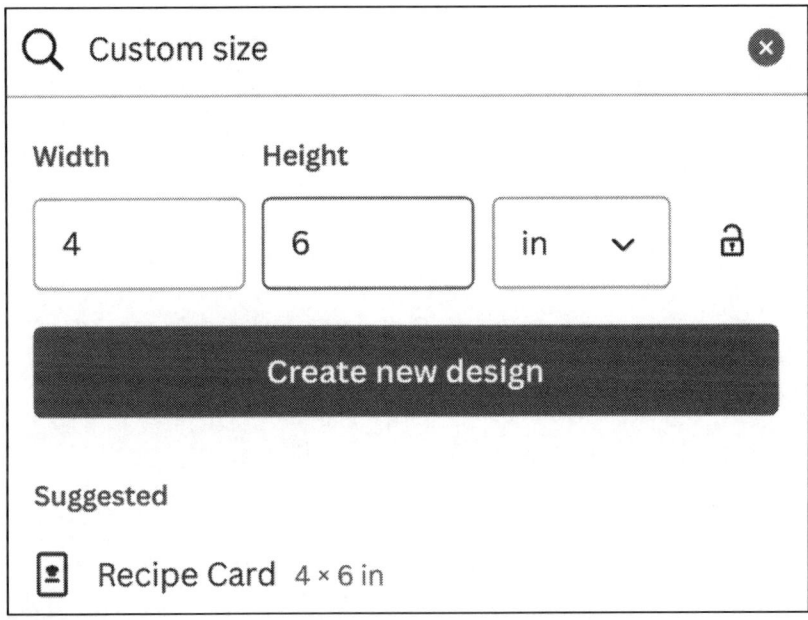

Figure 3.8

Now I have my new blank design ready to be edited. You can add additional pages as well if needed. When you click on the *Add page* button, a new page of the same size will be added below the current page.

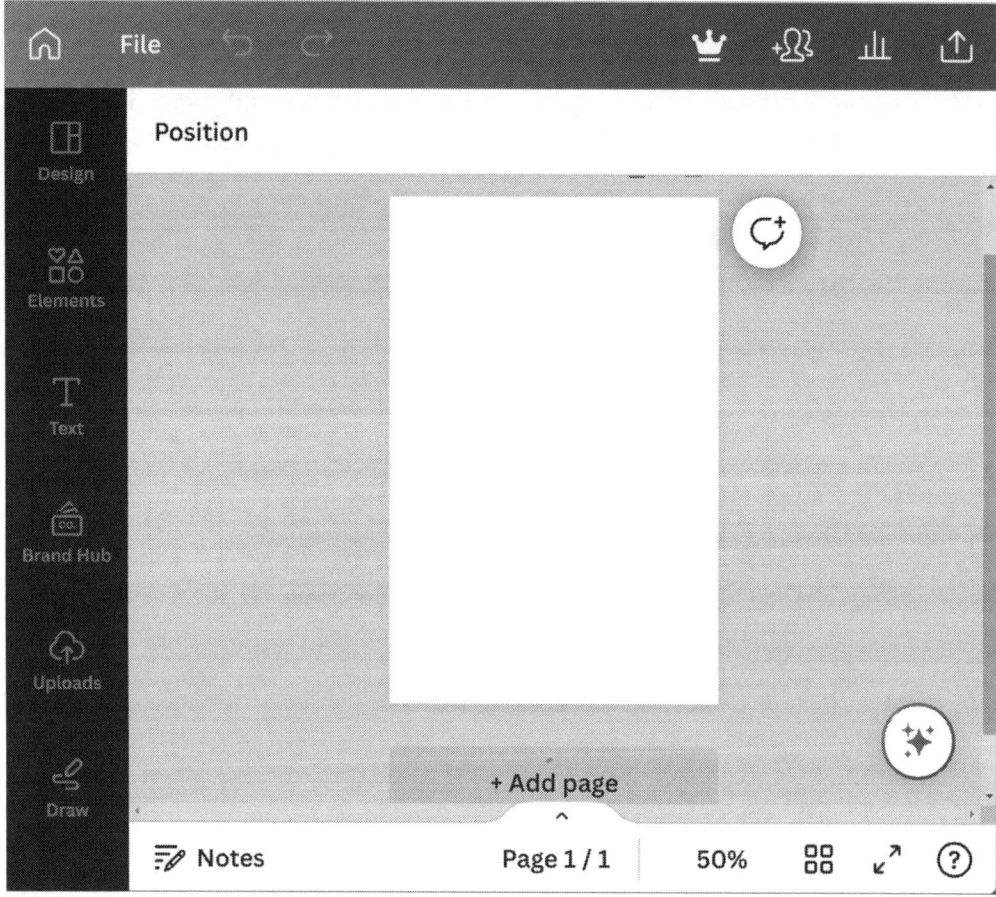

Figure 3.9

The Canva Toolbar

When working on any project in Canva, you will be using the toolbar at the left side of the screen to do things such as add graphics, videos, text and other design elements.

The *Design* section is where you can add templates or styles to the design that you are currently working on. You can use the search box to find templates or styles related to your project as well. Once you find what you are looking for, all you need to do is click on it and it will be added to your project.

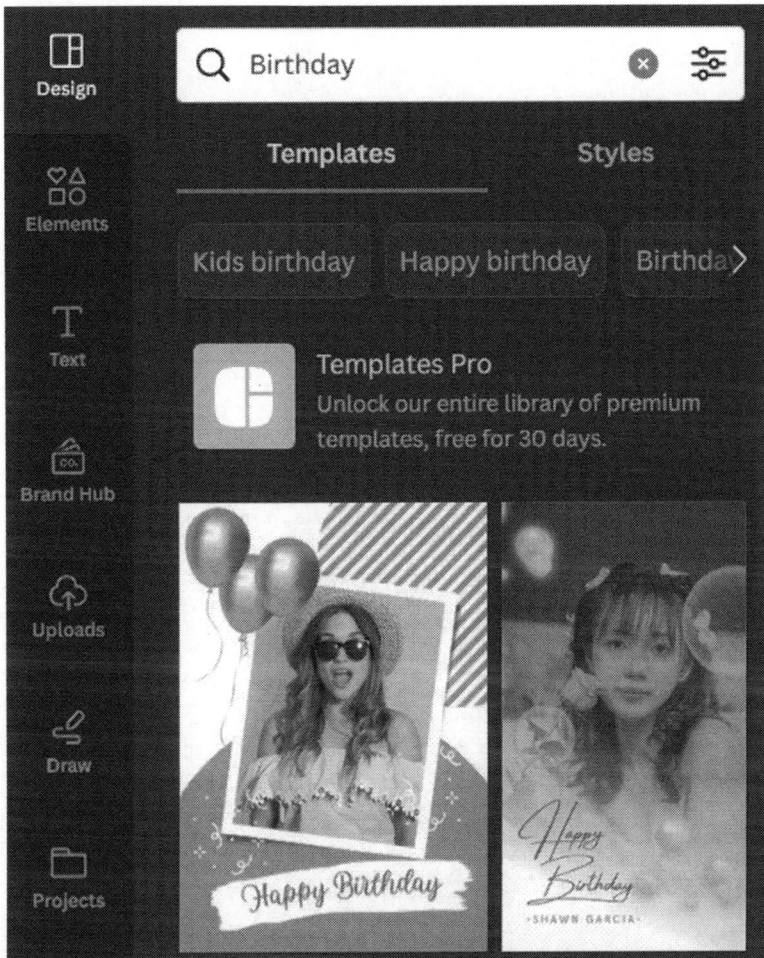

Figure 3.10

You will most likely find yourself in the *Elements* section quite a bit since this is where you can add things such as shapes, clipart, photos, videos, stickers and so on.

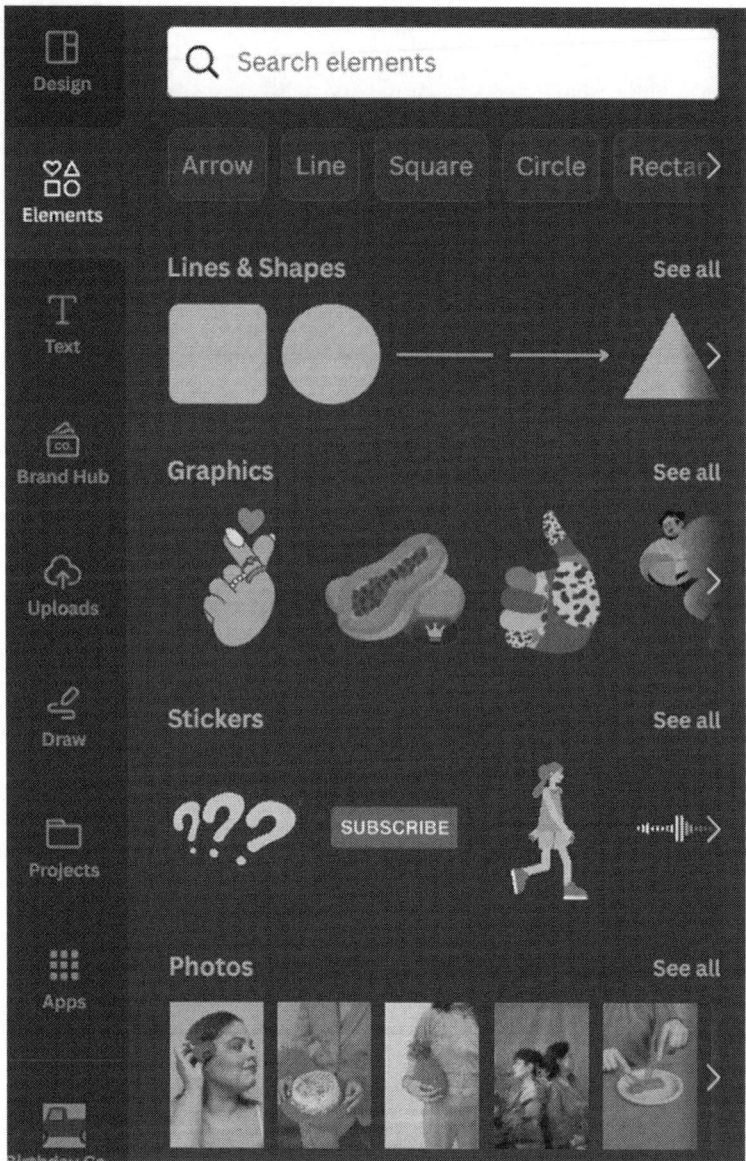

Figure 3.11

Once again, you can search here as well to help you find what you are looking for, so you do not need to sift through thousands of unrelated items. You can click on *See all* next to any category to view all the elements related to that specific type.

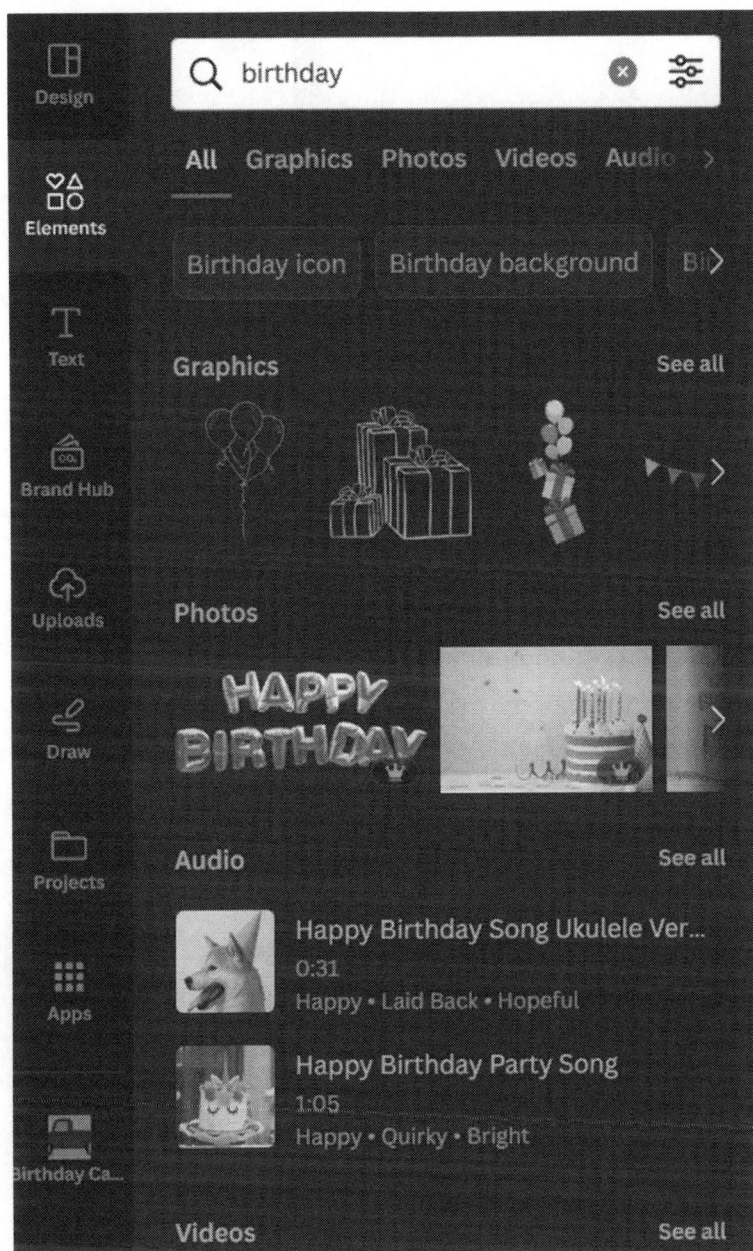

Figure 3.12

Adding text to your design is a common task and Canva makes it possible to add basic text in the form of a text box or to add general header style text as well as colorful graphic style text as seen in figure 3.14.

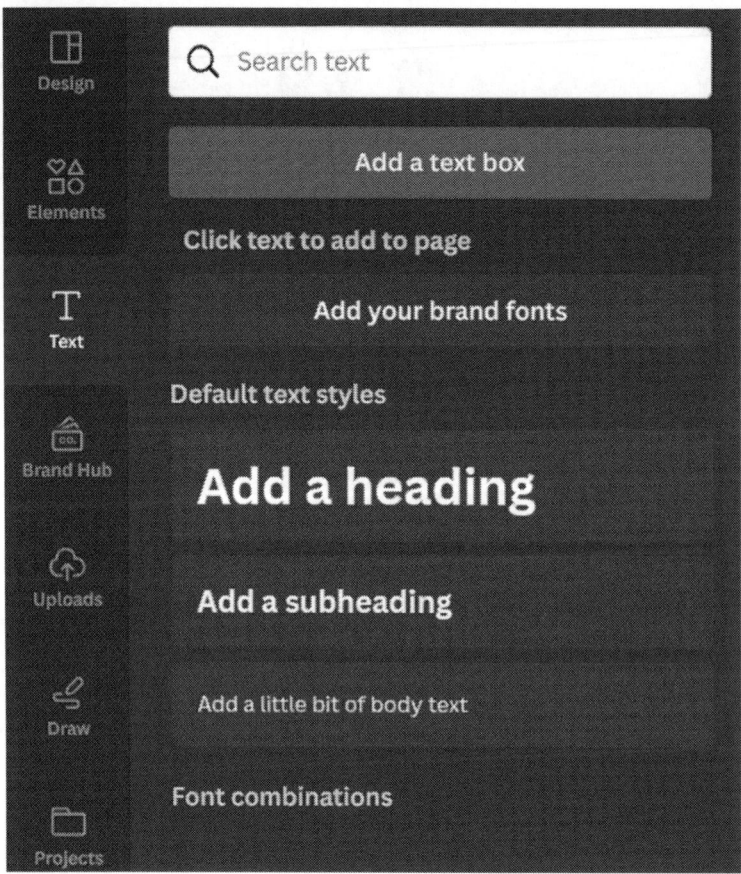

Figure 3.13

Figure 3.14

If you are the artistic type and would like to try adding some freehand drawings to your design, you can use the pens and markers from the *Draw* section. You can also choose your own colors and line thickness for the pens.

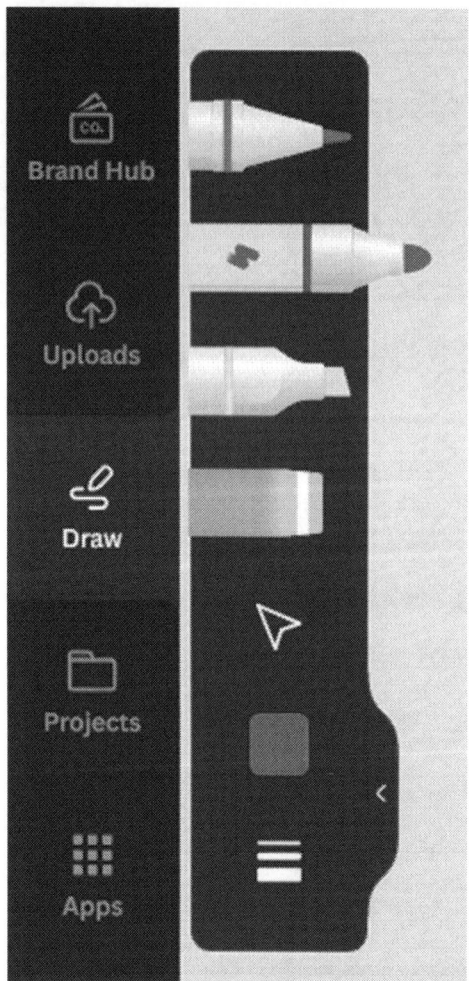

Figure 3.15

Once you start creating several designs, you will be able to find them in your *Projects* section in case you want to refer to a different project or switch over to another one to work on. The default view is to show all of your projects, but you can have it show only designs, folders or images to help narrow things down. And of course, you can search your projects as well by using the search box.

Figure 3.16

One other section I wanted to point out that is not related to the toolbar is the *File* menu at the top of the page. You can come here to start a new design, rename the current design, import files, save your project to a different folder, make a copy of your project, and also download it if needed.

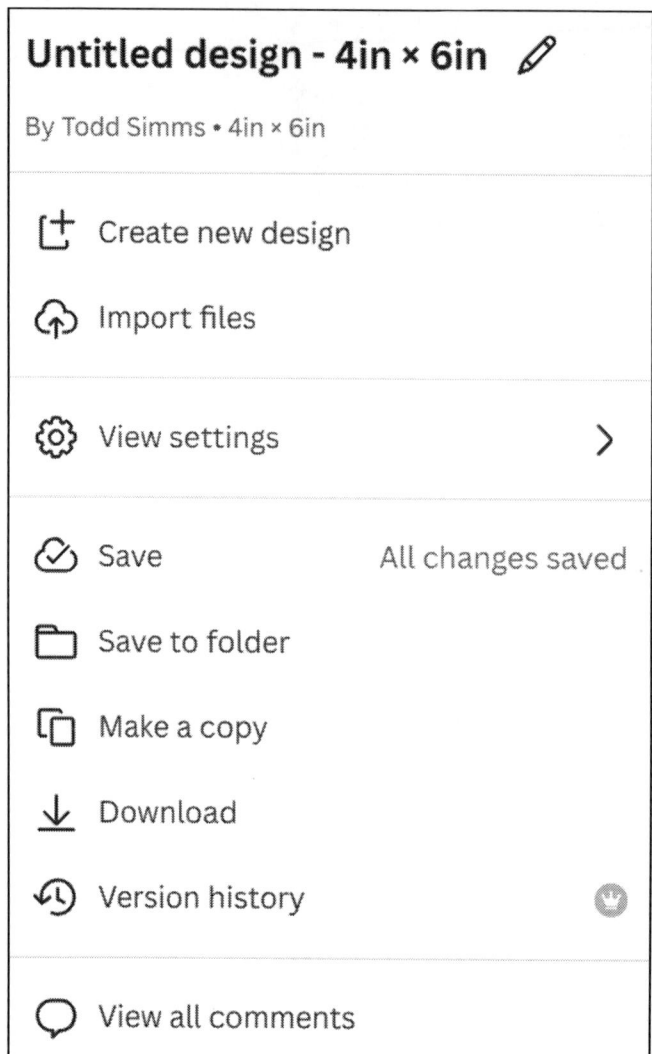

Figure 3.17

Adding and Editing Elements
If you have played around with Canva for any amount of time, you most likely know that there are thousands of ways to customize your project and it might be a bit overwhelming to try and take it all in.

I wouldn't worry about what you don't know how to do with Canva and focus on what you need to know to make your designs work for you. As I mentioned at the beginning of this book, Canva is simple yet very involved since there is so much you can do with it and there is no way to cover every aspect of it.

In this section, I will be working on the birthday card that I will be making from a blank design rather than a template. Then later on, I will create a new project from a template and show you how to edit it to make it your own.

To begin the process, I will go to the blank design that I created earlier and then go to the Elements section and do a search for *happy birthday banner.* Figure 3.18 shows the results of my search and as you can see, many if not most of the banners are not something I can use with the free account since they have the gold crown icon next to them. If you plan on using Canva on a regular basis, you might want to consider upgrading to the Pro plan so you will have access to everything you need.

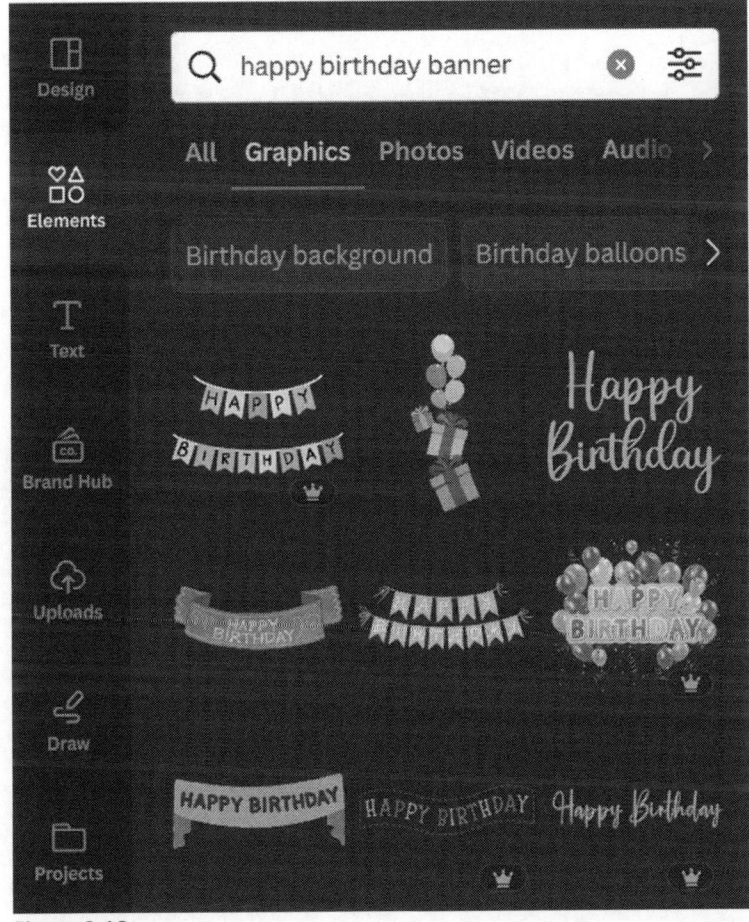

Figure 3.18

While browsing design elements, you can narrow down the results by clicking the filter button to the right of the search box. Then you will be able to choose to see graphics etc. that match a certain color, have a particular shape and are animated or static. The *Cut-outs* option will show you results that have a transparent background in case you are placing the element on top of something else or if you have a background color in your design.

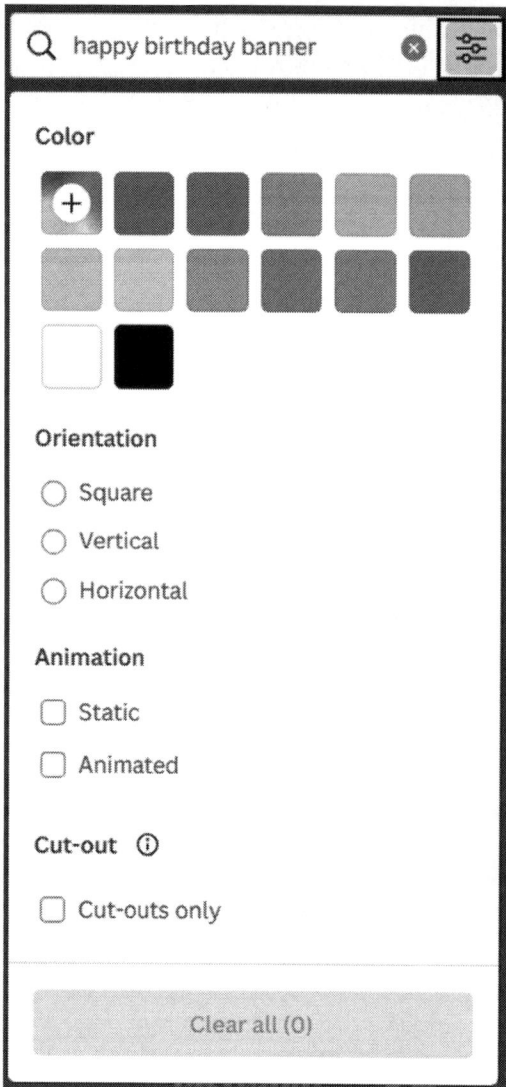

Figure 3.19

Since I cannot find a free banner that I like, I will insert one that I have previously uploaded to my Uploads folder.

Figure 3.20

Now that my image is placed in my project, I can do things such as make it larger or smaller, duplicate it, rotate it or even delete it if I change my mind.

Figure 3.21

Clicking on the ellipses by the trash can delete button will bring up some additional options that I can use with this image as seen in Figure 3.22. Most of them should be self-explanatory but there might be a few that need a little explanation.

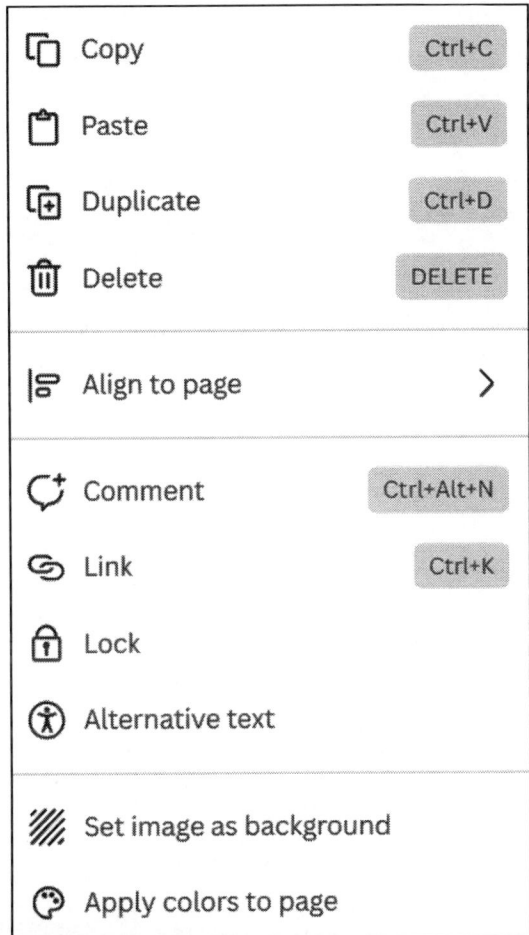

Figure 3.22

The *Align to page* option can help you to quickly align the element to the center, middle, top, bottom, left or right of the page so you do not have to guess and hope that you have it positioned exactly right.

The *Link* option can be used to add a link to a website so that when someone clicks on that element, they will be taken to that site. Keep in mind that links will only work with certain types of files such as PDF files when you export your project.

The *Lock* option can be used to lock an element in place so it can't be accidentally moved or deleted. You can unlock it as needed by clicking on the lock icon that appears after you lock the element.

Alternative text is used to enable screen readers and assistive technology to describe what is conveyed in the elements used in your project.

If you have an element that you think would look good as a background image, you can choose the *Set image as background* and Canva will make that element take up the entire page and then you can add additional elements on top of it.

The *Apply colors to page* option will take colors from whichever element you have selected and try and make all the elements and the background match the colors that make up that primary element.

Next, I will add some text to my card so I can put the name of the person who it will be going to underneath the happy birthday banner. I will choose one of the text effects that come with Canva and when it's added to my project, it will use the text that comes with the example.

Figure 3.23

Now I just need to change the text from WOW to the name of the person who will be receiving the card. I have also added a birthday cake graphic that comes included with the free Canva account.

Figure 3.24

Now I want to add some design elements to the corners of my card so I will search for corner borders and choose one that fits my design. If you take a look at Figure 3.25, you can see that I have added it to the lower left corner and also have duplicated the element so I can use it for the lower right corner as well.

Figure 3.25

You might have noticed that this corner design is not facing the right way and if I click on it to select it, there is a rotate button that can be used to spin the element as needed. Unfortunately, this will not solve my problem so I will need to use the Flip option at the top of the page and then choose *Flip horizontal*. Figure 3.26 shows the results and as you can see, it's now facing the right direction.

Figure 3.26

I will now add one more element to my project so I can show you how you can layer your graphics as needed to make sure everything looks the way you would like it to. I will add a present image to the bottom corners of my design but as you can see in figure 3.27, it's covering up my flower corner border which is not the look I am going for.

To fix this, I will select the present graphic, right click on it and choose *Layer > Send backward* to have it put behind my corner border. I can also select the corner border and choose *Send forward* to have it put in front of the present graphic. The results are shown in figure 3.28. You can also use the *Send to back* and *Bring to front* options to have elements placed all the way in the back or all the way in the front if you have multiple graphics on top of each other.

Figure 3.27

Figure 3.28

Now that I have all my elements in place, my birthday card is complete and ready to be printed or emailed. When creating designs, it's always good to remember that sometimes less is more because it's easy to get carried away by adding more and more elements to your project.

Figure 3.29

Editing an Existing Design or Template
As I previously mentioned, you might find yourself working with templates and pre-created designs more than you will be creating projects from a blank canvas. When going this route, it's always best to consider which way will result in less work for you.

If you do end up using a template, all you need to do is browse or search for the type of design you want to customize and then once you find what you are looking for, you can then start working on it. For my example, I will be editing a preconfigured collage poster and adding the pictures from my Hawaii trip to replace the photos that come included with the template.

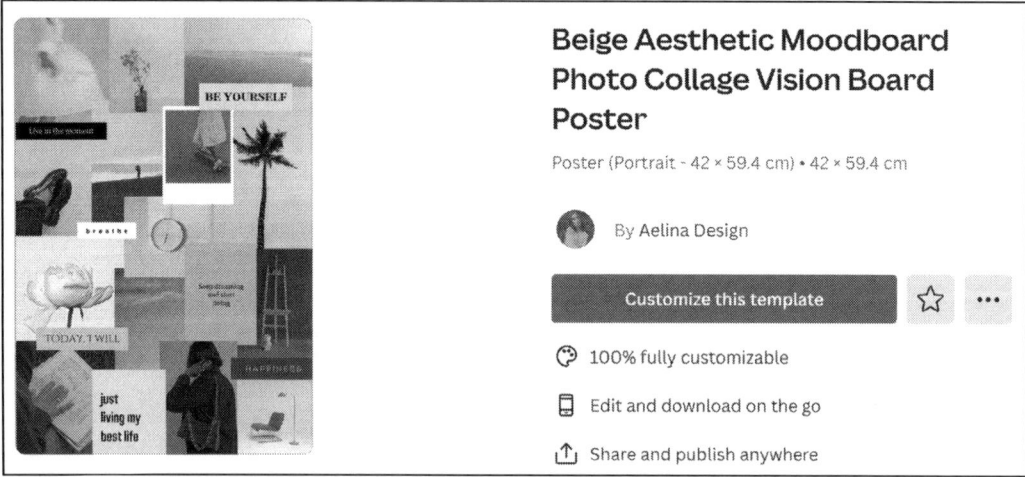

Figure 3.30

As you can see in Figure 3.31, I can select any photo or text box and then do things such as delete, move or edit it. I can also add any new elements as needed. But before I get started, I will upload my Hawaii photos to my Canva account so I have easy access to them when I am ready to insert them into my project.

Figure 3.31

Canva makes it easy to customize the templates to save you time and frustration trying to tackle it on your own. For this template, all I had to do was drag my Hawaii photos from my Uploads on top of an existing photo in the template and it was automatically placed there and resized to match the previous image. Then I simply changed the text to fit my pictures, changed the colors of some of the text boxes and that is all there is to it (Figure 3.32). Of course you can also do things such as add additional elements, add borders, rearrange the photos and so on.

Figure 3.32

Creating Animated Designs

For my last two examples, I created projects that would most likely be printed out or maybe even saved as image files so they could be emailed to other people. There is another type of project you can create that has the potential to be a bit more eye catching because it involves adding animated elements to the design.

If you have ever used Microsoft PowerPoint or Google Slides, you have probably applied animations to things such as text or graphics in an effort to keep your viewers attention for more than five minutes!

You can create similar effects in your work with Canva by applying animations to your design and also by adding elements that are already animated to begin with.

For this example, I will be going back to my birthday card and adding some animations to make it a little more exciting for the recipient. Once I have the project open, all I need to do is select which element I want to animate and then click on *Animate* in the bar at the top of the page. I will then have options to either apply an animation to just that element or to the entire page.

The Canva animation presets are broken down into photo animations and page animations. Figures 3.33 through 3.35 show the choices for photo animations while Figures 3.36 through 3.38 show the choices for page animations.

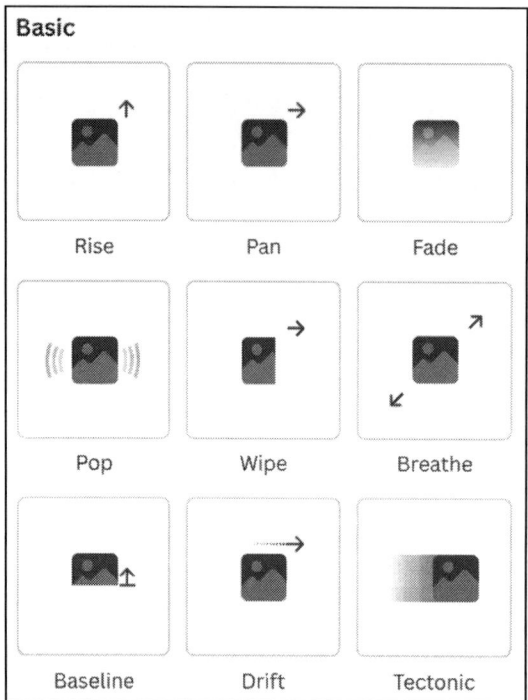

Figure 3.33

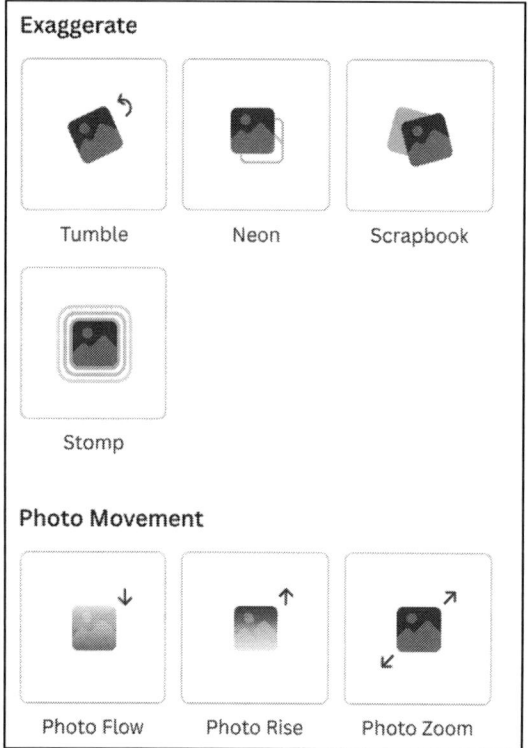

Figure 3.34

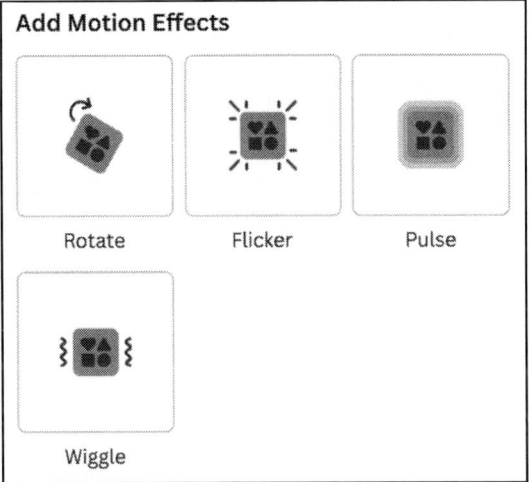

Figure 3.35

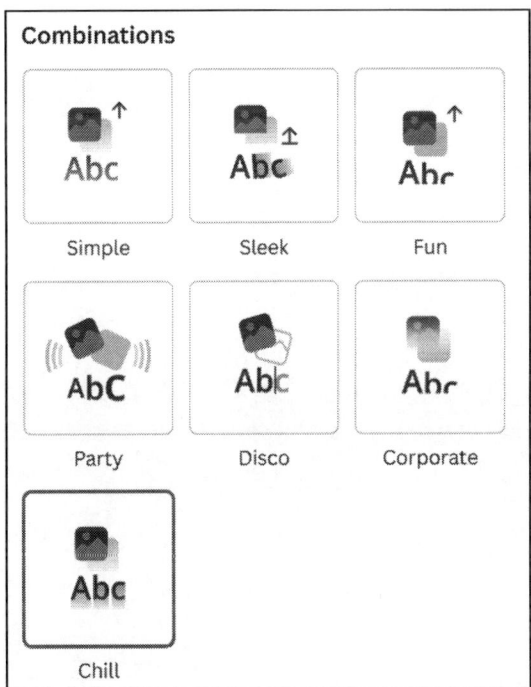

Figure 3.36

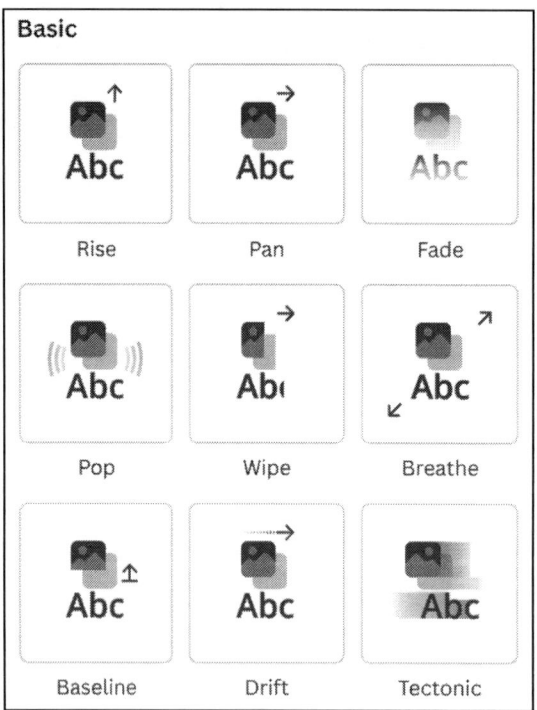

Figure 3.37

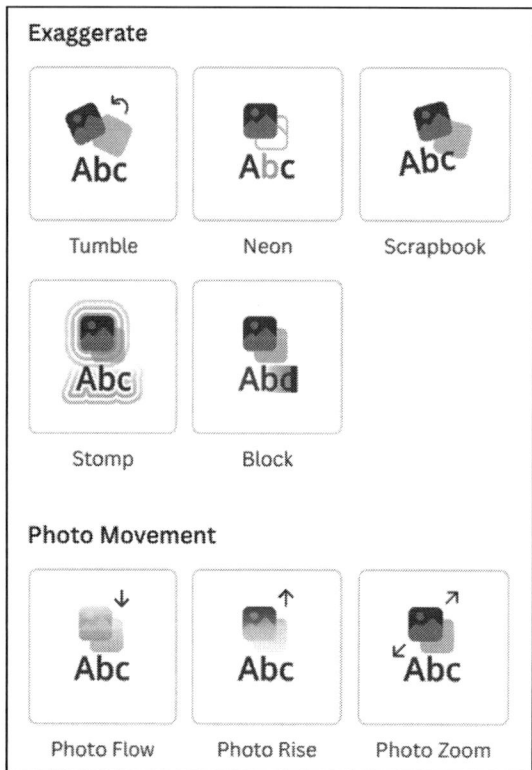

Figure 3.38

Once you apply an animation to an element or to a page, you will be shown a preview of how it will look. You can also click the play button at the upper right corner of the screen next to the Share button if you would like to see the animation again.

Figure 3.39

Some of the animations will have settings that can be adjusted such as the order the animation happens, the speed, the direction and so on. As you can see in Figure 3.40, some of the settings are for Pro accounts only. If you want to remove the applied animation, you can click the *Remove animation* button.

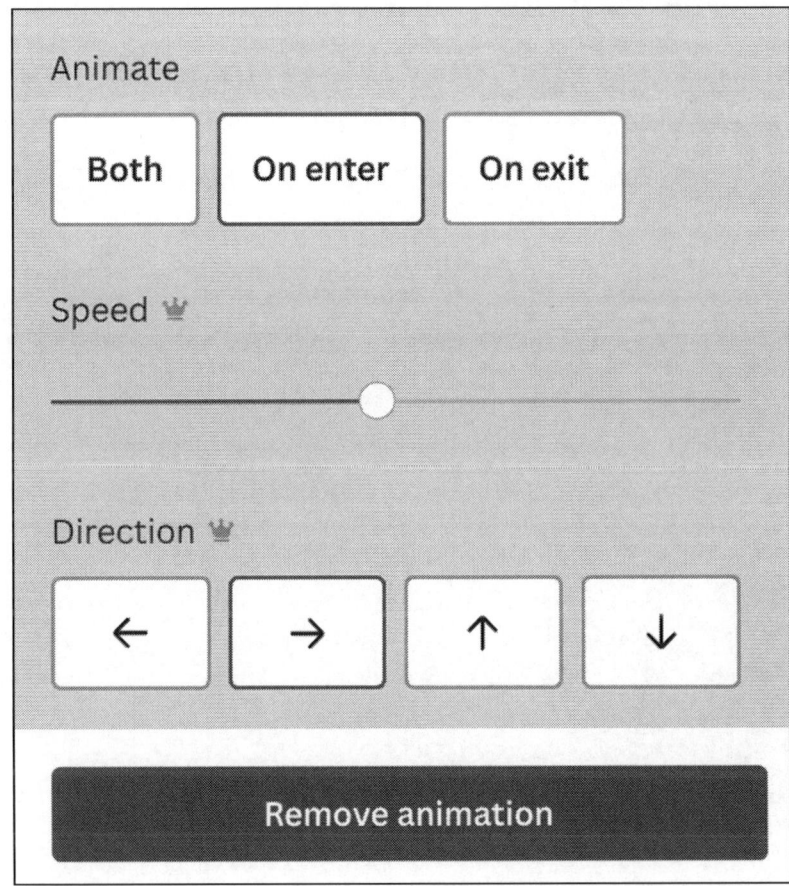

Figure 3.40

Canva has another nice feature where you can create your own animated path by dragging an object around the page to create a custom animation.

Create an Animation

Drag elements around the canvas to create your own animations.

Figure 3.41

Figure 3.42 shows that I have dragged the cake element around the page in the shape of a heart. Then once I release my mouse, that will set the path that the animation of the cake will follow.

Figure 3.42

After you apply a custom path, you can then make adjustments to how the element will move.

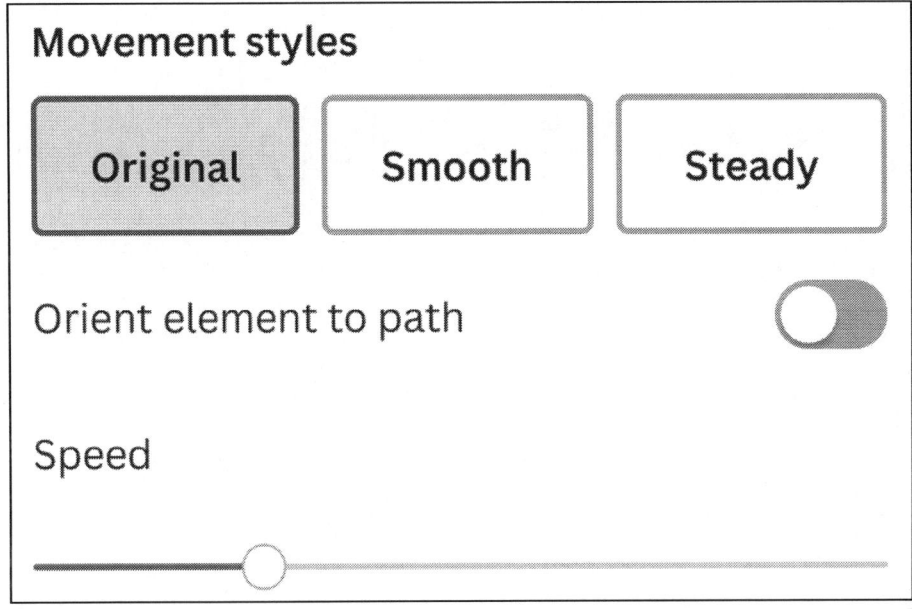

Figure 3.43

Since you cannot see the applied animations in a book, you will have to take my word for it when I say they look great!

When exporting or downloading animated designs, keep in mind that you will need to download them as a movie or animated GIF file in order to see the animations. I will be discussing the download process later in this chapter.

Creating a Presentation
One of the more commonly used designs of Canva is the presentation feature which is very similar to other presentation software such as PowerPoint and Slides. So if you have experience with those apps, you should be able to get the hang of the Canva version without any problems.

Just like with any other design, you can create a presentation from scratch or use one of the many built in templates that Canva offers. If you do go with a template, Canva will create the first slide for you and then give you the option to load all the other slides into your project as seen in Figure 3.44.

Figure 3.44

If you only want to use the first slide in the template, you can click on the + button to add another blank slide. Or you can click on the ellipses on the first slide and choose one of the options as seen in figure 3.45.

If your goal is to keep the current theme yet still create your own slides, you can choose the duplicate page option and then edit the new slide as needed.

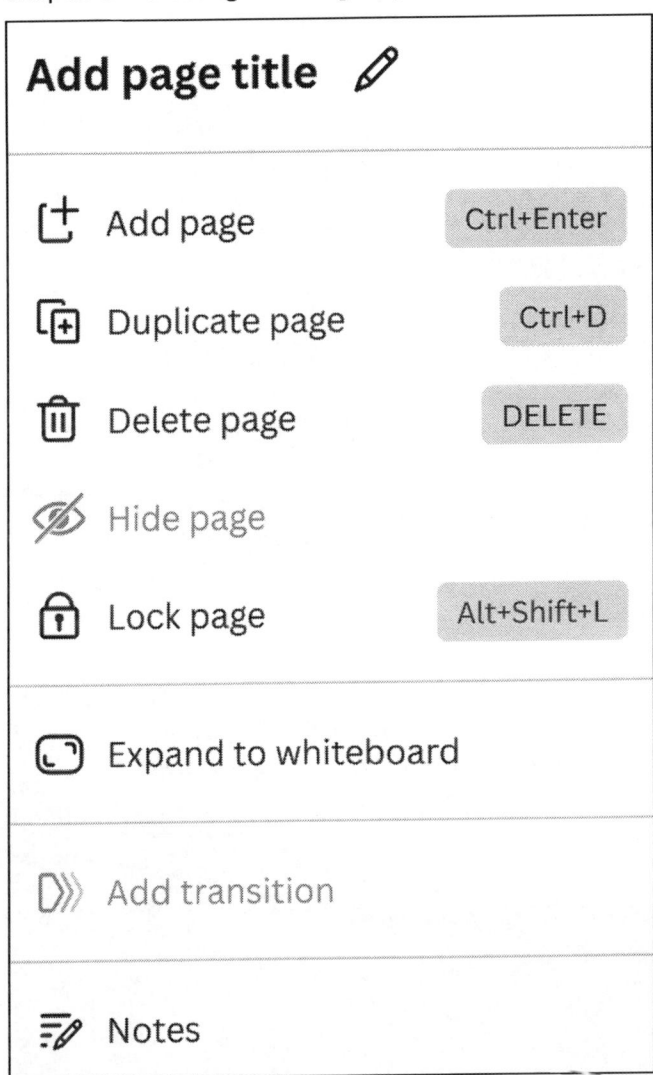

Figure 3.45

Once you click on an element such as text, graphics or photos, the toolbar at the top of the page will change accordingly to give you options based on the element you have selected. You can also toggle between the slides\pages by clicking the one you want to edit at the bottom of the page.

You can then add, remove or edit elements as needed to make the presentation fit your topic. You can also apply the same types of effects and animations to elements in a presentation just like you can with other types of projects.

Figure 3.46

At the bottom of the page, there is a button labeled *Duration* and when you click on it, you will then see a play button that you can click on to see how your slideshow will look regarding its timing. The default setting is to show each slide for 5 seconds but if you click on the time in the slide thumbnail, you can change it as seen in Figure 3.48.

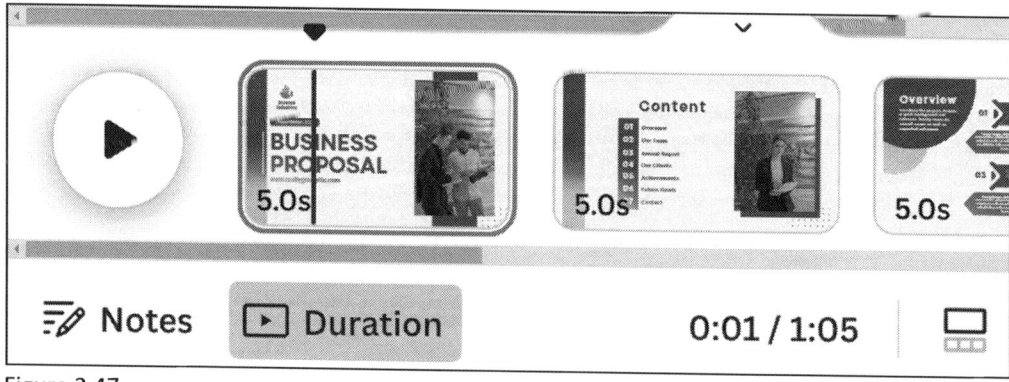

Figure 3.47

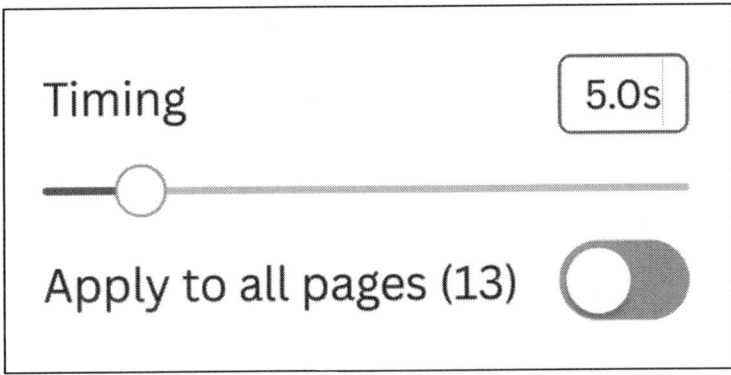

Figure 3.48

Once you have your presentation ready to go, you can then click on the *Present* button at the top right corner of the screen and choose how you want to present your slideshow.

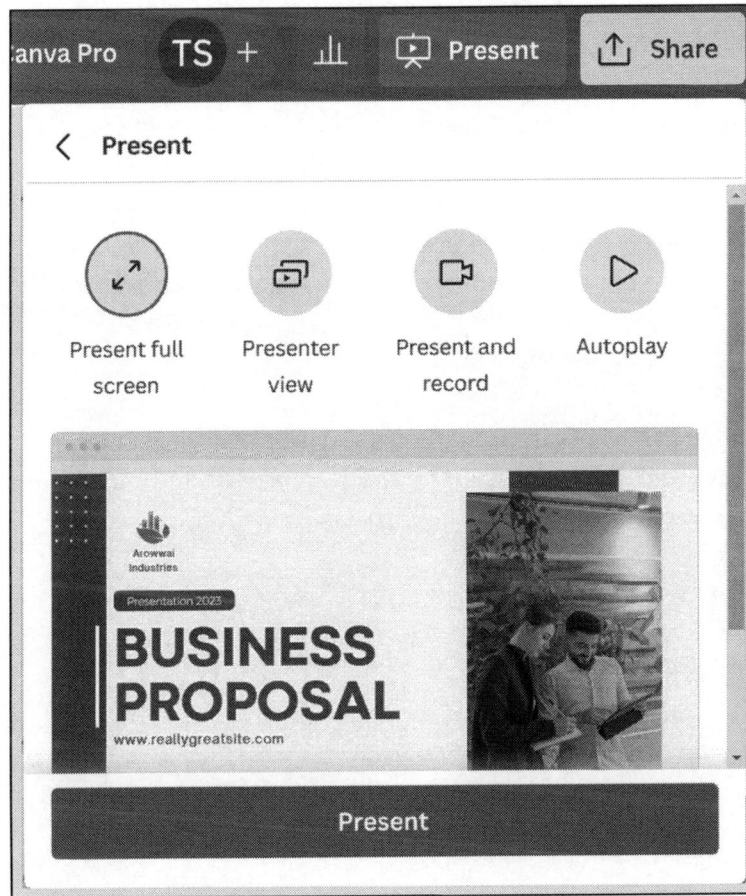

Figure 3.49

Present full screen will display your slides full screen and you can move between them using your mouse button or arrow keys on your keyboard. You can press the Esc key to exit presenter mode at any time.

Presenter view is used to show the slideshow on one screen that your audience will see and then you will have a separate screen where you can see things like your notes. This can be used when you are using a laptop with a projector or a separate monitor where you have two separate screens.

Present and record can be used to present your slideshow and make a recording of it at the same time. This way you can record your voice as you are discussing the slideshow and also record the screen as you navigate through the slides.

Autoplay is the process of having your slideshow play on its own and switch between the slides at the interval you select with the default being every five seconds.

Copying, Moving and Downloading Your Projects
Managing your projects is an important thing to know about since you will most likely be doing more than just creating and editing projects. In chapter 2, you learned about creating folders to help keep your projects organized, and in this section, I will take things to the next level and show you copy, move and download your projects.

Copying Projects
One reason you might have to copy your projects is so you can edit the copy while leaving the original intact. That way you do not need to worry about making any changes to the original that you might not be able to revert back to.

To make a copy of a project, simply find it in your list of projects and click on the ellipsis and choose *Make a copy*. If you have the project already open, you can go to the *File* menu and find the same option.

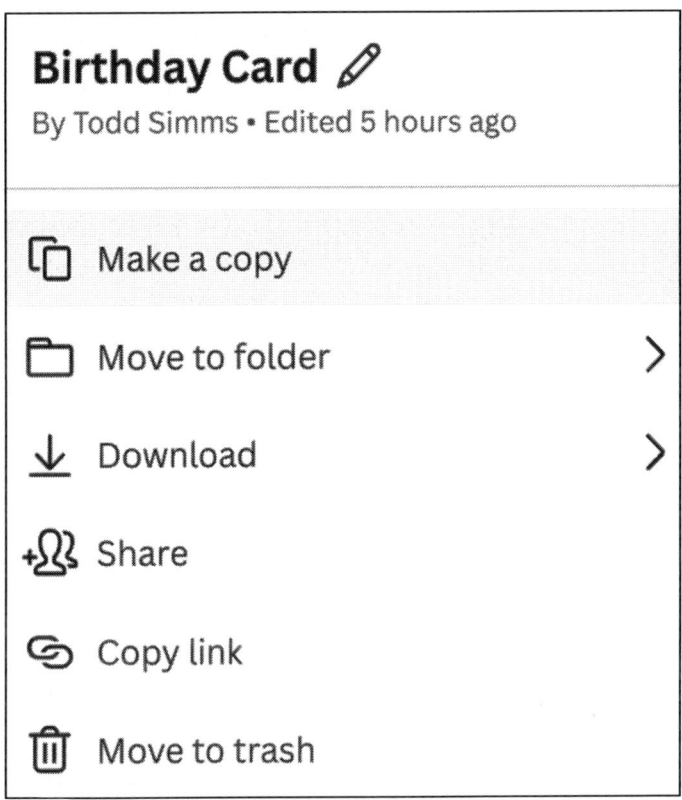

Figure 3.50

Once you click on Make a copy, you will not see anything happen or be asked to name your copied project but rather you will find a copy of your project with your other projects, and it will have the same name except it will have *Copy of* in front of it.

Copy of Birthday Card	--	4 x 6 in	a few minutes ago	•••
Green minimalist pro...	--	Presentation	4 hours ago	•••
Birthday Card	--	4 x 6 in	5 hours ago	•••

Figure 3.51

73

If you want to change the name of the copied project, you can click on the ellipses again and then change the name from there next to the pencil icon.

Moving a Project

If you want to keep your projects organized, you might find yourself wanting to move some existing projects into other folders so they are easier to keep track of. Since I made a copy of my birthday card project, I want to save it in a folder called Backups and maybe add other copied projects to this folder if needed.

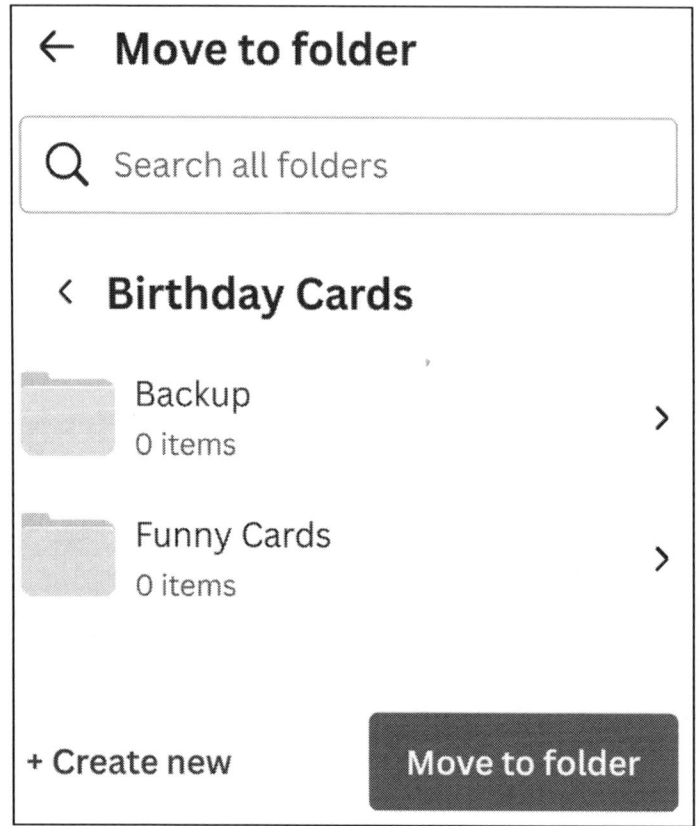

Figure 3.52

You can get to the *Move to folder* option from the same menu as you saw for the copy option but when you move a project, you get to choose where it is moved to. If you do not already have the folder created that you want to use, you can click on *Create new* to have a new folder added under the folder you are currently in. Then you can click the *Move to folder* button to have your project moved to the other folder. You will also get a popup message with an option to undo the move if you change your mind right away.

Figure 3.53

Downloading Projects

If you don't plan on sharing your designs with others via the sharing options that Canva offers, you can also download your projects in various formats so you can then use them with other applications or even email them to other people who don't have Canva accounts.

You will find the download option in the same place as you do the copy and move options. Once you click on Download, Canva will suggest a file type based on the attributes of your project. For example, since my birthday card now has animations, Cava will suggest that I download it as a video file so I will be able to see the animations when I open my file. If I click on the dropdown arrow, I can also choose other file formats such as animated GIF or JPG etc.

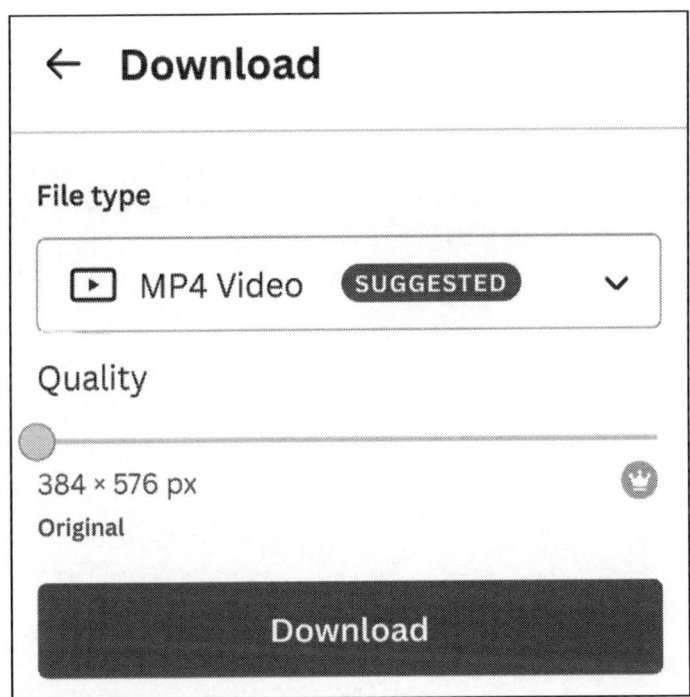

Figure 3.54

When I download my presentation, Canva suggests that I use the PDF format even though there is another option for a PPTX file which is a Microsoft PowerPoint document. So keep in mind that Canva might not always offer you the best suggestion for your download type.

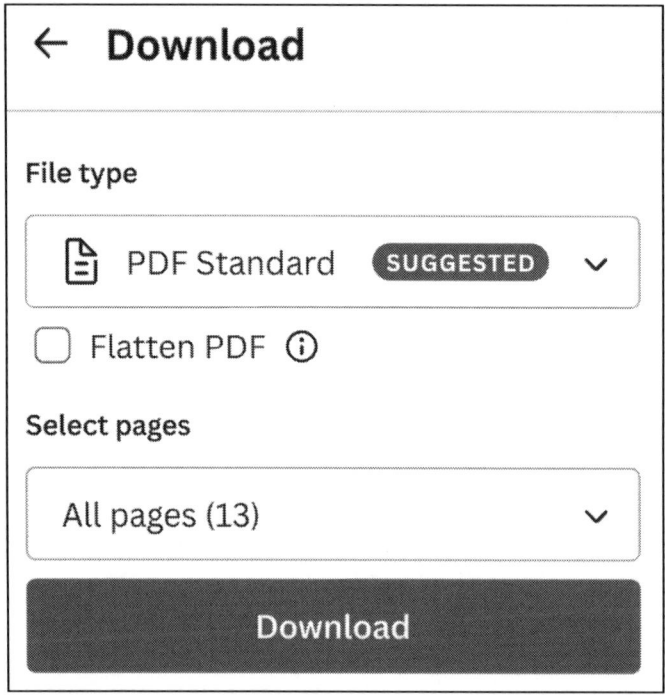

Figure 3.55

When you download a file, Canva may not ask you where you want to save it depending on the configuration of your web browser. If you are a Windows user, then you can check your Downloads folder to see if you can find it there. Figure 3.56 shows how my presentation project looks when saved as a PDF file and opened up with the Adobe Reader app.

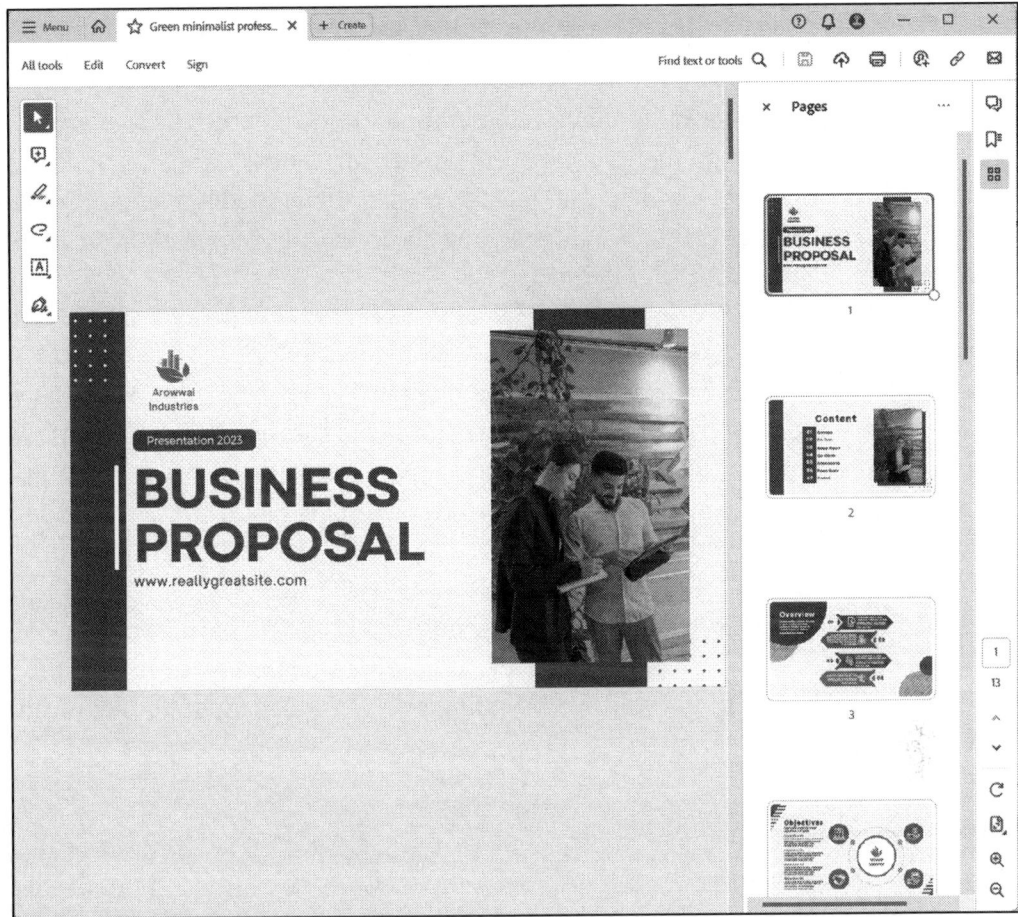

Figure 3.56

Chapter 4 - Sharing and Social Media

If you have had a smartphone for any period of time, then you know how everyone likes to share everything they do with everyone they know! And Canva is no different since a lot of its features are geared toward social media and sharing. In this chapter, I will show you some things you can do to get your work noticed by the world... or at least your friends.

Sharing

While working on your projects, you have most likely noticed the large Share button at the top of the page. This can be used to share your designs in multiple ways. You can share it with certain people and assign certain access levels, publish it on a website, share it on social media, save it to an online cloud storage account, send it via a messaging service and so on.

Figures 4.1 through 4.8 show all the sharing options you can use when you click on the Share button. As you can see, there are more ways to share your design than you ever thought possible! I will not be going over all these options but rather some of the more popular ones.

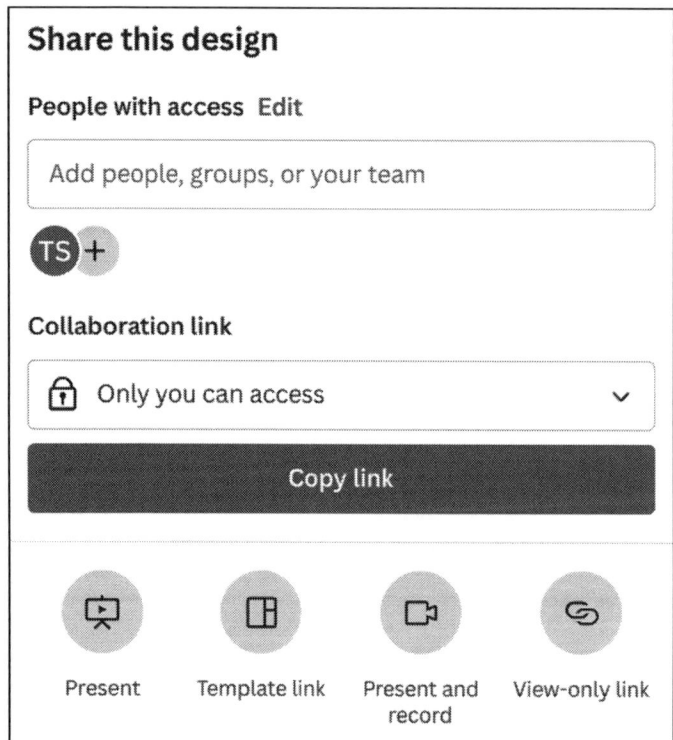

Figure 4.1

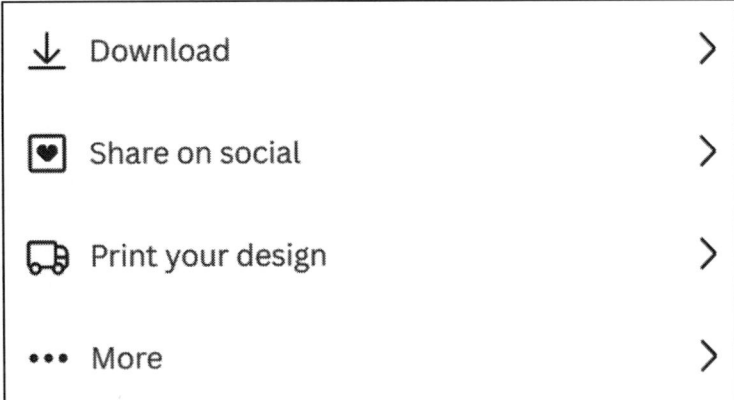

Figure 4.2

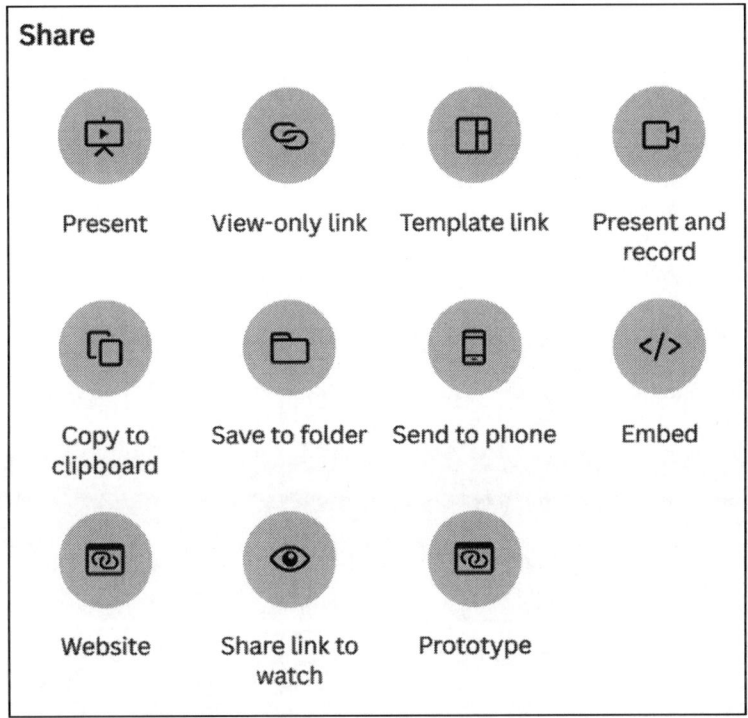

Figure 4.3

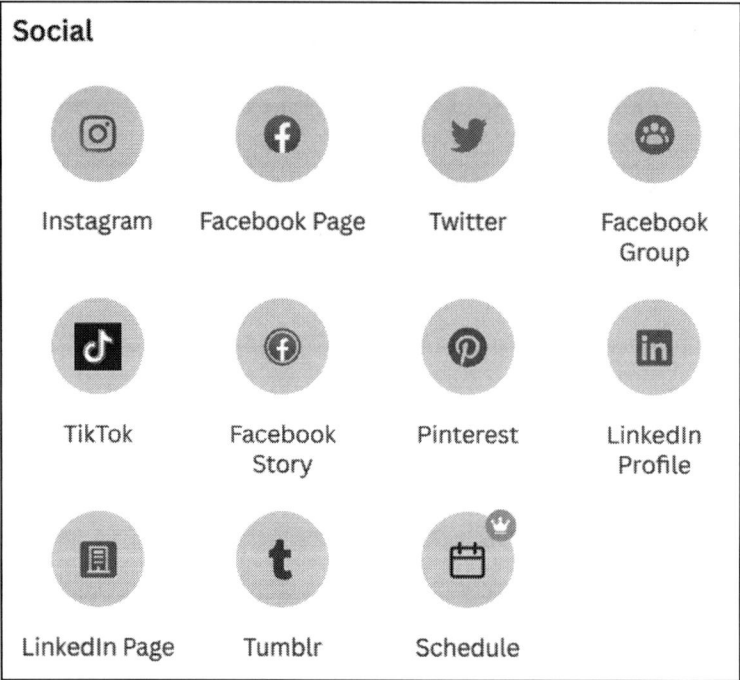

Figure 4.4

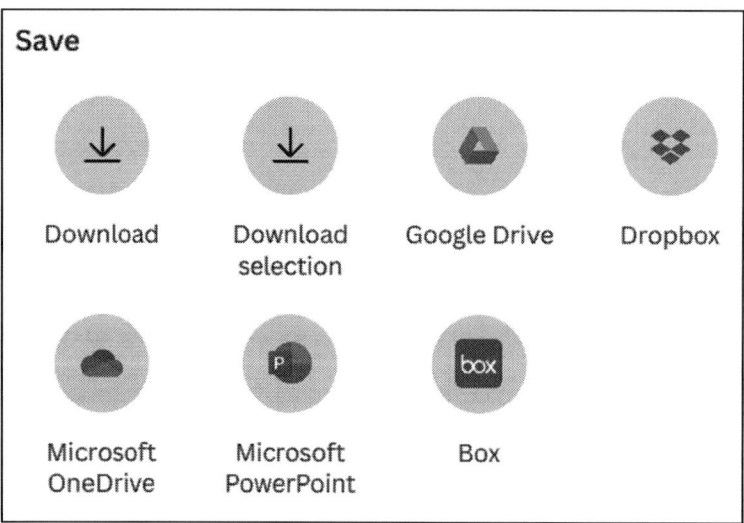

Figure 4.5

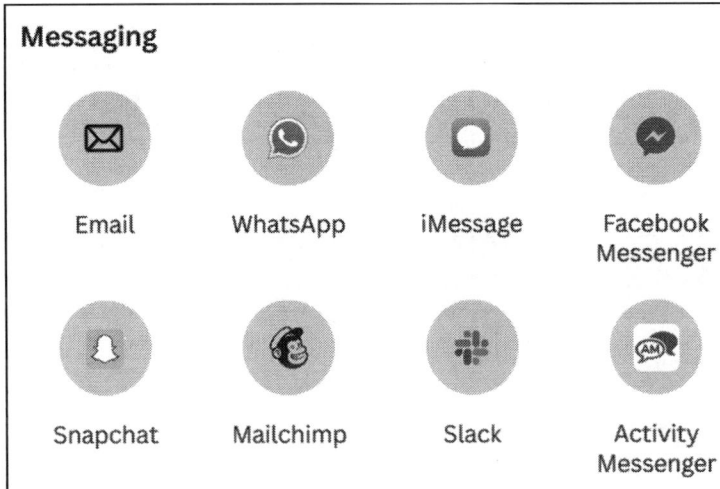

Figure 4.6

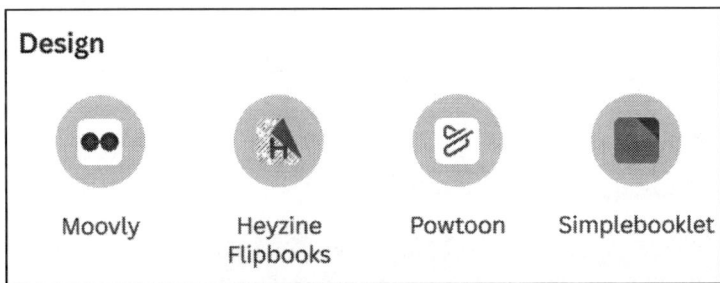

Figure 4.7

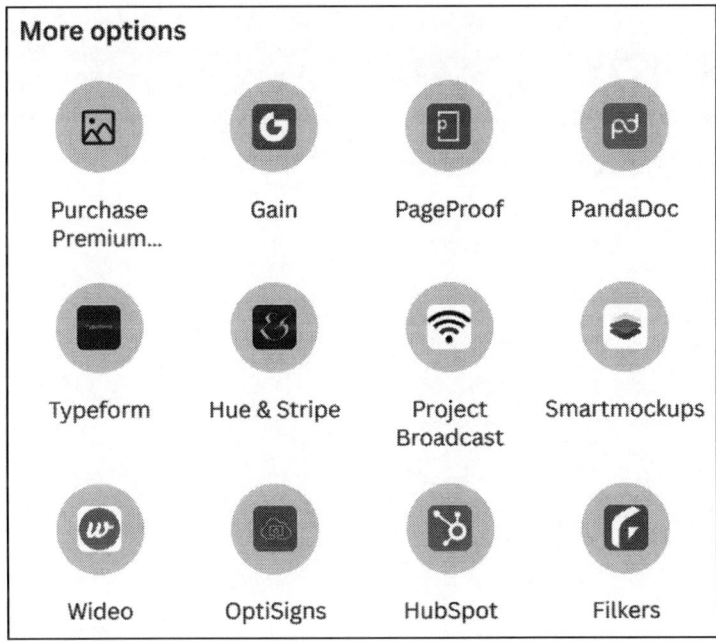

Figure 4.8

Many people like to share their work with specific people so one way you can do that is to use the first option and type in their email address in the *People with access* section. The default permission level is editor, but you can change that to commenter or viewer if needed. You can also add a personal note as shown in figure 4.9.

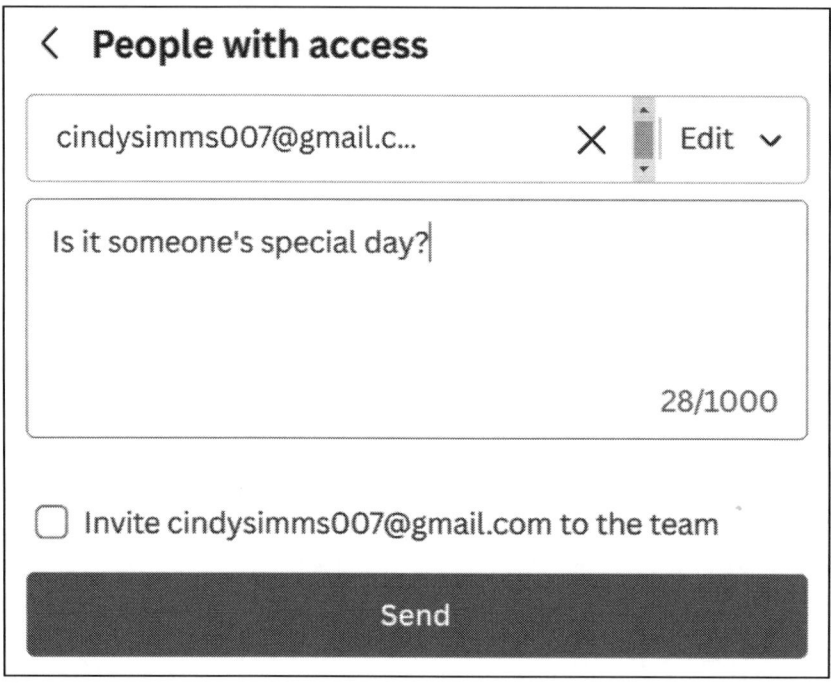

Figure 4.9

Once you send the invitation to view your shared project, you will then notice that the invited person will have their initial alongside yours and anyone else's that you have shared the design with if you go back to share it again.

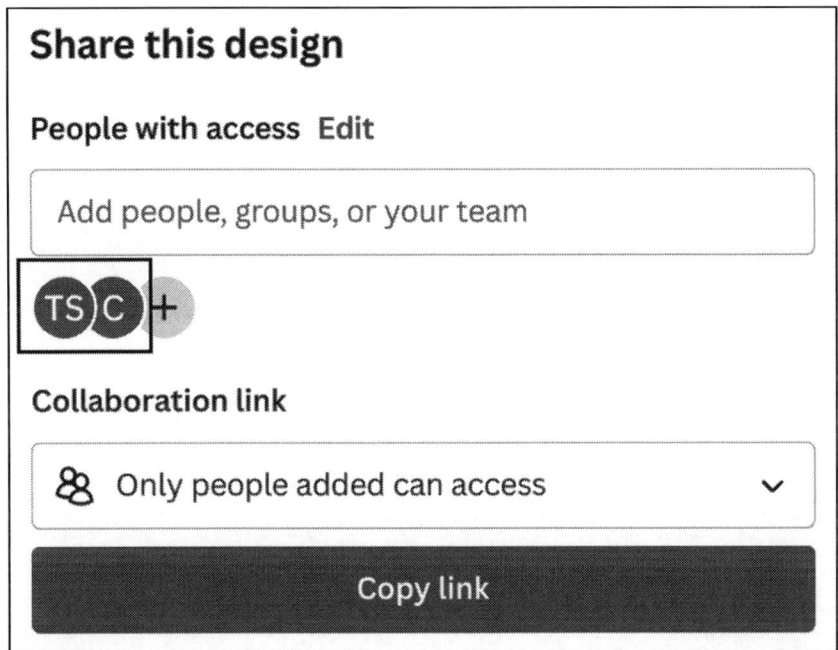

Figure 4.10

When the recipient receives the email, they will have a link to view the design in Canva (Figure 4.11). But if you left the access level set to *Only people added can access* as shown in Figure 4.10, they will not be able to view your design unless they have a Canva account.

Todd Simms would like you to take a look at the design titled "Birthday Card"

Is it someone's special day?

Todd Simms

Open in Canva

Figure 4.11

If you changed the access level to *Anyone with the link* and chose an access level of view, comment, or edit, then they would not need a Canva account to view your design. They will still most likely get prompted to sign up for an account but that can be bypassed and then they can go directly to the design.

At any time, you can go back to the sharing settings and click on *Edit* to change what level of access they have as seen in figure 4.12. You will also notice under Cindy's email address that it says *Pending invitation* because she has not signed up to view the design yet.

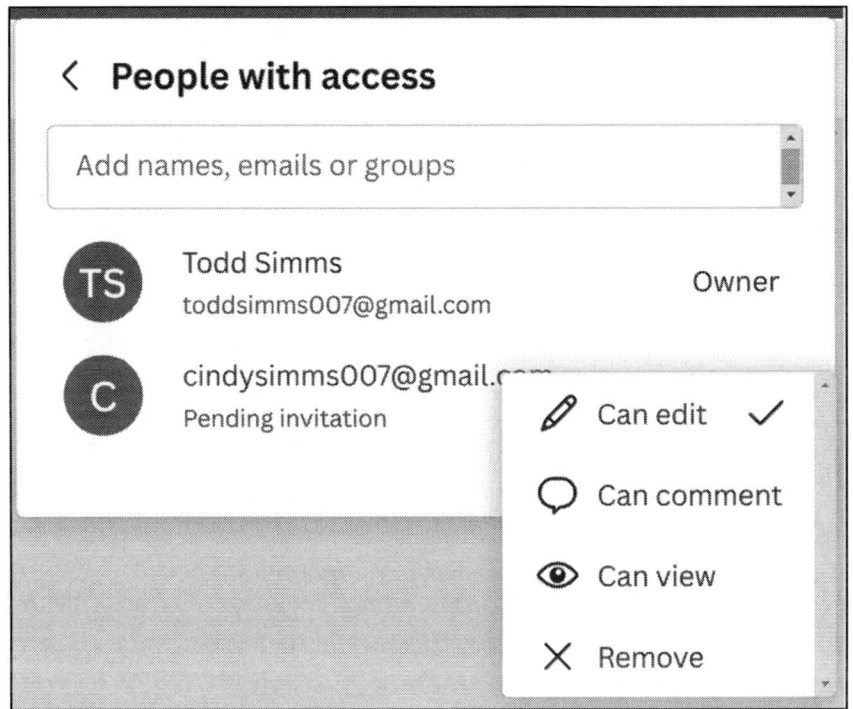

Figure 4.12

Another great sharing option that Canva offers is the ability to share your project as a template. That way others can take advantage of all the hard work you put into your design and then use it for their own projects. Once you click the *Template link* button, you will be presented with a link that you can copy and send off to others and they will be able to open it in Canva. They will need to have a Canva account to use shared templates though.

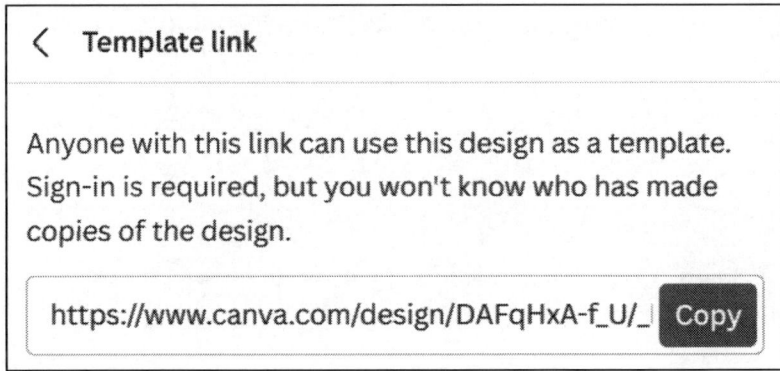

Figure 4.13

View only links are a great way to quicky share your work with anyone since all you need to do is create the link and send it out to as many people as you like. Then these people can view your design without needing a Canva account.

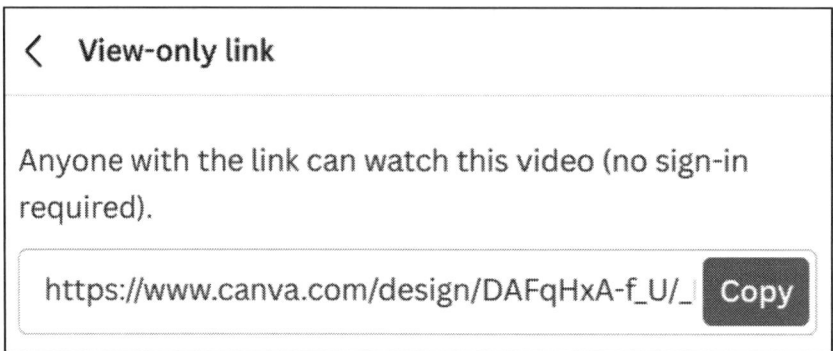

Figure 4.14

One sharing option you might find handy is the *Share as website* choice. When using this option, you will have several ways to share your project as a website. Figure 4.15 shows my presentation project as a web page with back and forward buttons as well as emojis that can be added to my slides.

Figure 4.15

Figure 4.16 shows the web page with navigation options that can be at the top of the page or over at the right side and clicking on any of the selections will take the viewers to the matching slide.

Figure 4.16

One of the other share options that I want to discuss is not really related to sharing but it is an option you will find when clicking on the Share button. If you scroll down to the *Save* section, you will find several choices to save your project to the major cloud storage platforms such as Google Drive, Dropbox, OneDrive and Box.

The first time you use one of these options, you will need to connect your Canva account to your cloud account to give it permission to access your files. Then once you choose the cloud sharing platform you want to save your project to, you will be able to browse your folders and save it to the one you want (Figure 4.17).

Then you can technically share your project from your cloud storage account just like you would any other file that you have stored there.

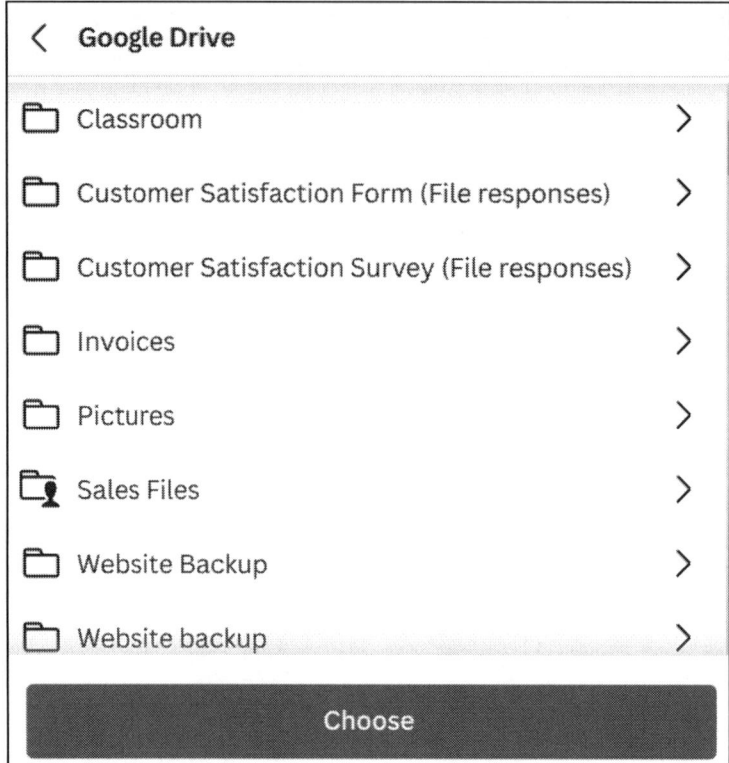

Figure 4.17

Social Media Templates

One of the main types of projects that people use Canva for is creating designs for social media accounts. Canva has templates for the more popular social media platforms such as Facebook, Instagram and LinkedIn but can also help you create designs for other platforms such as WhatsApp and YouTube as well.

If you go to the Social Media section in Canva, you will see design ideas and templates for these types of accounts which will allow you to easily create professional looking designs for your posts. And of course, you can always search for the social media platform you are looking to make a design for.

Figures 4.18 through 4.20 show some examples of what you will find when browsing the social media templates. Then if you decide to use one of them, you can simply open it and edit it just like any other template. Figure 4.20 shows how you can apply filters to your results to narrow them down so you can find what you are looking for.

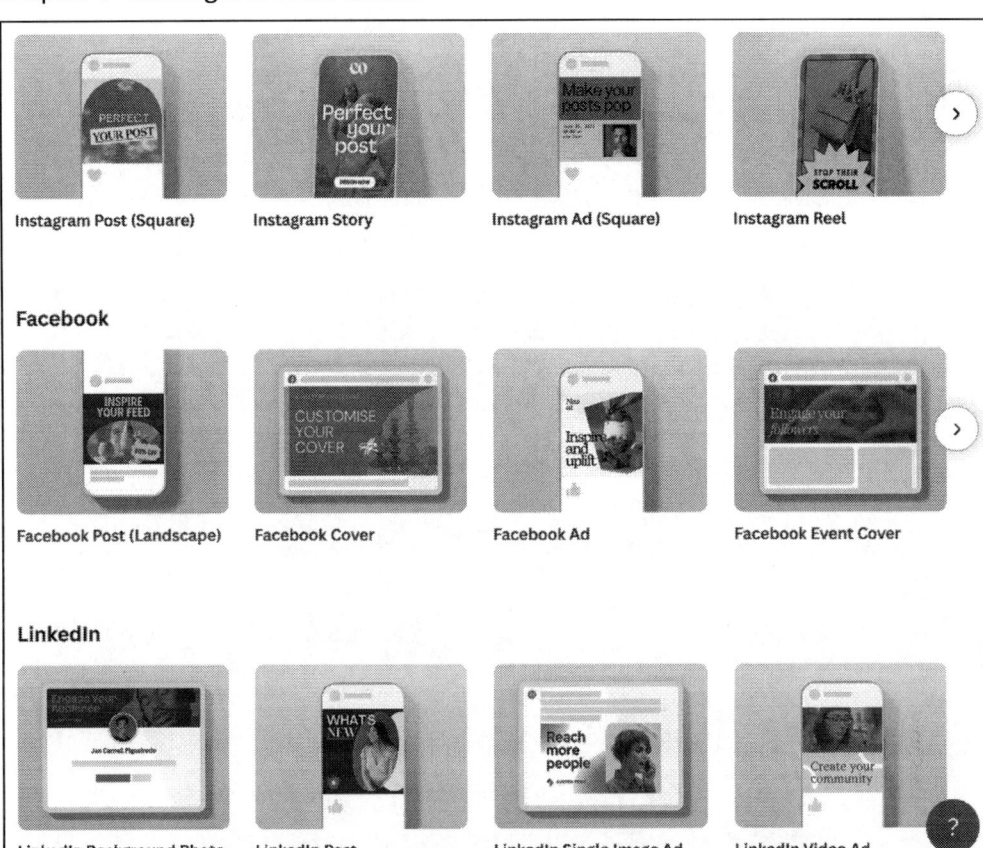

Figure 4.18

Figure 4.19

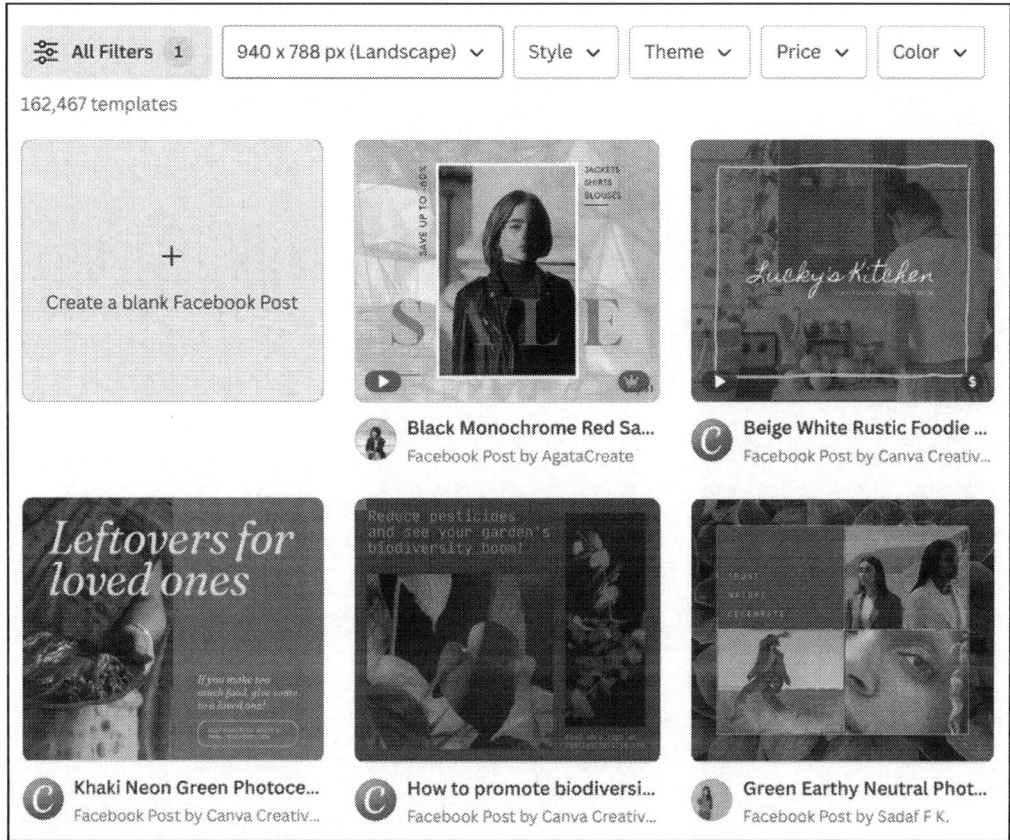

Figure 4.20

Connecting Social Media Accounts for Posting

When you create a design for a social media post, you can download it as whatever type of file you need and then upload or post it to your social media account like you would any other photo or video. Or you can link your social media account to your Canva account so you can post right from Canva itself.

I designed a quick Facebook post about my Hawaii vacation as seen in Figure 4.21 and rather than download it from Canva and then upload it to Facebook, I will link Canva and Facebook so I can post directly from Canva as needed. This is a one-time process so once it's complete, you will not need to go through it again, unless of course you are linking to a different social media account such as LinkedIn for example. Just keep in mind that the process for linking to social media accounts will vary depending on which one you are trying to connect to.

Figure 4.21

To connect to my Facebook account, I will click on the *Share* button and as you can see in Figure 4.22, it recognized that I was using a Facebook template so it gives me a *Facebook Page* option right at the top, so I do not need to go find it within all the possible options.

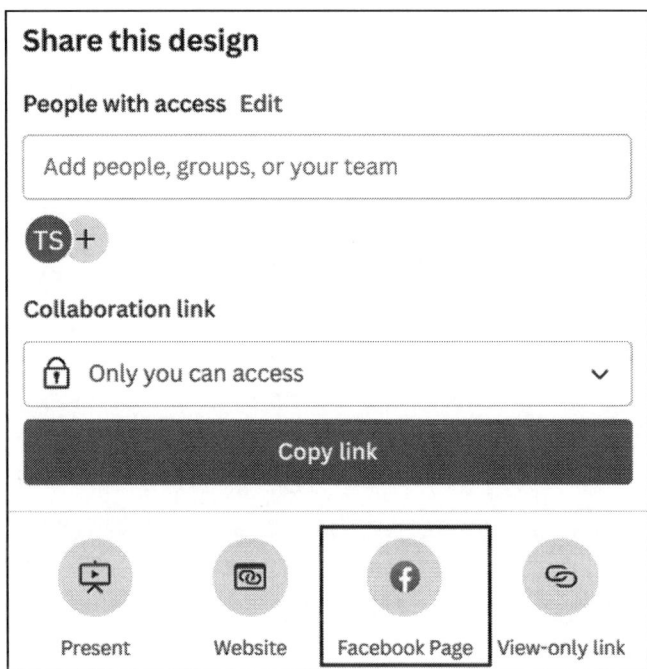

Figure 4.22

Next, I will click on the *Connect Facebook* button that appears on the next screen.

Figure 4.23

If I am not logged into my Facebook account, I will be prompted to do so.

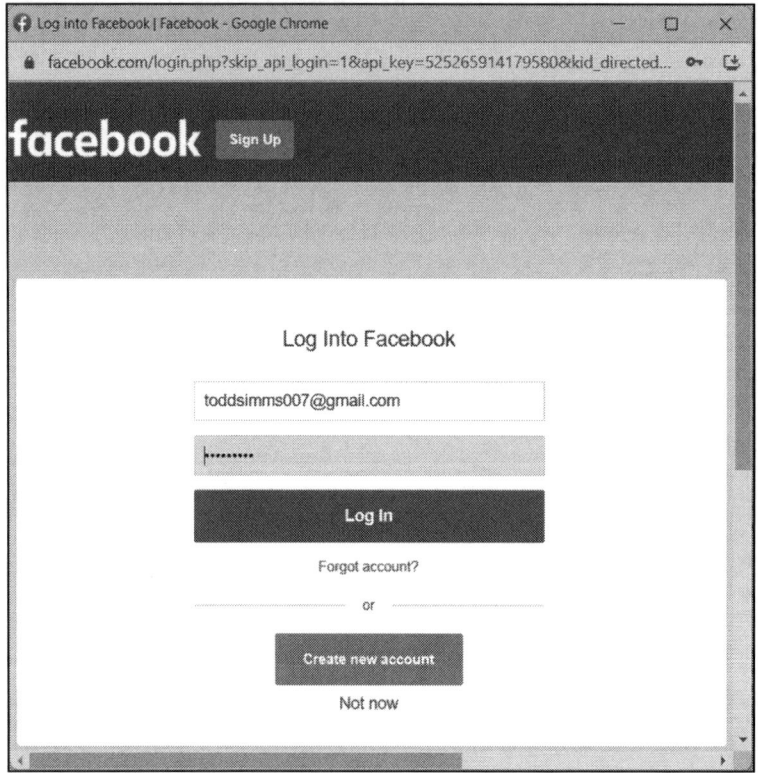

Figure 4.24

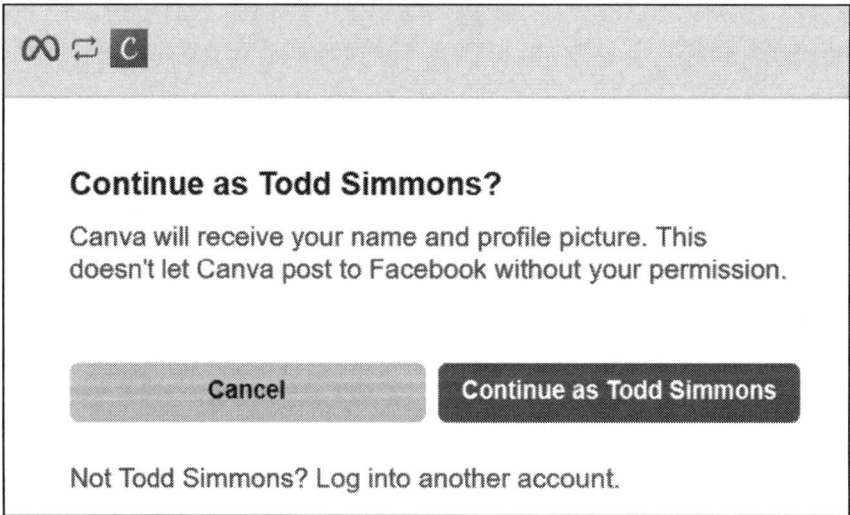

Figure 4.25

Canva will then want to know what page you want to post this on. If you do not have any pages configured in your Facebook account, you can continue but you might get a message saying Canva doesn't have enough information to connect to your Facebook account. You can also click the *Create a Page* button and make a page to post your design on.

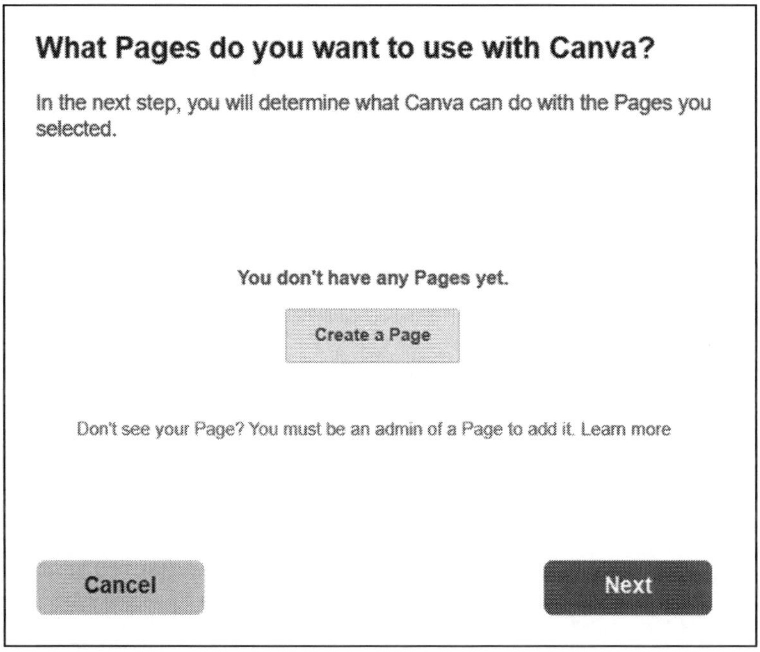

Figure 4.26

Once you decide what page you want to connect to your Canva account, you can select it from the next screen.

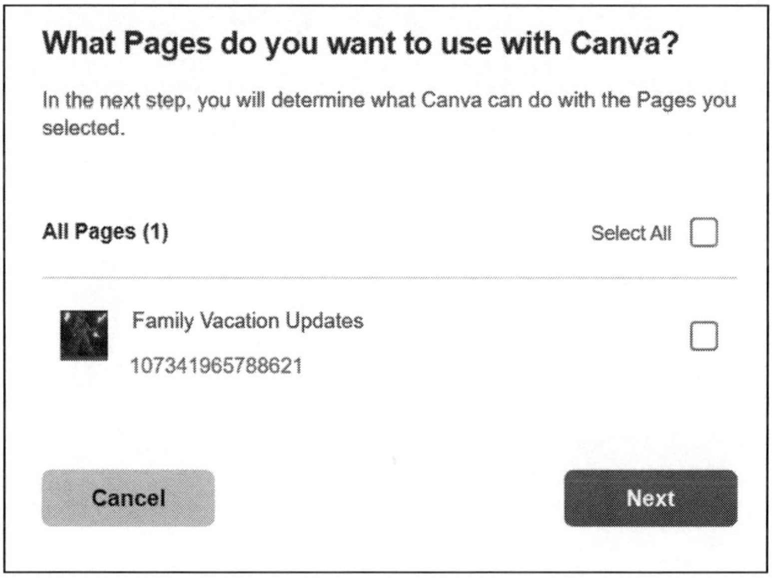

Figure 4.27

Then you will need to decide what permissions you want to give Canva regarding posting to your Facebook account.

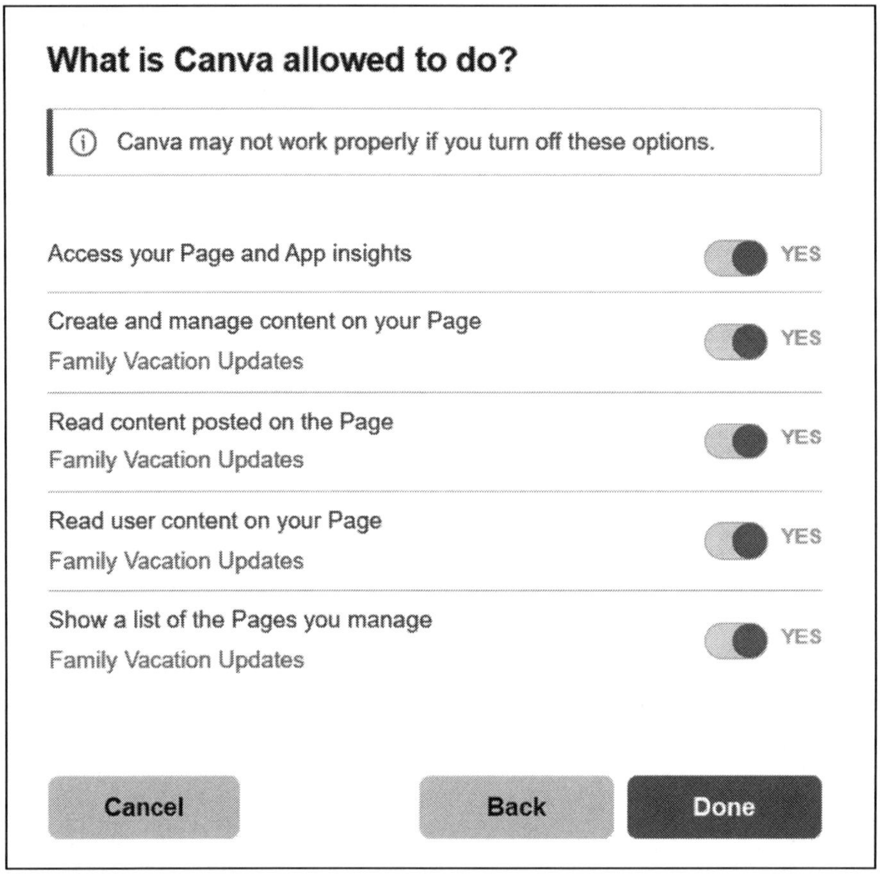

Figure 4.28

Once the connection is complete, you should see a message telling you that things are ready, and you may have a link that will take you to your Facebook settings if you need to edit any permissions or even remove the connection from your account (Figure 4.30).

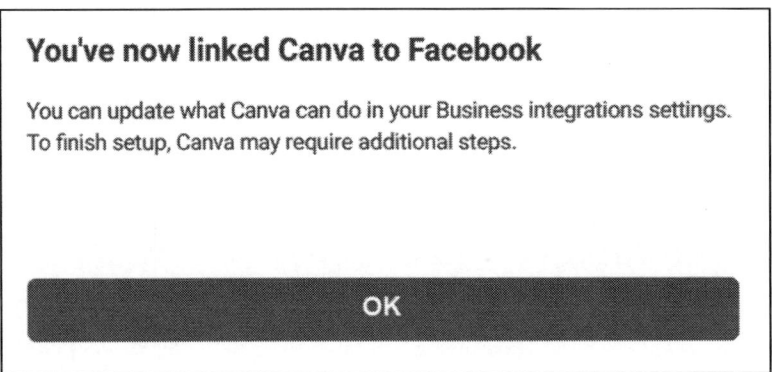

Figure 4.29

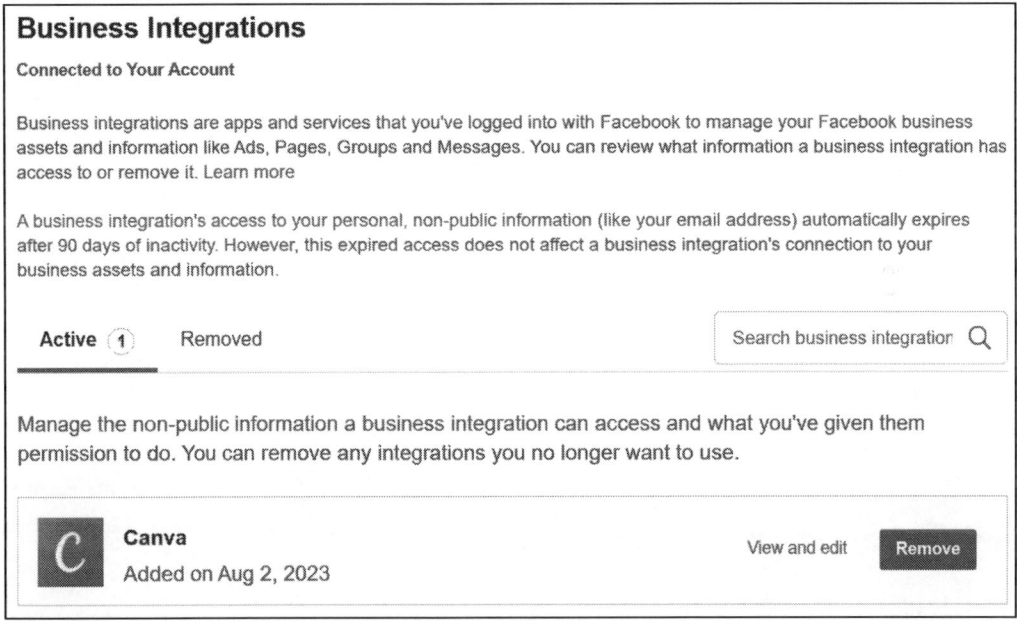

Figure 4.30

Next, I will choose the page that I have added the connection for from the list of available pages (I just have the one). You can also add another Facebook account from this section if you have a Pro account.

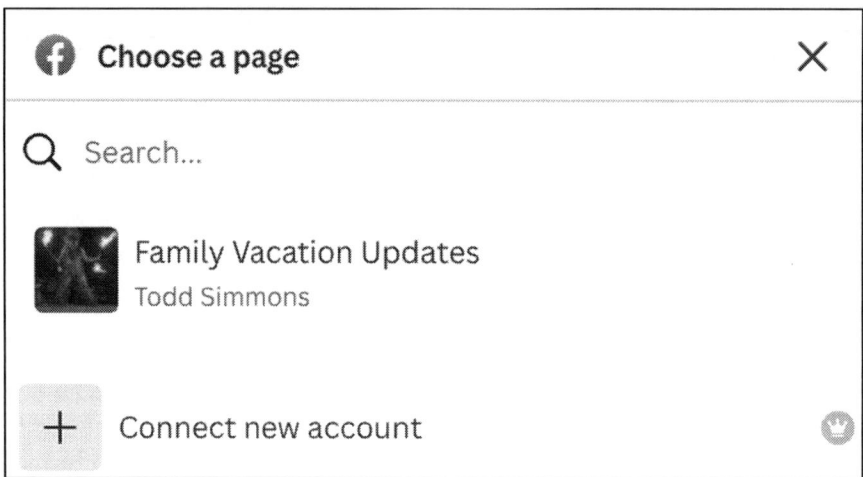

Figure 4.31

When you choose the page you want to post on, you can also add a message to the post which will appear on your Facebook page.

Figure 4.32

Then you should get a message telling you that your post was published. You will also have buttons to see your post or view your post history.

Figure 4.33

Figure 4.34 shows how my post looks after it is on my Facebook page.

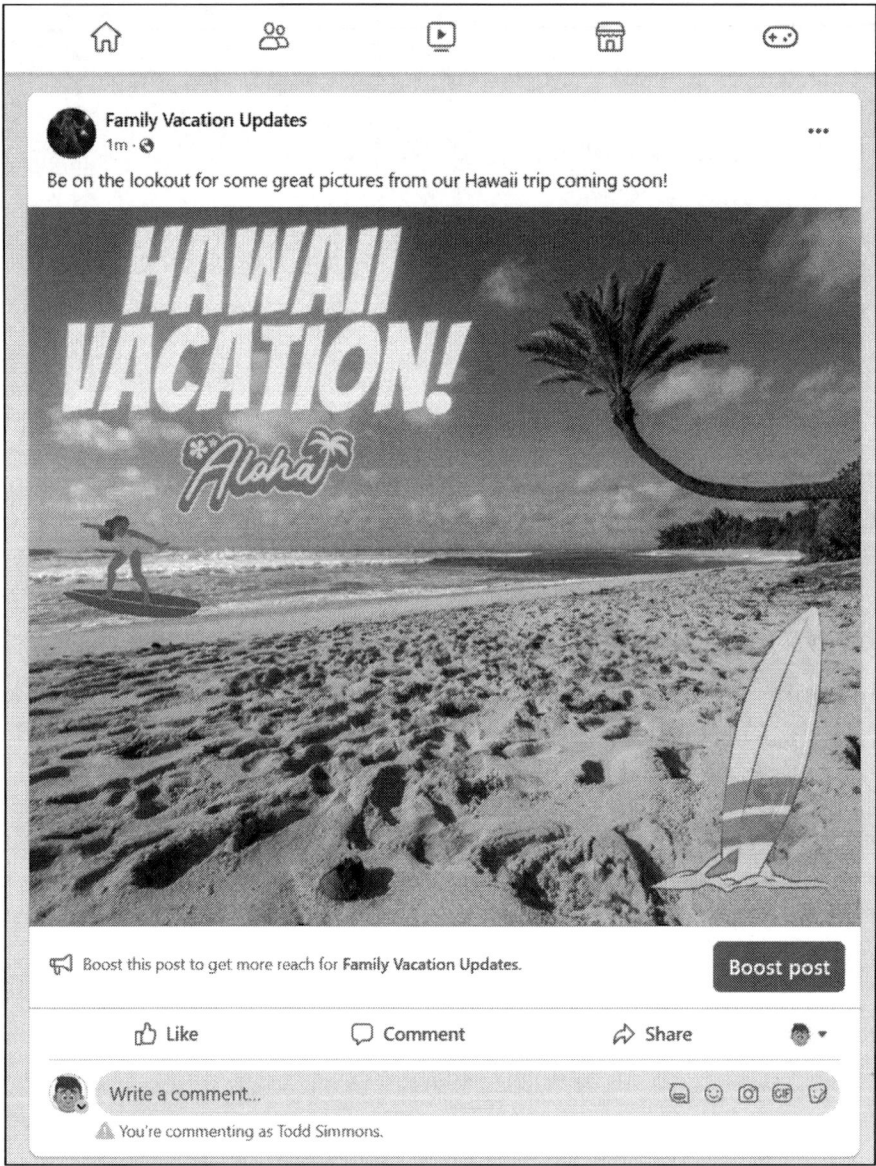

Figure 4.34

Canva Whiteboard

Another handy feature that you can use with Canva is their online whiteboard tool. This allows you to create whiteboards that are accessible to anyone that you share them with. Then they can view your whiteboard in real time and even participate by adding their own content.

One of the best features of the Canva whiteboard is that there are no limits to its size. So, you never have to worry about running out of space because it will keep growing as you add more content.

If you don't want to create your whiteboard from scratch, you can use one of the available templates designed specifically for whiteboards.

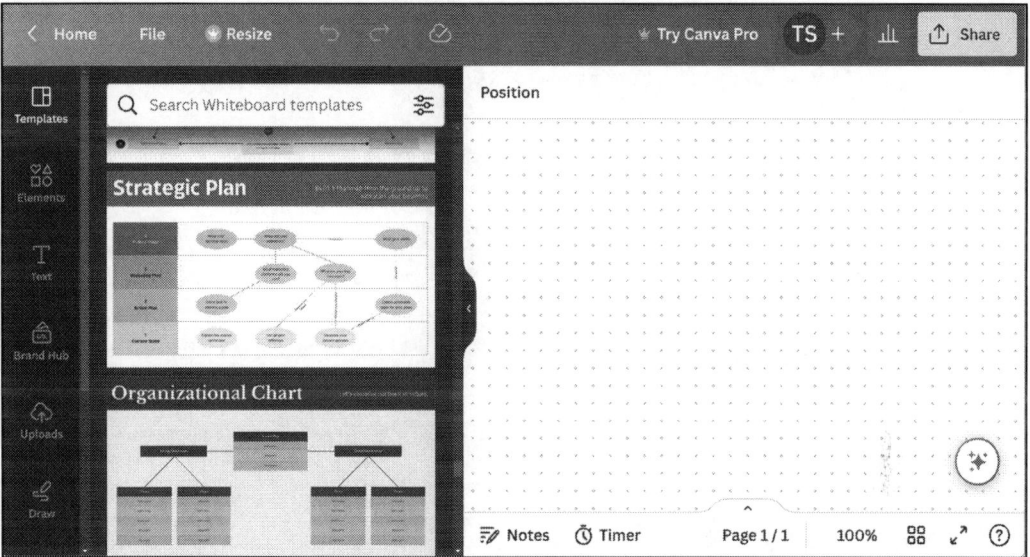

Figure 4.35

You will also notice that when you go to the Elements section on the left, you will find whiteboard specific graphics and other objects that you can use with your new project.

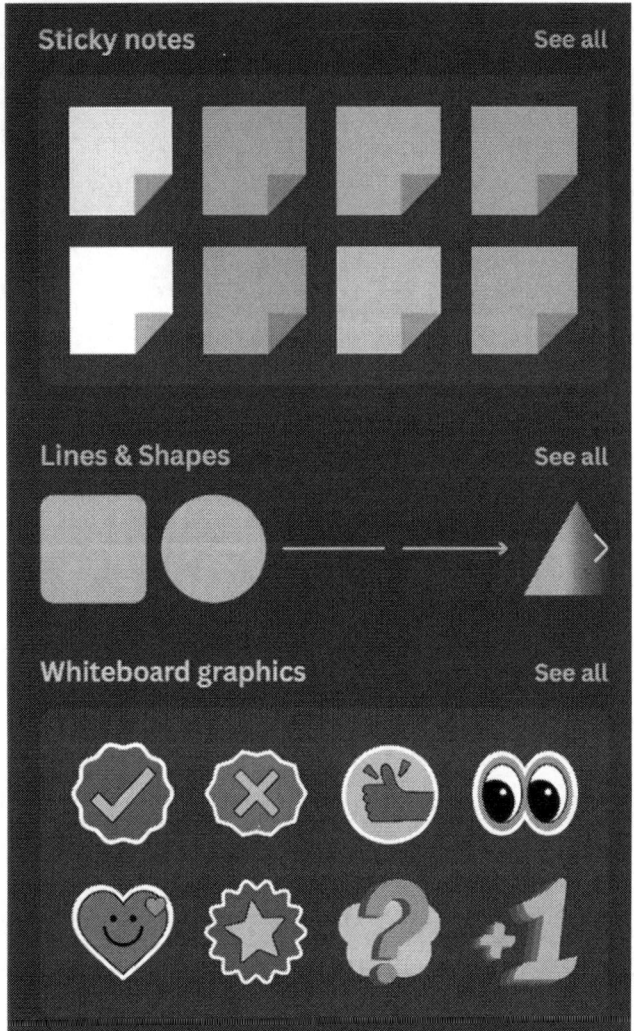

Figure 4.36

To allow others to view your whiteboard, all you need to do is share it by adding the email addresses of the people you want to see it, or you can create a link so those without Canva accounts can participate as well.

Once you have multiple people viewing your whiteboard, any changes that are made will be displayed with that person's initials next to the object that was changed.

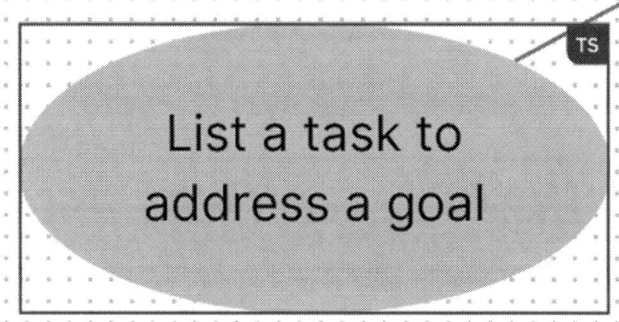

Figure 4.37

If you ever see any animal icons rather than initials or profile pictures at the top of the page, this means that there are people viewing your project that do not have Canva accounts or are not signed in.

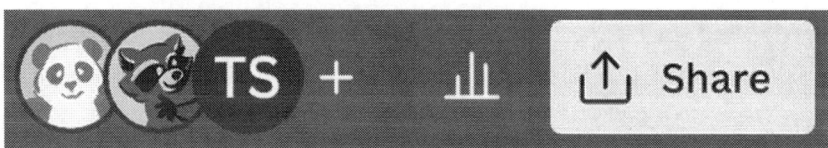

Figure 4.38

If you want to see what a particular person is doing on your whiteboard, all you need to do is click on their profile picture, initials, or animal icon to be taken to the area on the whiteboard where they are working and then your screen will follow them until you tell it to stop. Also, when you are hosting the whiteboard, you should be able to see other participants' mouse movements with their name (or animal) as they move around your whiteboard.

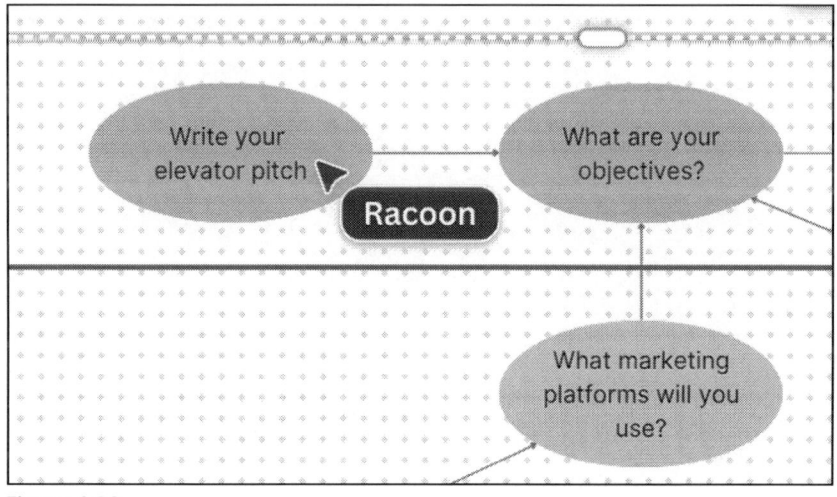

Figure 4.39

When other people join your shared whiteboard session, you will get a brief popup on your screen telling you who has joined.

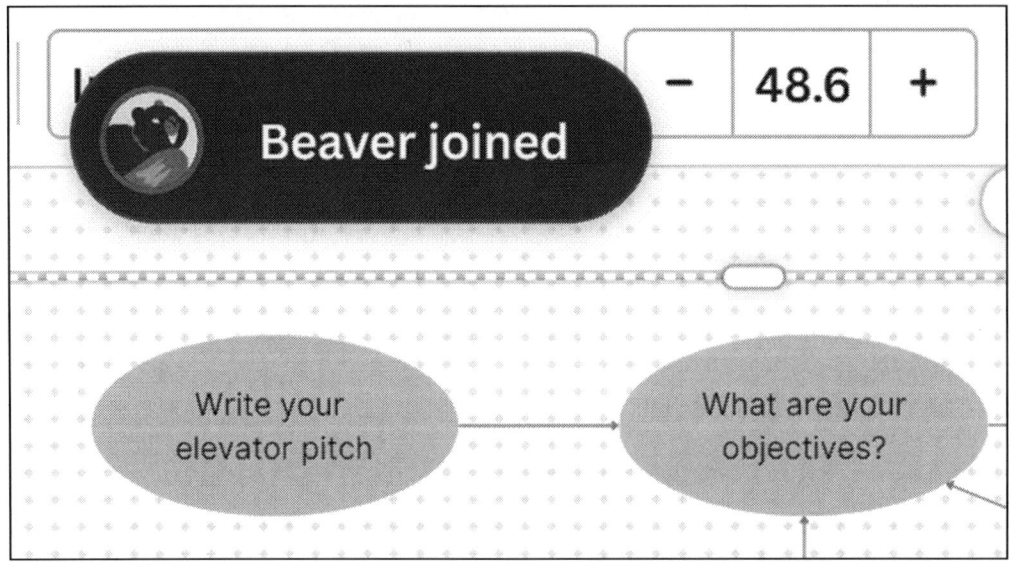

Figure 4.40

Using Comments

When you are working with shared projects, you have the ability to add comments to do things such as help the people you are collaborating with see your ideas or changes that you might want to suggest to them. You can even assign tasks to another Canva user via a comment.

You probably have noticed the speech bubble icon at the upper right corner of the page while in a project. This is what you would click on to add a comment to that specific page.

Figure 4.41

Once you click on the comment button, you can add a general comment for everyone to see or you can start typing the @ symbol and then someone's name to direct a comment to a specific person as shown in figure 4.43.

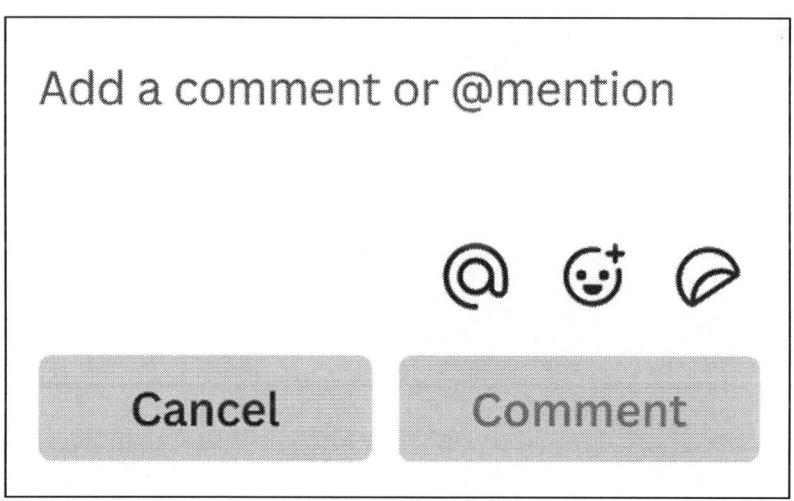

Figure 4.42

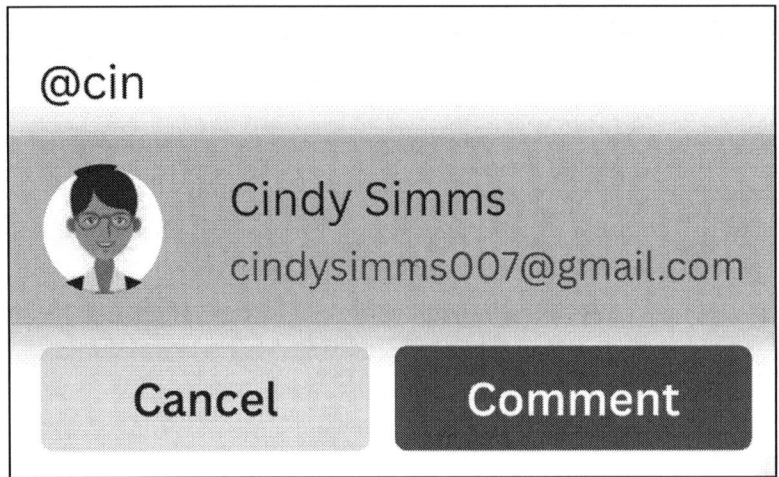

Figure 4.43

You can also add emojis and stickers in your comments to convey how you feel about them or simply to add a fun touch to them.

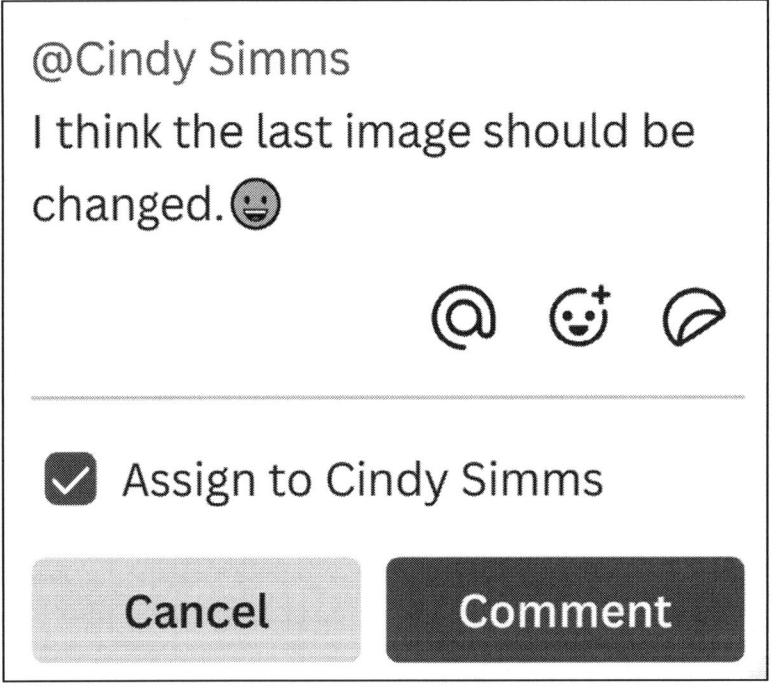

Figure 4.44

When you direct a comment toward a specific person, they will receive a notification in their Canva account at the top of the page.

Figure 4.45

They can then see the comment and then click on it to take action on it if needed.

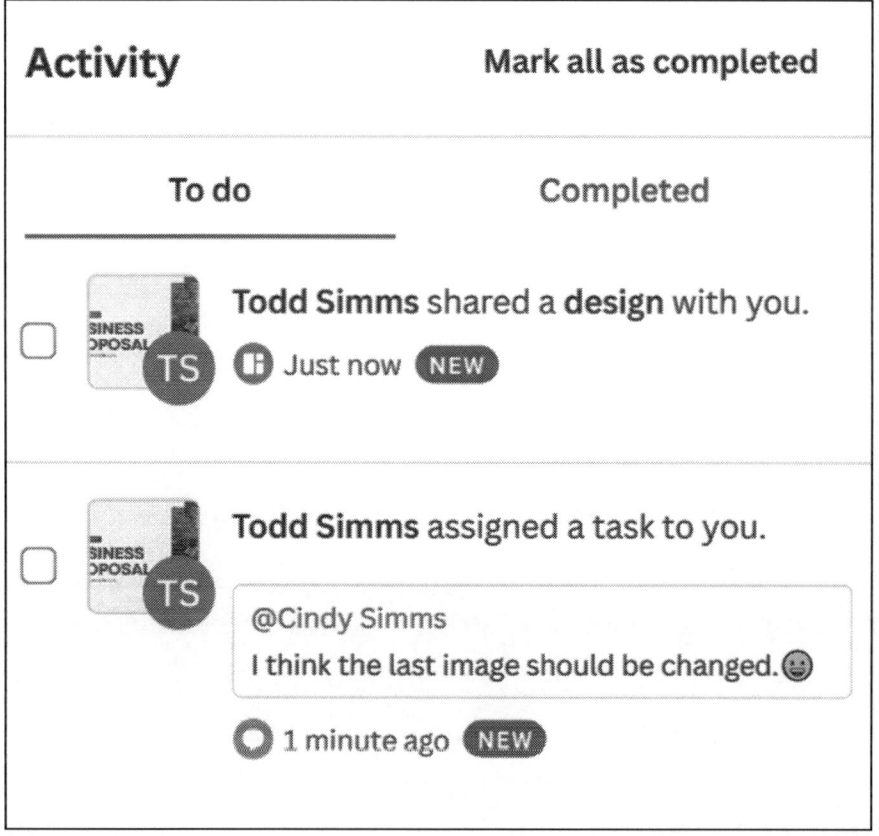

Figure 4.46

When a comment is assigned to a person, they will have a *Resolve Comment* check mark that they can click on to mark it as resolved. They can also add their own comment to your comment if needed.

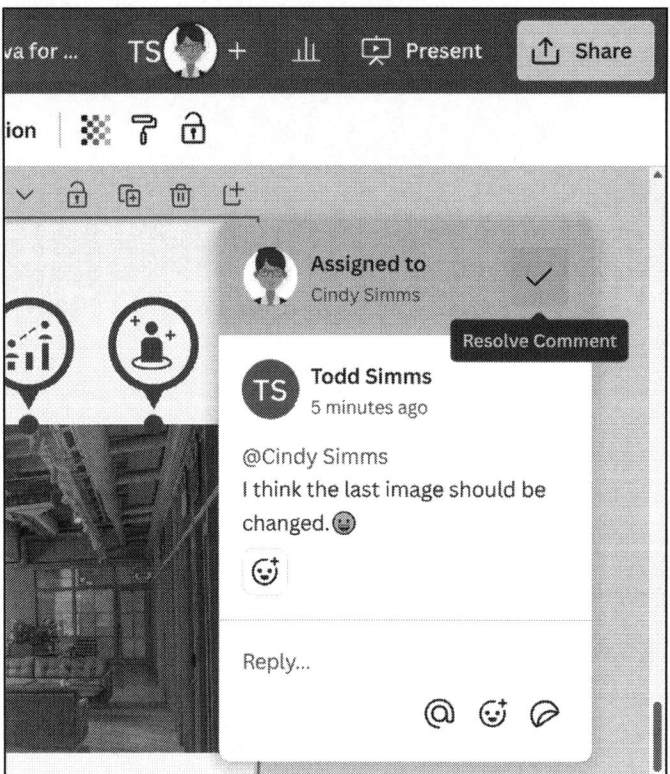

Figure 4.47

Once they mark the comment as resolved, you will then get a notification letting you know that it's complete.

Figure 4.48

Chapter 5 – Photo, Video and PDF Editors

Not only can you create designs for virtually any application in Canva, but you can also edit existing items such as photos, videos and PDF files using the built in editing tools that come included with the Canva app.

Using the Photo Editor
Canva has a built in photo editor that can be used on a photo that is already in a project or on one that you have in your uploads or even stored on your computer. If you go to the Canva photo editor upload webpage, you can simply upload a photo from your computer right into the editor.
https://www.canva.com/photo-editor/

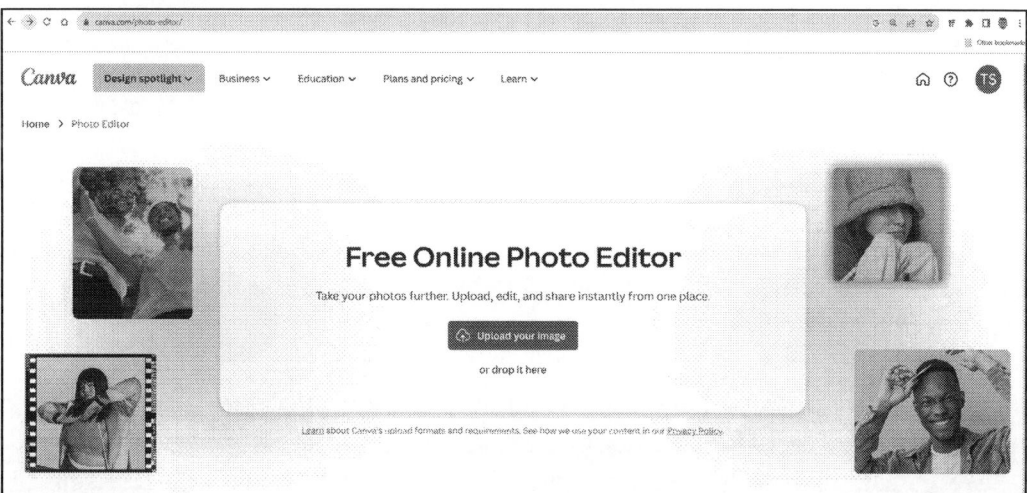

Figure 5.1

After uploading your photo, it will be opened in the Canva photo editor where you can make edits using the effects, adjustments and cropping tools as seen in Figures 5.2 through 5.4.

After you make your edits, you can click on the *Use in a design* button to have your edited photo opened in a new Canva project and then you can use it just like any other project you have worked on before. There is also a *Save* button which will have a download option to let you save your changes as a file on your computer.

The *Effects* section is broken down into three categories labeled Tools, Filter and Effects. You will notice that the background remover and magic eraser tools are for the Pro versions of Canva so you will not be able to use them on the free version.

109

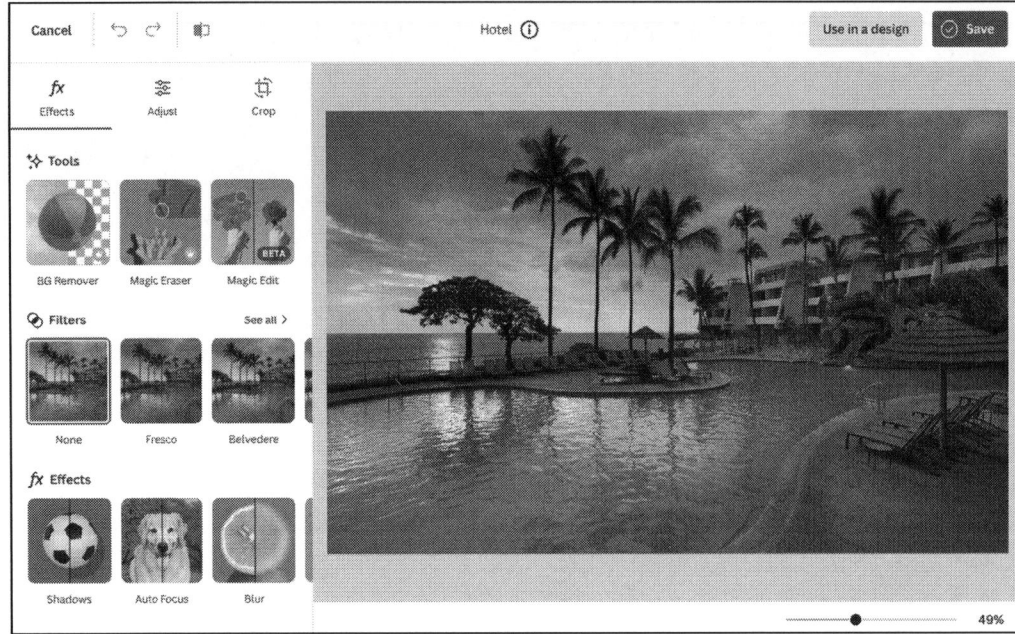

Figure 5.2

At the top of the photo editor, you will also find an undo and redo button if you want to revert any changes you have made. The *Compare* button is used to toggle back and forth between the change you have made and the original to help you see the difference your changes have made.

The *Adjust* section has a large variety of tools that you can use to adjust attributes such as brightness, color and sharpness (Figure 5.3). You can also choose to apply these adjustments to the whole image, foreground or background by using the dropdown menu at the top of the adjustment screen. If you want to see what Canva can do to improve the look of your photo, you can click the *Auto-adjust* button and see if you like the results.

Chapter 5 – Photo, Video and PDF Editors

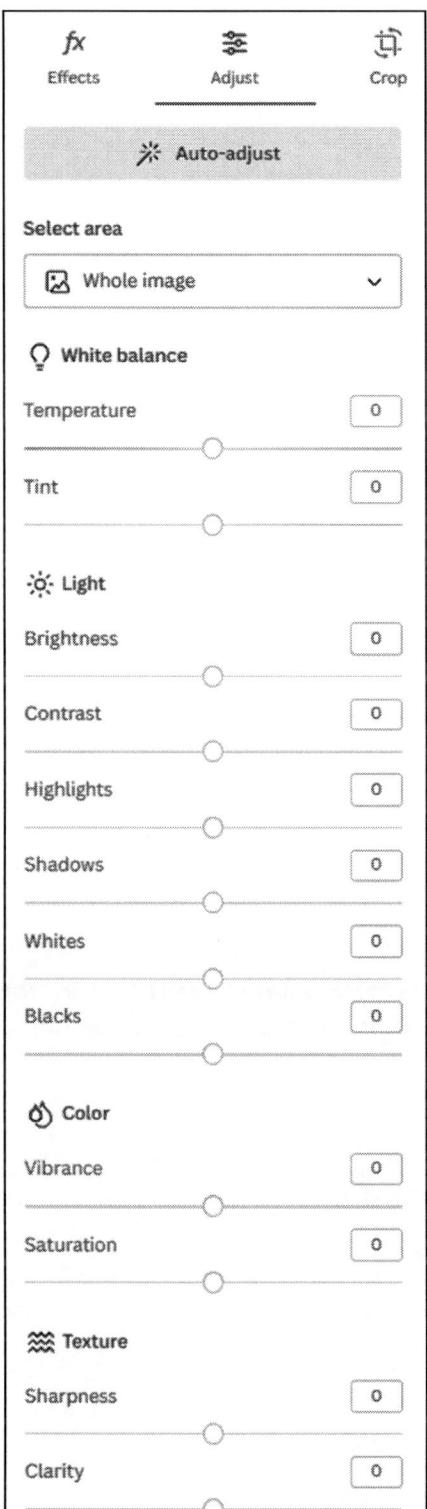

Figure 5.3

If you need to crop your image you can do so using one of the cropping tools. You can also rotate your image from here by using the slider or by typing in a positive or negative number for the degree of rotation you wish to apply.

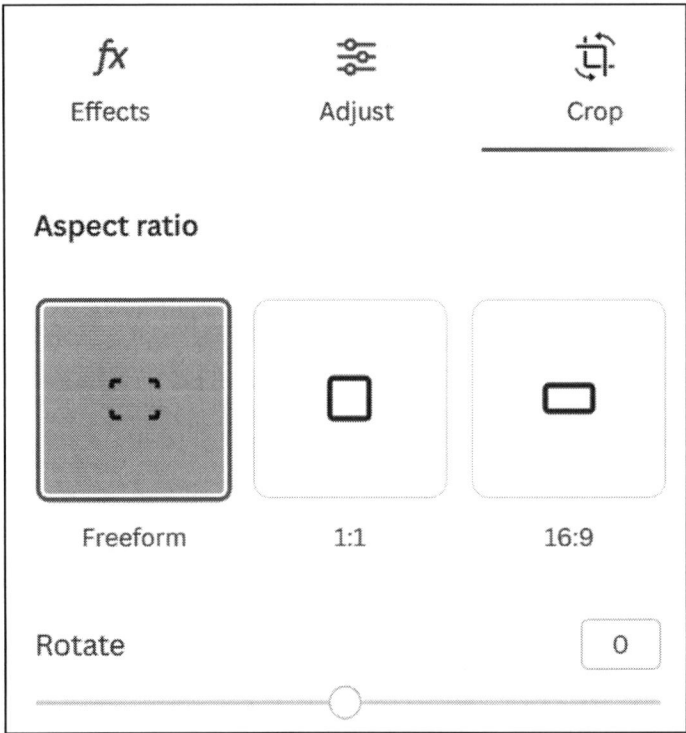

Figure 5.4

If you want to edit a photo that is already in a project, then you can click on the picture to select it and then you will see an *Edit photo* button appear in the bar at the top of the project window.

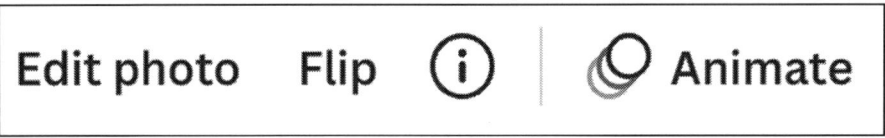

Figure 5.5

You can also open a photo from your uploads by clicking on it and it should automatically be opened in the photo editor.

Editing Videos
Not only can you edit your photos with Canva, but you can also edit videos that you have in your uploads or on your computer. If you want to edit a video stored

on your computer, you can either upload it to your Canva account or go to the Canva video editor website and upload it there which will actually add it to a new project as well as your uploads once it's finished uploading.
https://www.canva.com/video-editor/

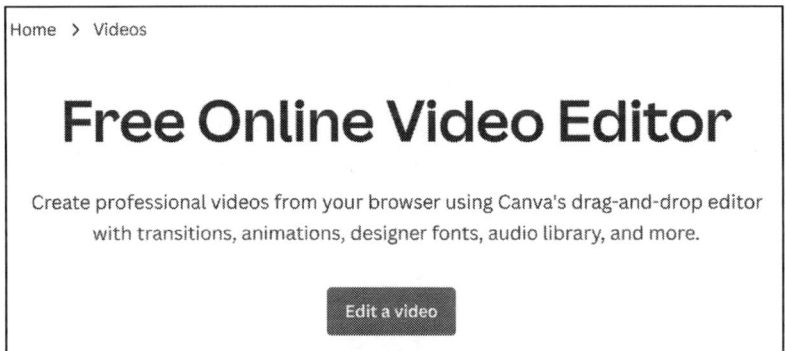

Figure 5.6

To edit a video, you will need to add one to a project from your uploads. This works the same way as adding a photo or element etc.

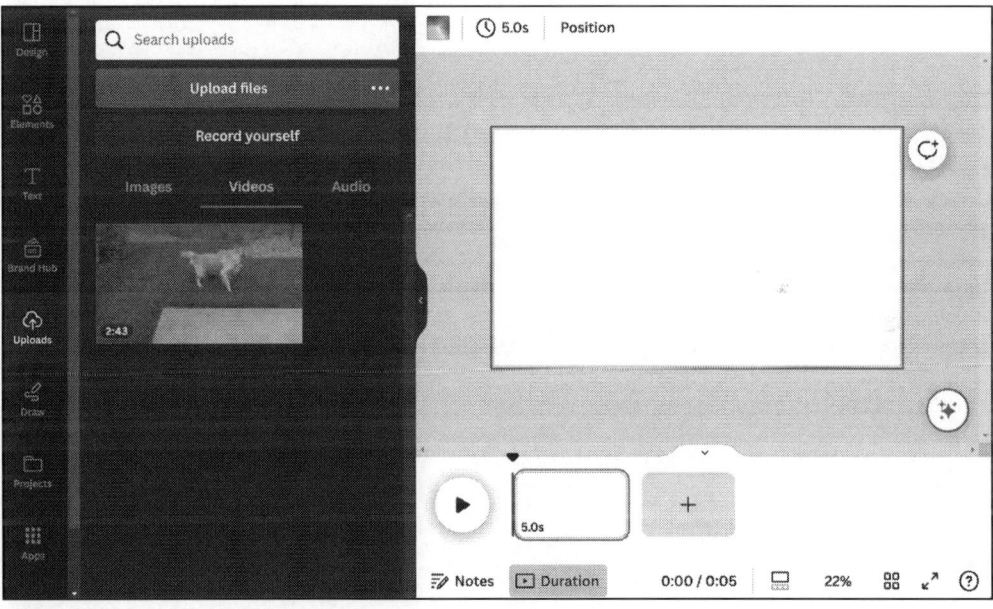

Figure 5.7

Once the video is in your project, you can click on it to select it and then you will have some editing options at the top of the screen. Many of these you will have seen before while working on your other projects.

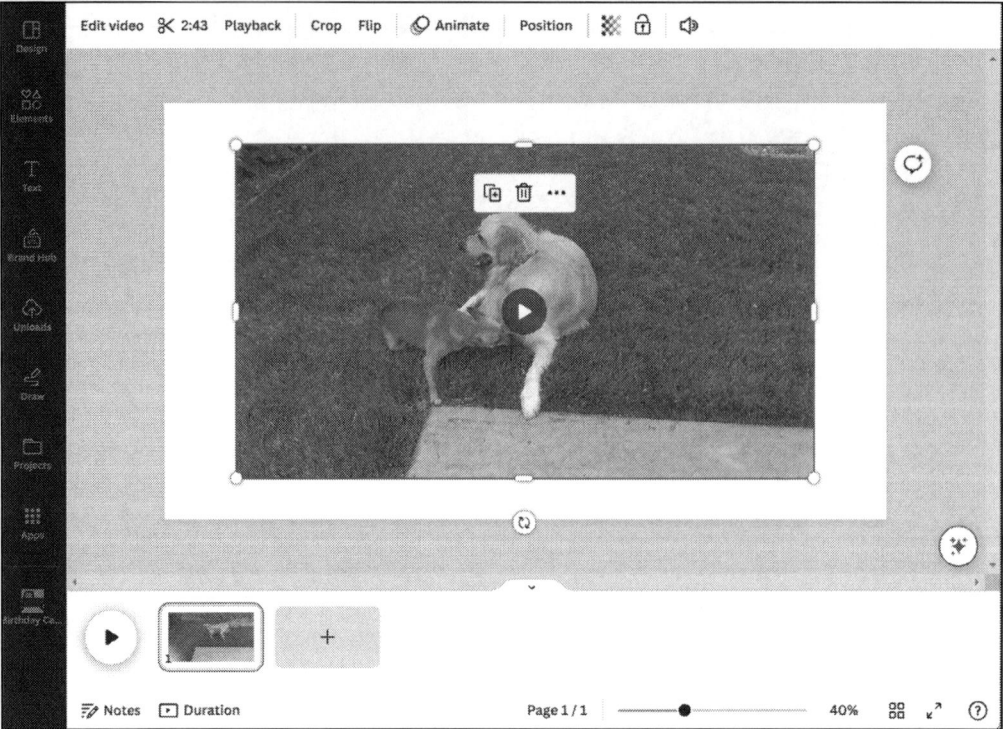

Figure 5.8

Clicking on the *Edit video* button will bring up the effects and adjustments settings as seen in Figures 5.9 and 5.10. These are similar to the adjustments you can make for photos.

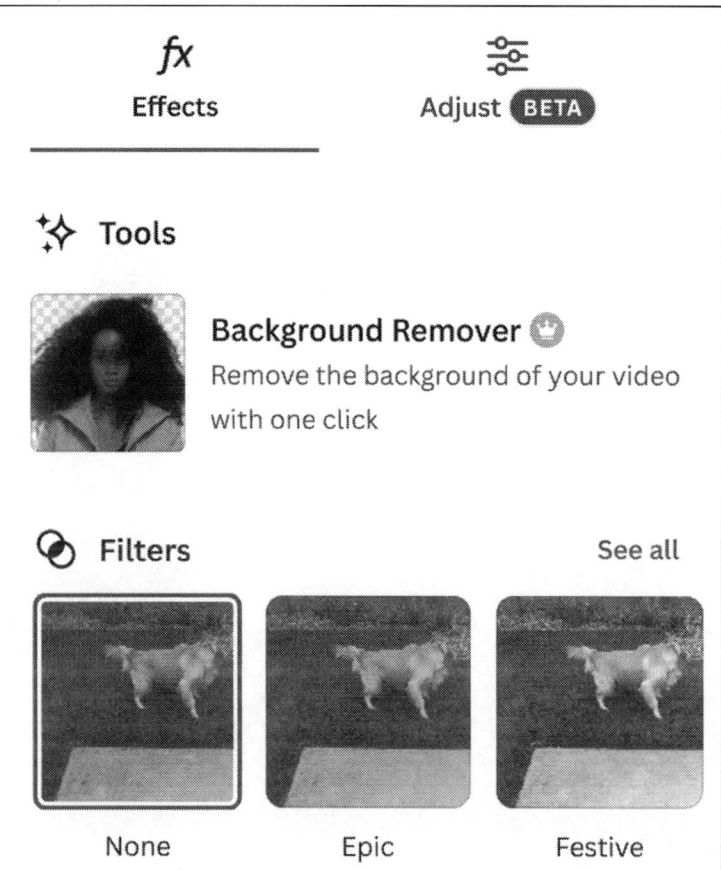

Figure 5.9

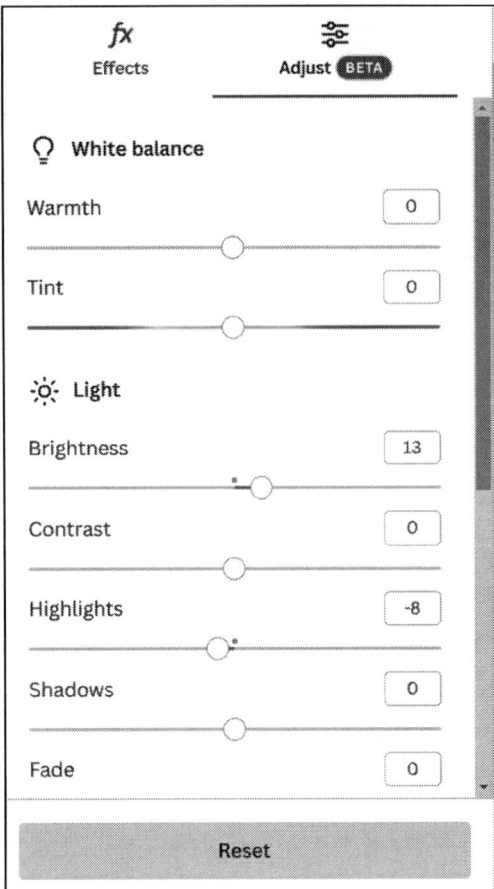

Figure 5.10

You can also adjust the video speed as well as make your video constantly loop when used in a presentation. That way it will not simply stop when it's finished in case you want to leave it on the screen for a while.

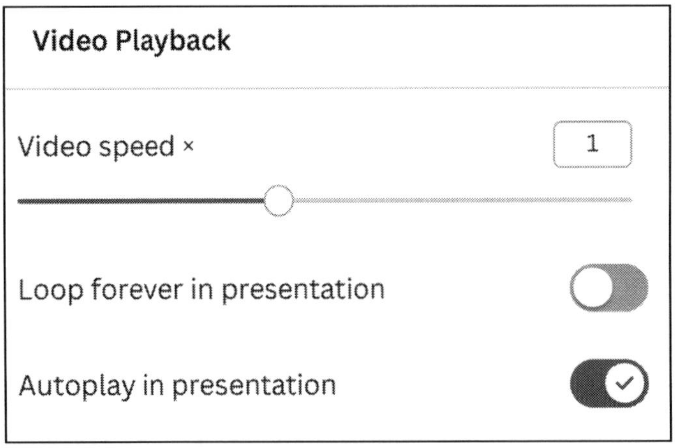

Video Playback

Video speed ×   1

Loop forever in presentation

Autoplay in presentation

Figure 5.11

Clicking on the ellipses next to the trash can delete icon will bring up the same types of options you do for photos such as copying, deleting and aligning your video to various sections of the page. If your video contains someone talking then you can enable the captions option from here so others can read what they are saying.

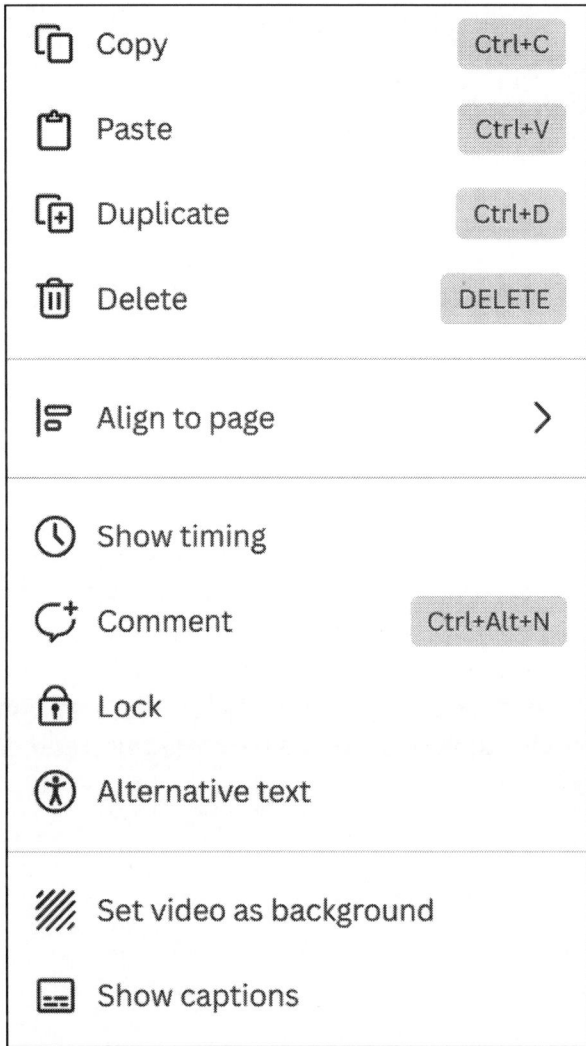

Copy	Ctrl+C
Paste	Ctrl+V
Duplicate	Ctrl+D
Delete	DELETE
Align to page	>
Show timing	
Comment	Ctrl+Alt+N
Lock	
Alternative text	
Set video as background	
Show captions	

Figure 5.12

Clicking on the *Duration* button at the bottom will show your video on a timeline in 5 second increments which can help you find a part of the video you are looking for so you can add elements that appear for a certain part of the video.

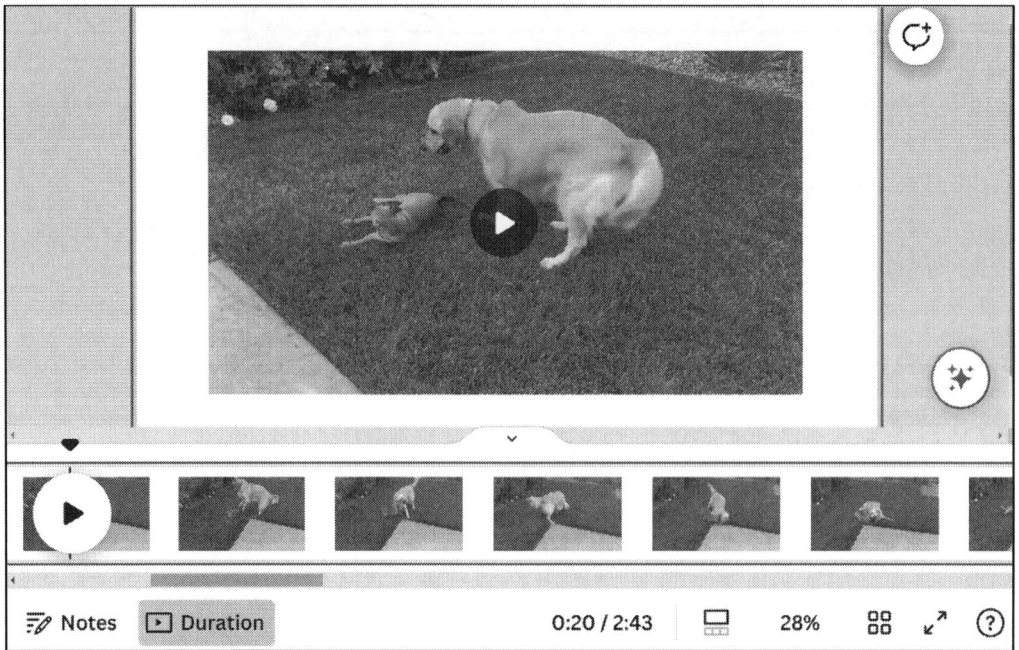

Figure 5.13

Figure 5.14 shows that I have added a bone graphic and some text to my video, but I do not want this to be shown for the entire length of the video. To adjust the time the elements are shown on the screen, I can right click one of them and choose *Show timing*. This will then place a marker on the timeline for that element that I can drag to change the position or duration that the element will be shown in my video. If you want to make your video a bit more fancy, you can add animations to your elements to do things such as make them fly into the scene or appear out of nowhere for example.

Figure 5.14

Canva makes it possible to combine videos simply by clicking on the new page button and then selecting another video from your uploads to be placed on this new page.

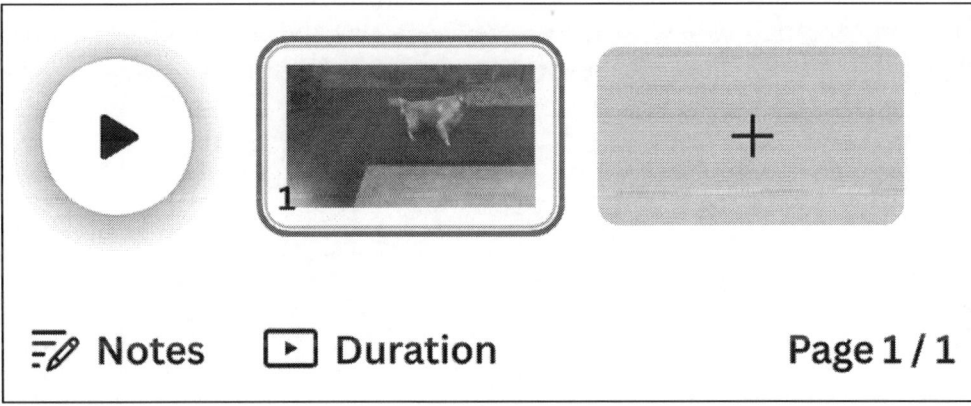

Figure 5.15

Then you can edit the video on the second page separately from the first page but when you play the video, they will be combined into one video.

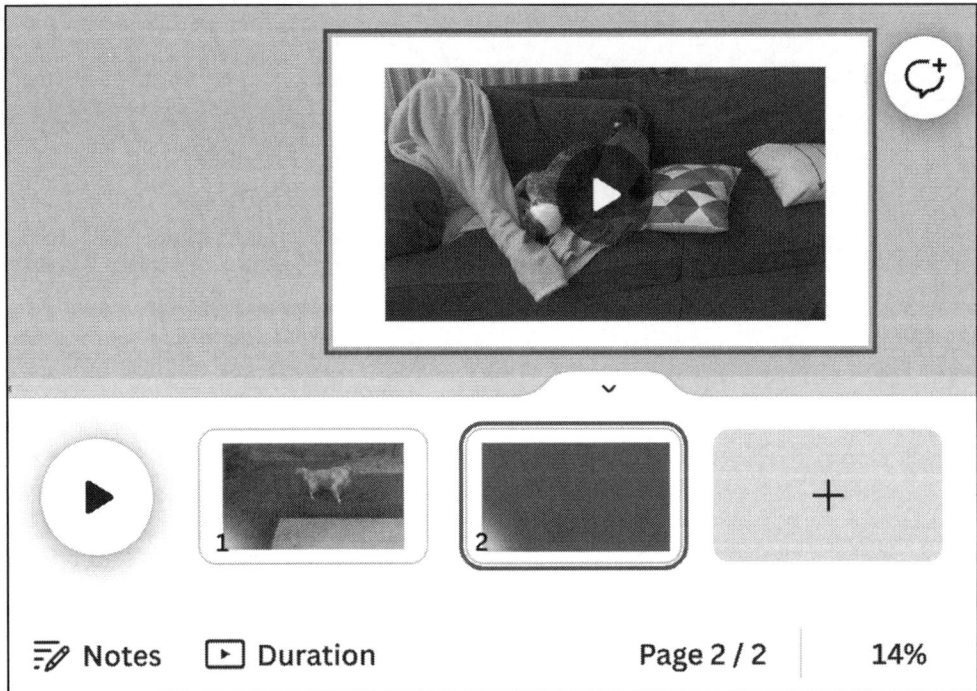

Figure 5.16

Once you have everything looking good, you can save your video to your computer by clicking on the *Share* button and choosing the *Download* option. You can then choose the file type which will most likely be MP4 since that is a common video file format. If you have the Pro account, you can increase the resolution from the maximum 1080p that you get with the free version. You can also have the pages be downloaded as separate videos with the Pro version.

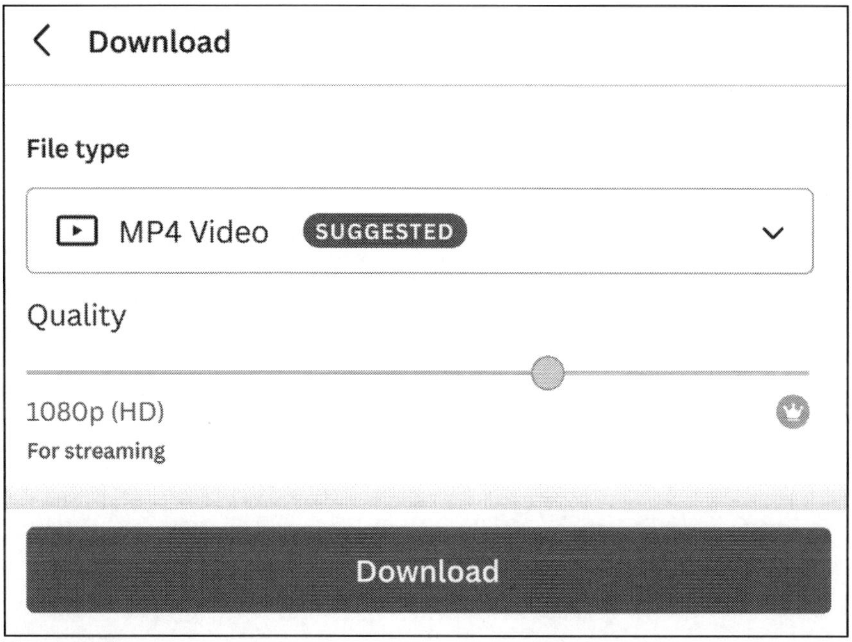

< **Download**

File type

▶ MP4 Video SUGGESTED ⌄

Quality

1080p (HD)
For streaming ♛

Download

Figure 5.17

Editing PDF Files

Another handy feature that comes included with Canva is the ability to edit PDF (Portable Document Format) files directly from Canva itself. This way you can do things such as edit or add text and also add other elements such as pictures and clipart to your PDF files.

To edit a PDF file, you can upload one to your account and then open it in a project or you can go to the Canva PDF editor website and upload your file right from there.
https://www.canva.com/pdf-editor/

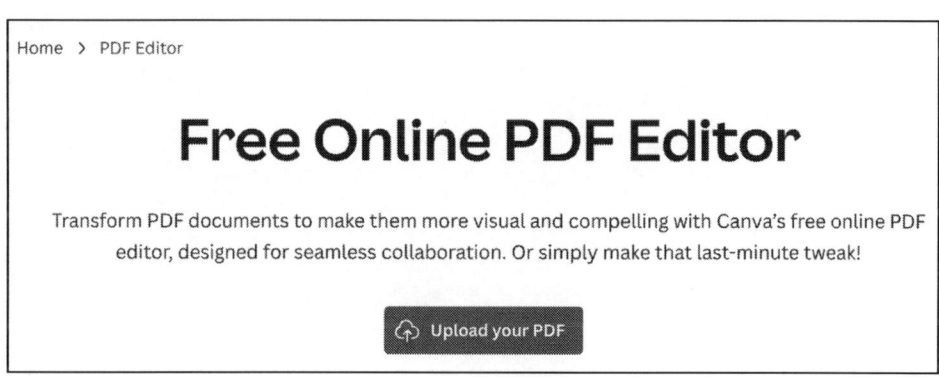

Home > PDF Editor

Free Online PDF Editor

Transform PDF documents to make them more visual and compelling with Canva's free online PDF editor, designed for seamless collaboration. Or simply make that last-minute tweak!

⌂ Upload your PDF

Figure 5.18

Once your PDF file is uploaded, you will see each individual page and be able to do things such as move, insert and delete pages as well as add new blank pages.

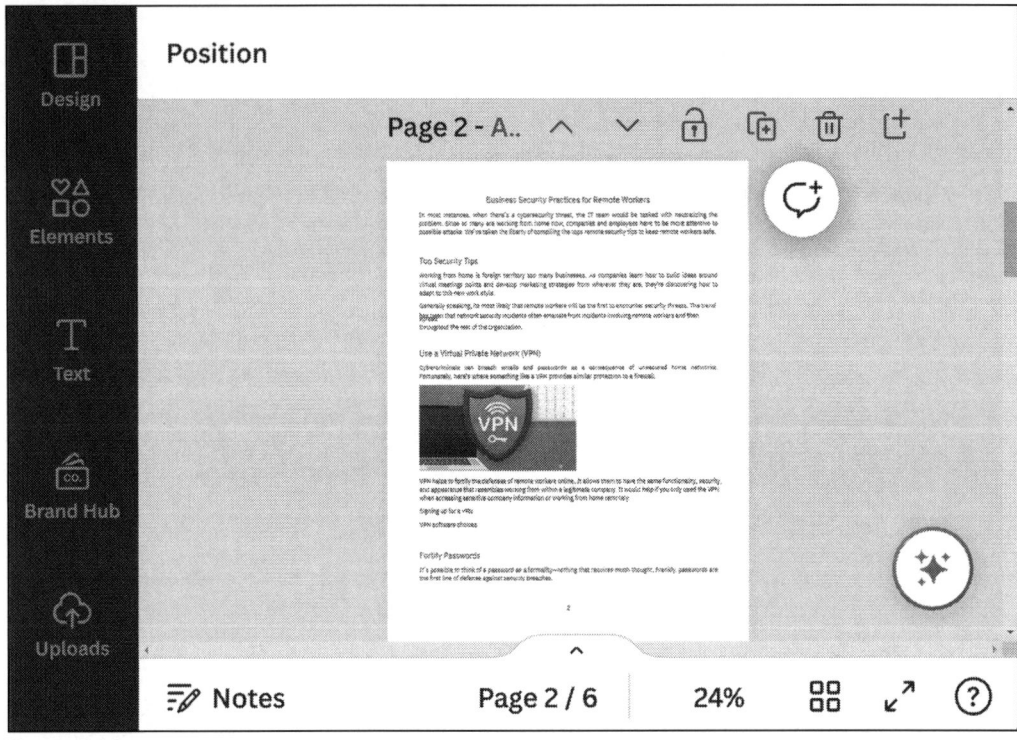

Figure 5.19

If you want to find the uploaded PDF file, you will most likely find it in your Projects under Designs since it will most likely not be kept with your image or video uploads.

Figure 5.20

You can then zoom into your PDF file and edit text such as changing the font, color or size. Another nice feature is the ability to create a link to another page in your document or an external website by highlighting any text and clicking on the link button (Figure 5.21).

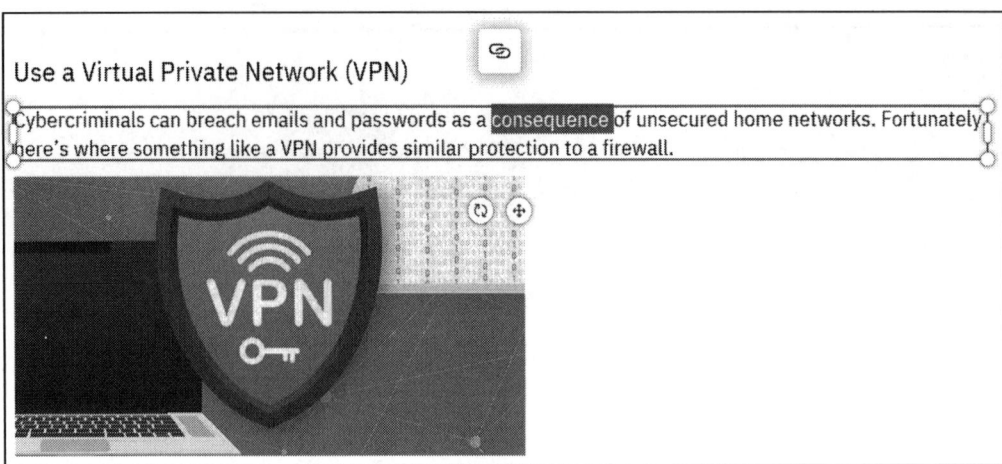

Use a Virtual Private Network (VPN)

Cybercriminals can breach emails and passwords as a consequence of unsecured home networks. Fortunately, here's where something like a VPN provides similar protection to a firewall.

Figure 5.21

If you have any images you would rather use, you can delete the image within the file and replace it with a new one.

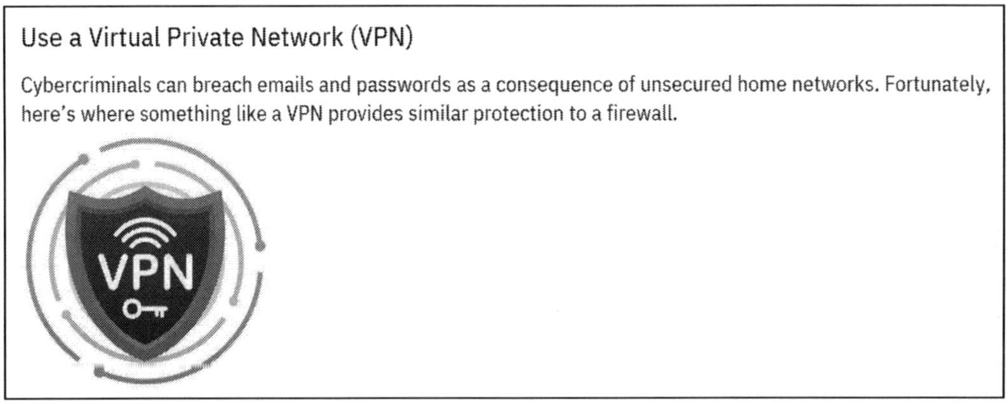

Use a Virtual Private Network (VPN)

Cybercriminals can breach emails and passwords as a consequence of unsecured home networks. Fortunately, here's where something like a VPN provides similar protection to a firewall.

Figure 5.22

Chapter 6 – Extra Features

As I mentioned at the beginning of this book, Canva has so many features that it's impossible to cover everything in one book. Plus they are constantly adding additional functionality to the app to make it even harder to keep up!

In this chapter, I will be covering some of the extra features that I think you might find useful and may want to try out for yourself. For the most part, you can use these features in your daily work to add a little flair or to make things easier on yourself.

Magic Design Templates

Just like with everything else, Canva is implementing AI (Artificial Intelligence) into their app with their Magic Design feature. They have applied this technology to their templates, and they call this new feature Magic Design Templates.

If you go to the templates section you should be able to find the Magic Design area but if not, you can simply do a search for it and then you should see a screen similar to figure 6.1.

The way Magic Design templates work is that you add some media from your Canva account, or you can upload a file from your computer. Then you can filter the template design by things such as category, style and theme etc.

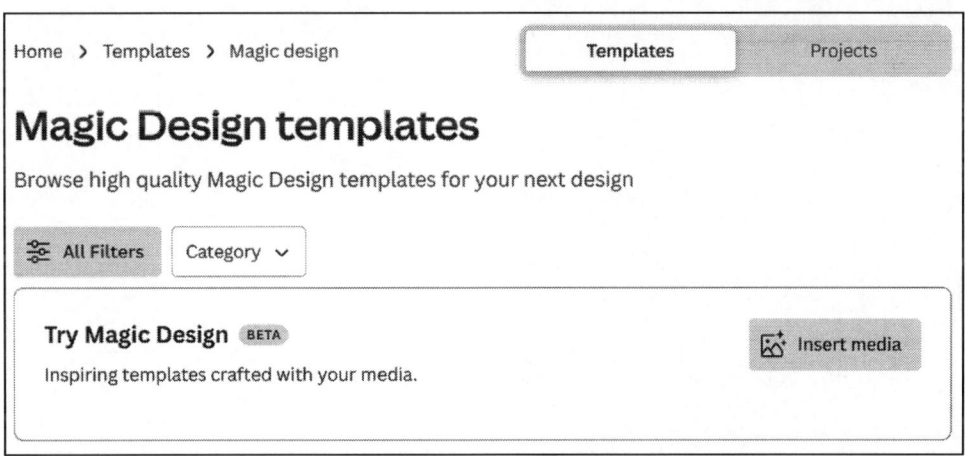

Figure 6.1

For my example, I will be using the photo shown in figure 6.2 as my media.

Figure 6.2

Canva will then show me some designs based on the categories I have chosen as shown in Figures 6.3 through 6.5.

Flyer

Figure 6.3

Chapter 6 – Extra Features

YouTube Thumbnail

Figure 6.4

Invitation

Figure 6.5

If you want to fine tune how your templates look, you can choose from some built in style features from the *Style* drop down menu.

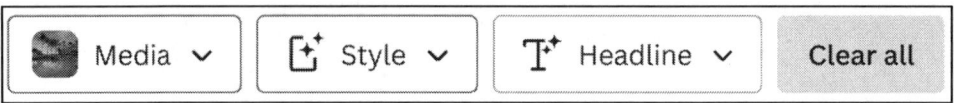

Figure 6.6

You can choose a color and font style and then one or more vibe\theme attributes to have applied to your template.

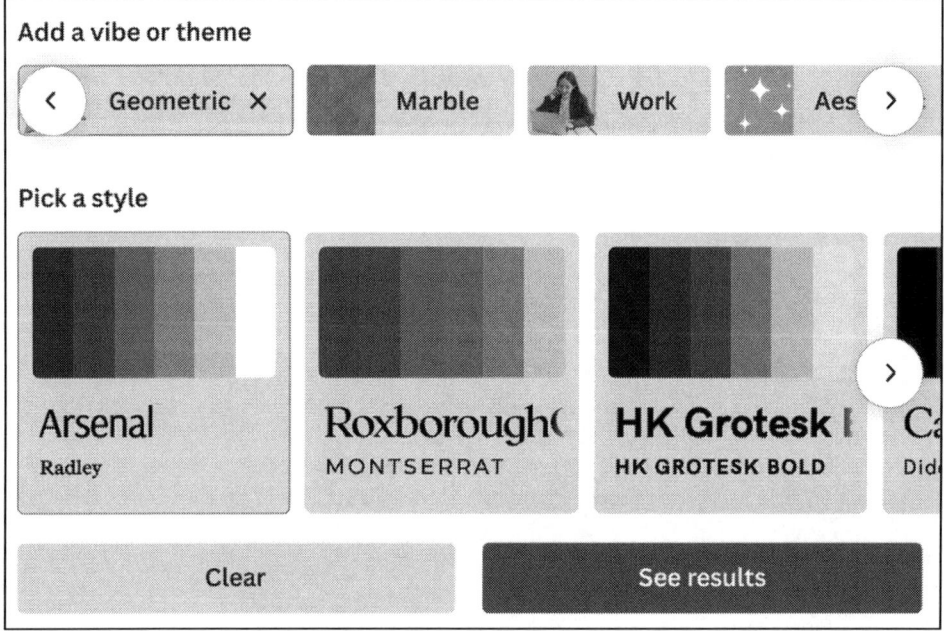

Figure 6.7

If you want to have some text automatically added to your template, you can click on the *Headline* button and type in your text.

Now that I have added a style and vibe to my Magic Design template, I will see some different options after clicking the *See results* button.

Figure 6.8

Once you find a template you want to use, you can then click on the ellipses next to it and choose *Customize this template* to open it in the Canva editor.

Figure 6.9

Canva Desktop App

If you would rather not have to use your web browser when working in Canva, you can try the Canva desktop app which is available for Microsoft Windows and macOS. There is even a version for Android and Apple smartphones and tablets. When you go to the Canva desktop app website, you can choose your operating system and download the version that is right for you.

https://www.canva.com/help/canva-desktop-app/

Figure 6.10

You can then install the Canva desktop app just like any other software on your computer. You will need to log into Canva with your web browser to complete the installation.

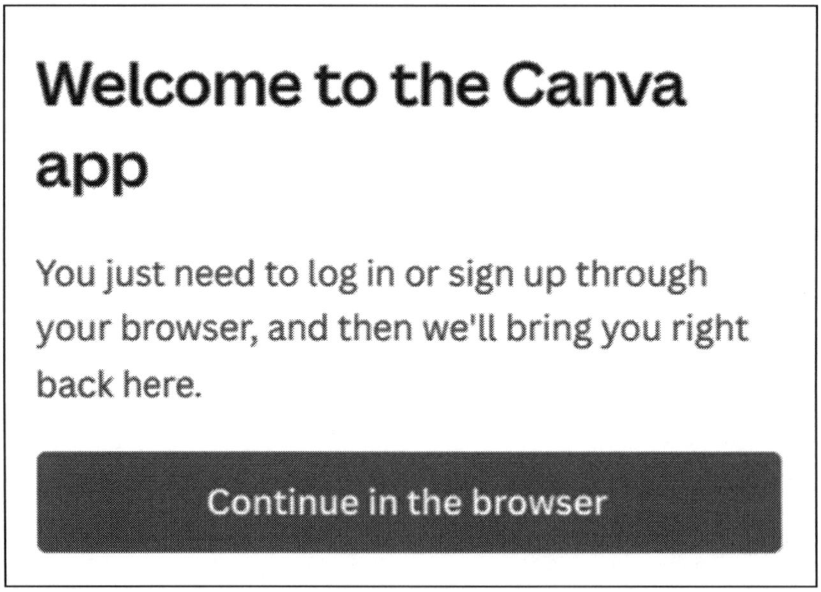

Welcome to the Canva app

You just need to log in or sign up through your browser, and then we'll bring you right back here.

Continue in the browser

Figure 6.11

Figure 6.12 shows how the Canva desktop app looks. As you can see, it's almost identical to the web version except you have a different bar on the top of the app.

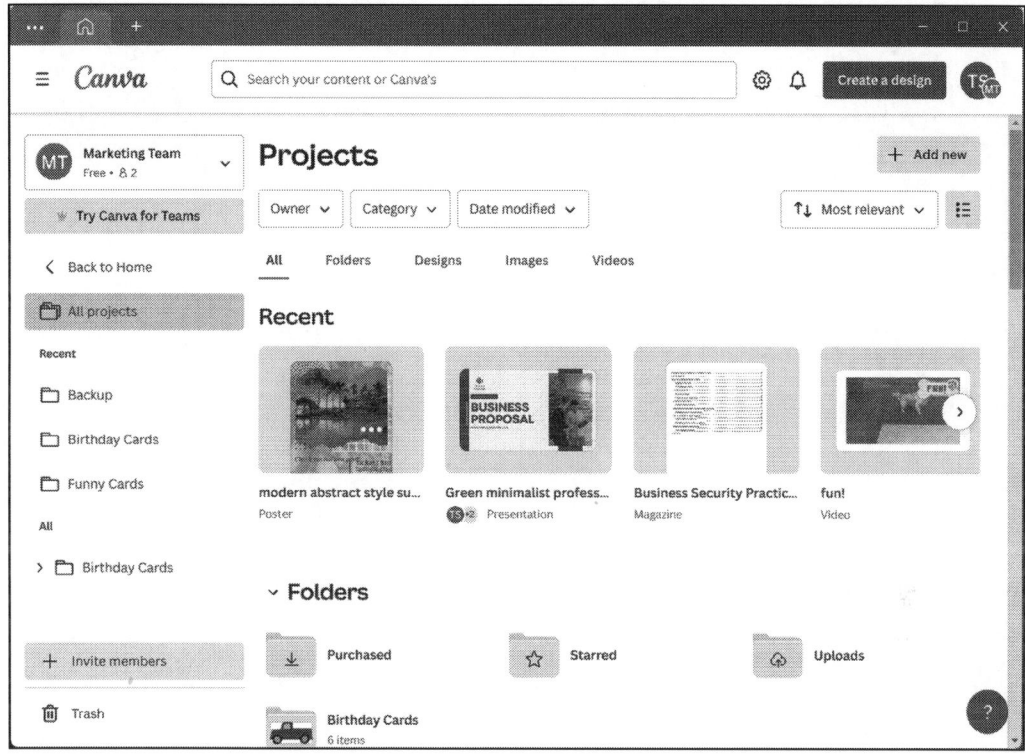

Figure 6.12

This bar lets you open different projects in their own tab like you can do in your web browser. You can click the + button to add a new tab and you can also drag the tabs around to change their order.

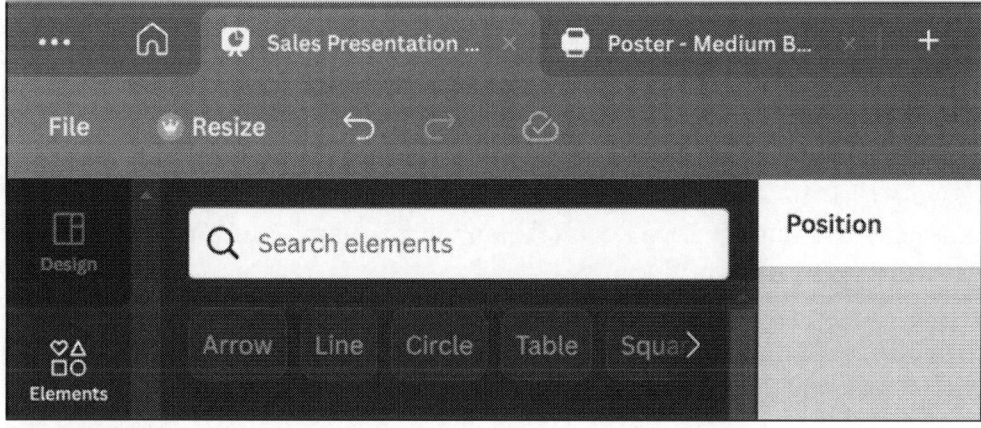

Figure 6.13

You can right click on a tab to see additional options.

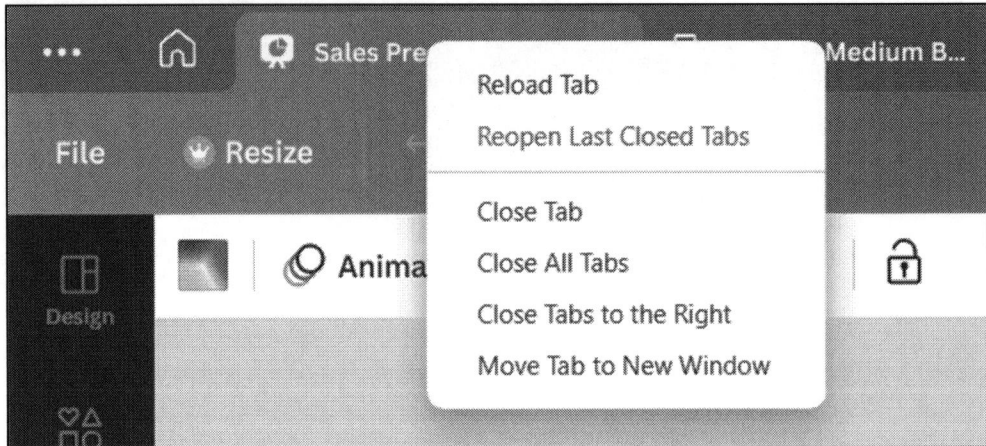

Figure 6.14

Canva Assistant

You might have noticed the round icon with the stars in it next to your page when working on a project and wondered what it does. This is used to start the Canva Assistant which can help you out with ideas for your design if you are having trouble with your creativity for example.

Figure 6.15

Once you click on the Canva Assistant icon, you will be shown a listing of recommended actions that you can take on your project. You can also search for ideas at the top of the window.

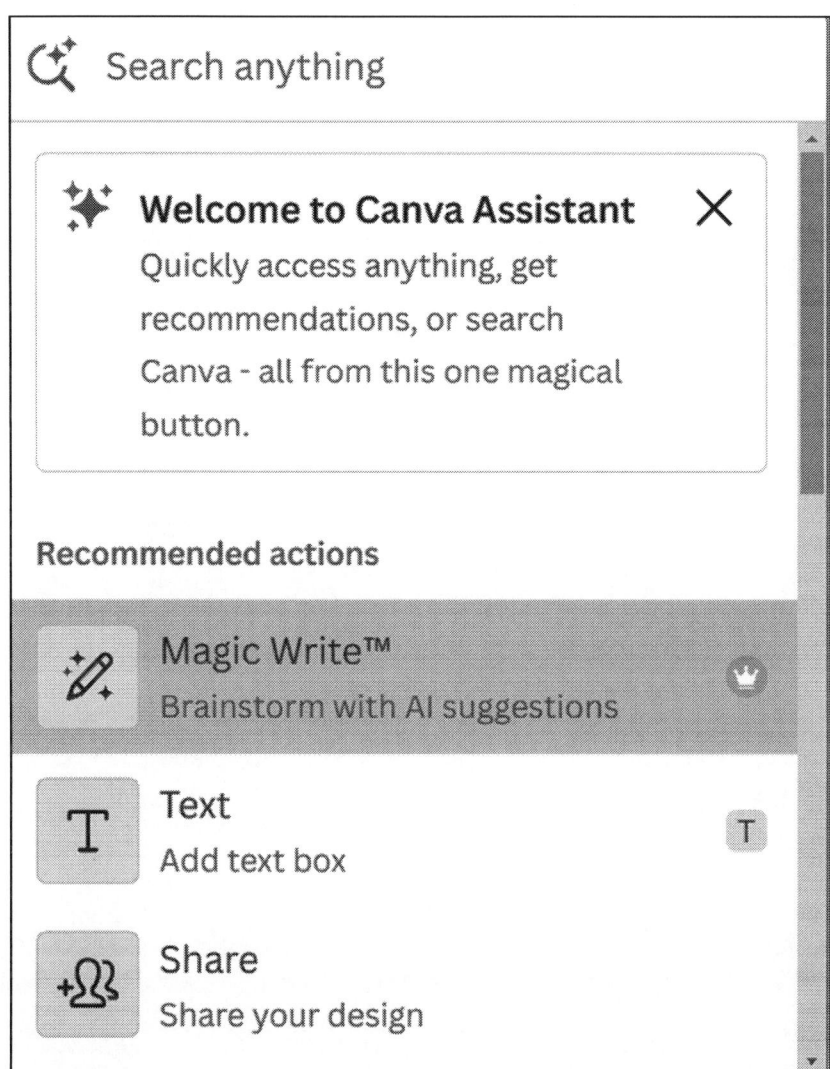

Figure 6.16

As you scroll down the list of recommendations, you can click on any of them to use that particular tool. You will also notice that some of them are for the Pro accounts only so keep that in mind.

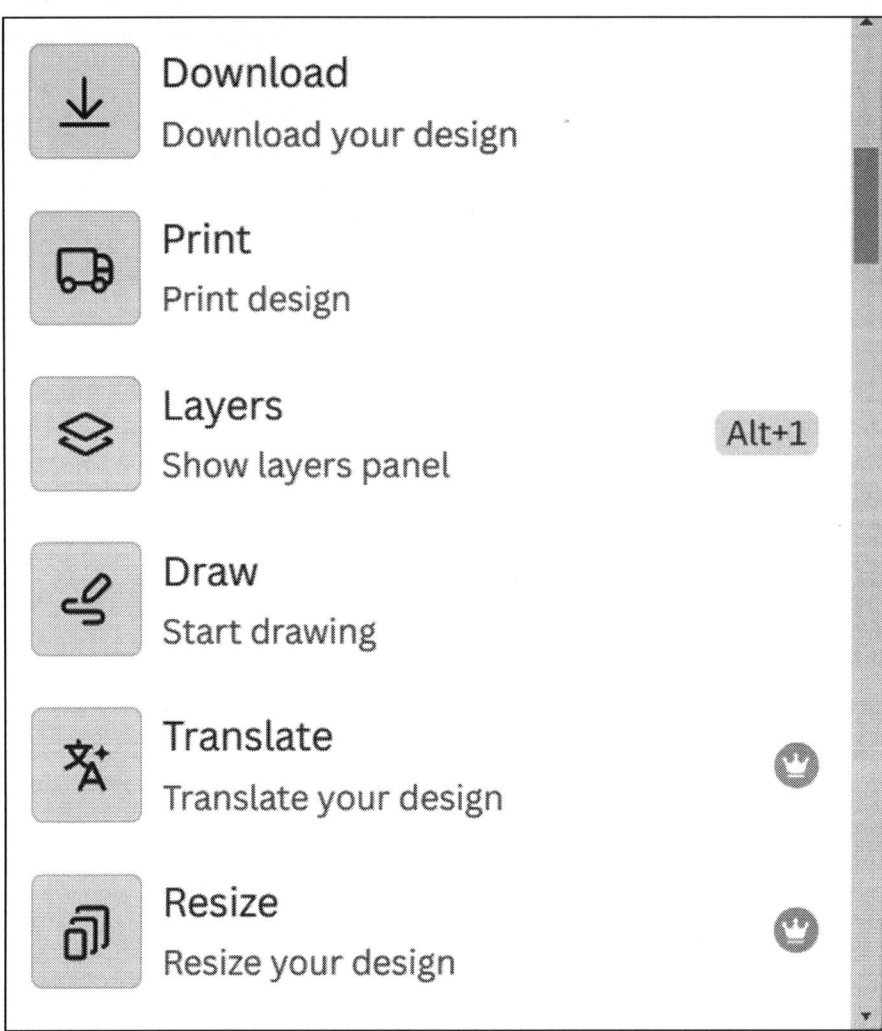

Figure 6.17

At the bottom of the list, you will also be shown some graphics and photos that you might want to use with your project. If you like any of the suggestions, you can simply click on one to have it added to your project.

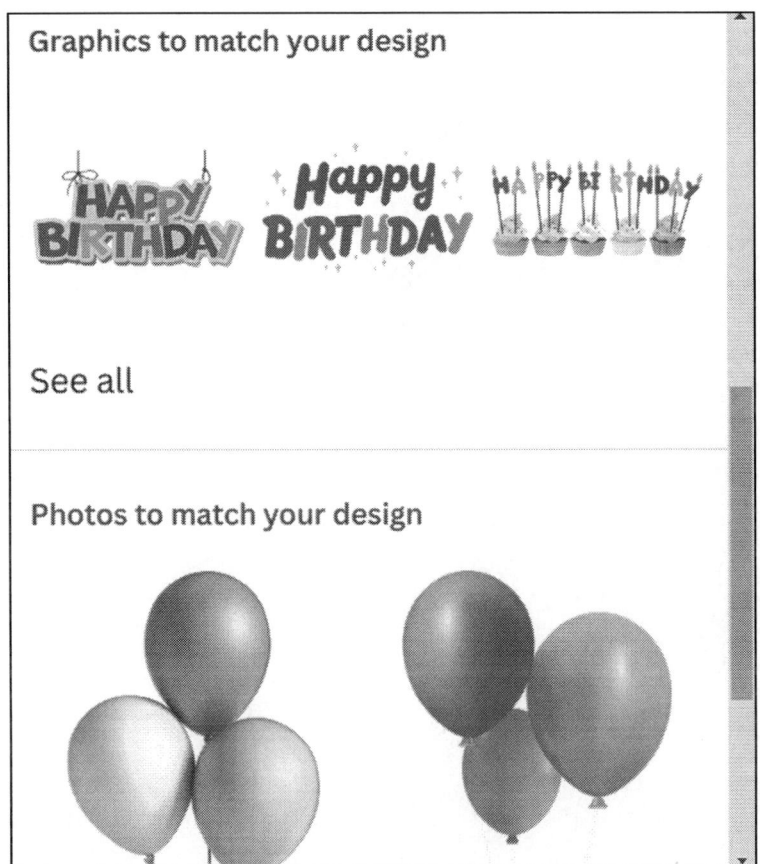

Figure 6.18

Also at the bottom of the list, you should see an option that says *See all*. When you click on this option, Canva will open the Elements panel to the left with multiple suggestions all in one place (Figure 6.19).

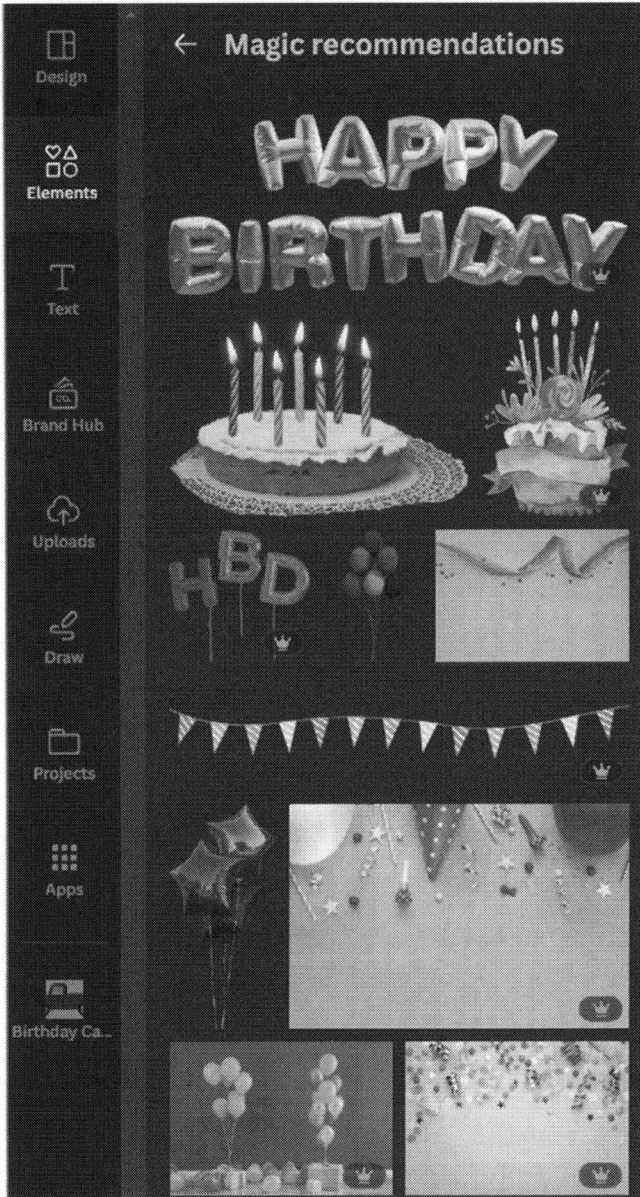

Figure 6.19

Canva Print

You have probably figured out that you can print any of your designs on your printer at home simply by downloading them and printing them like any other document. You can even send them out for professional printing if you are looking for a better quality printing job.

But if you want to have your design printed on unique things such as mouse pads, notebooks, calendars, mugs, photo books, banners and so on, you can use the Canva print services to do so.

To start the process, you can simply go to the *Canva Print* website and click the Start printing button.
https://www.canva.com/print/

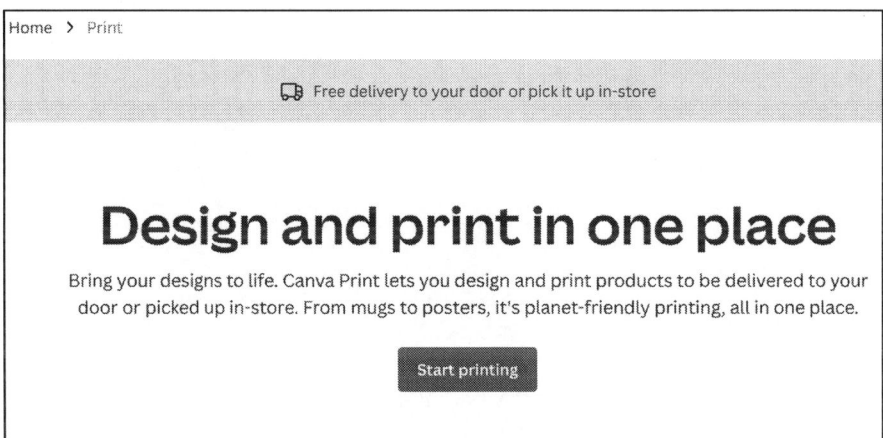

Figure 6.20

Next, you can browse through all the available categories until you find what you are looking for.

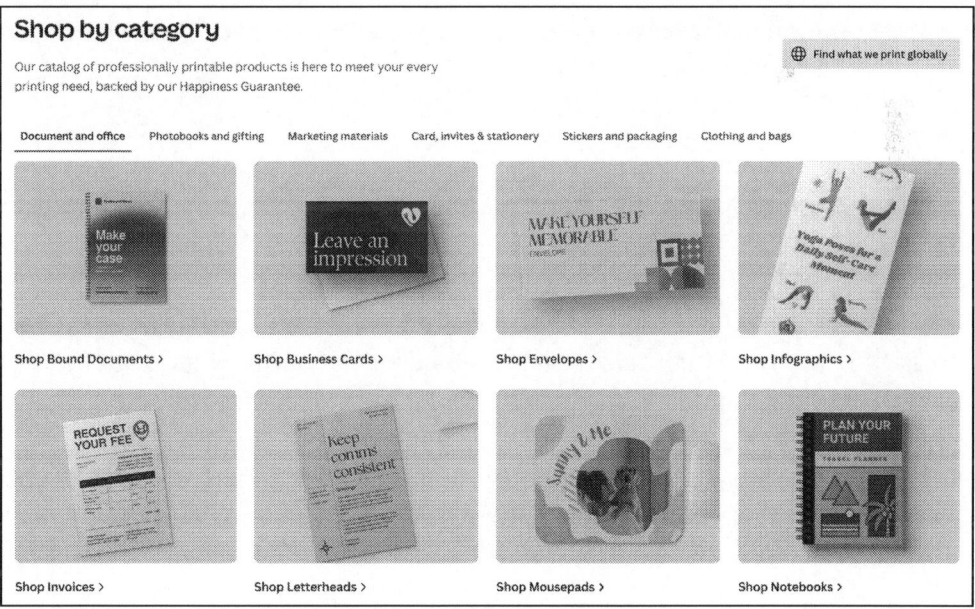

Figure 6.21

Let's say I wanted to create a mousepad from one of my designs. I would click the *Shop Mousepads* category and then I can add my design to the mousepad template as seen in figure 6.22. I can then edit my design like any other design if I need to make any changes.

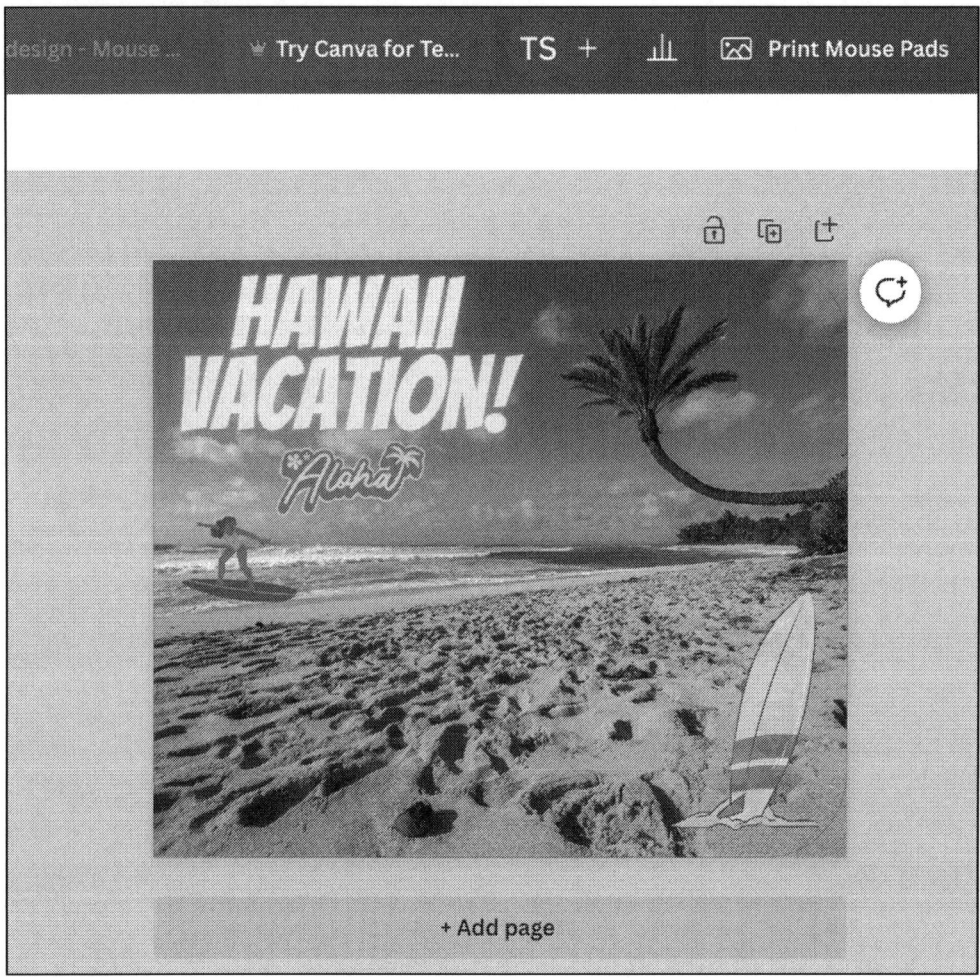

Figure 6.22

Once I have everything looking the way I like, I can click on the *Print Mouse Pads* button at the upper right corner. Then I will be able to choose what page to use if I have more than one and how many mousepads I want to have printed.

You can also scroll down on this screen to see if Canva found any issues with your design that might make it not print correctly (Figure 6.23). You can then fix these issues yourself or have Canva do it for you. Then you can download a sample of how the product will look by clicking the *Download PDF* button.

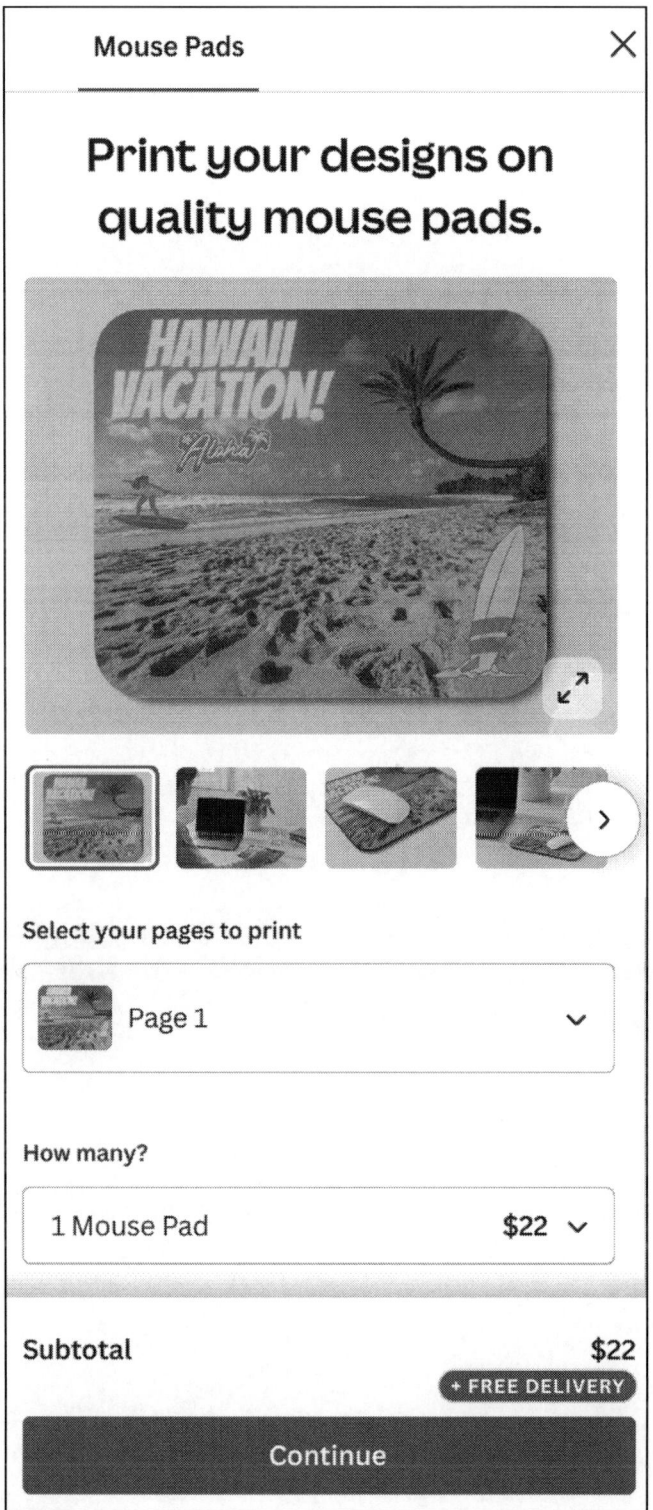

Figure 6.23

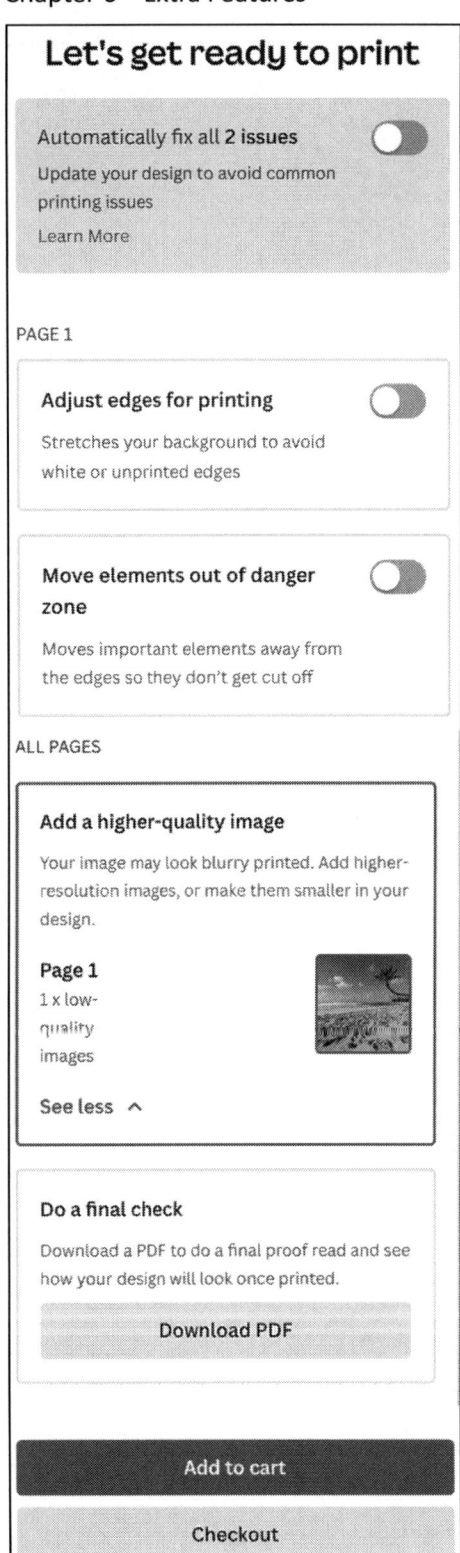

Figure 6.24

Then you can choose your shipping method and add your name and address to the form.

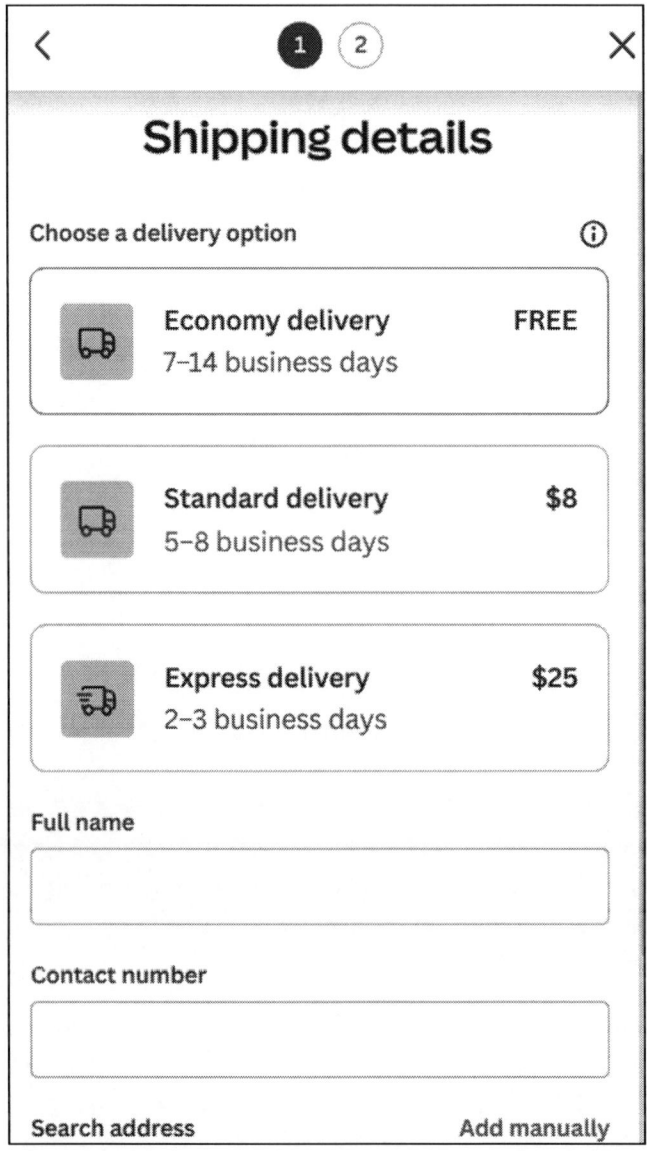

Figure 6.25

Finally, you can choose your payment method and place your order.

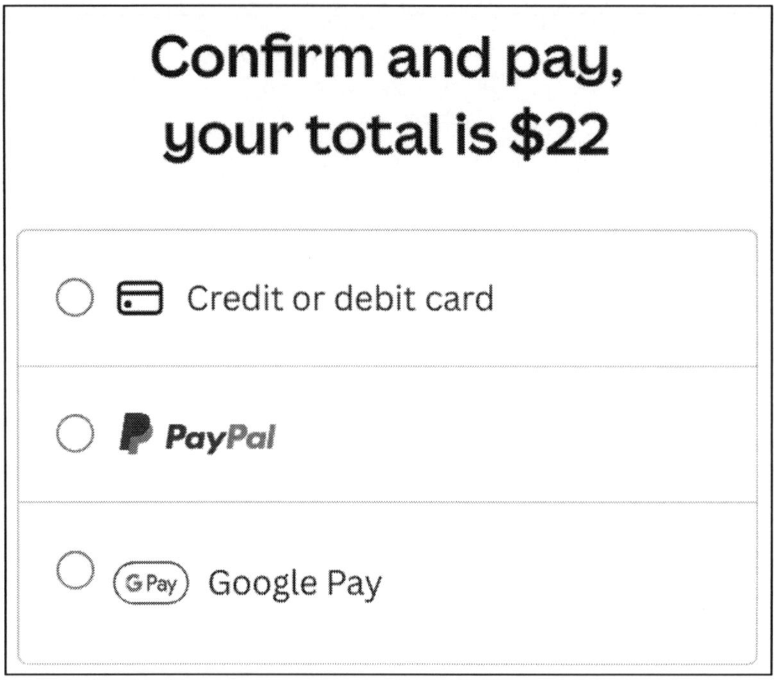

Figure 6.26

Canva Apps

Even though Canva is an app itself, there are additional apps you can use with Canva to enhance its functionality. It is similar to installing an extension or add-on in your web browser.

You most likely do not have any apps installed within Canva unless you have done so in the past. You can go to the Apps section on the left side of the screen to see what apps are available and also to search for a specific type of app.

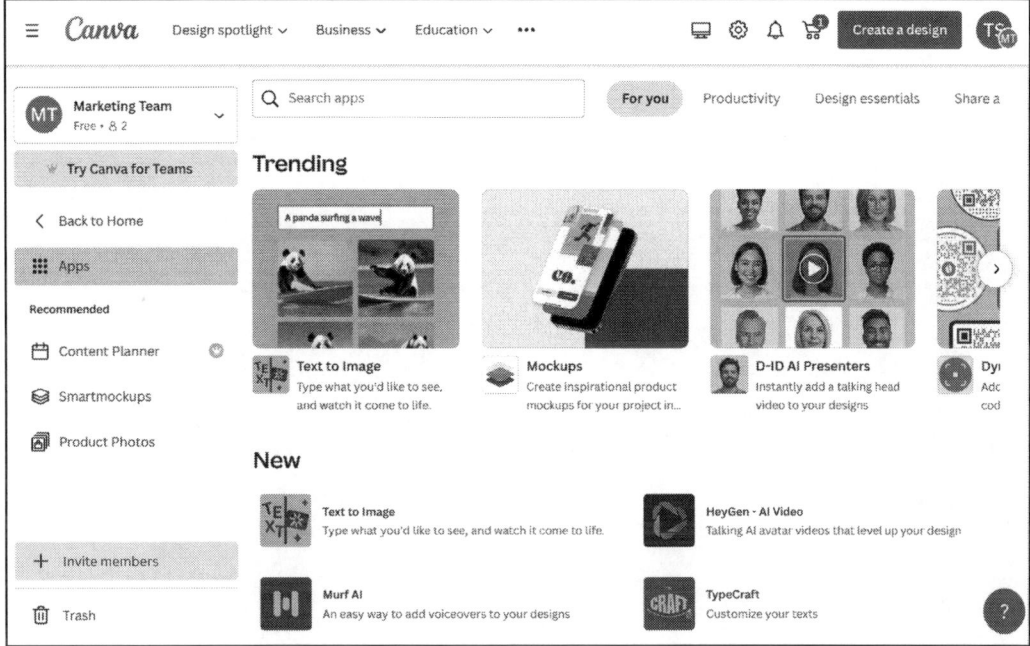

Figure 6.27

I will click on the *Text to Image* app under the Trending section and will then be asked if I want to use the app in an existing design or in a new one. I will choose the option to use it in a new design.

Figure 6.28

When my new design is opened, I can then go to the Apps section in the toolbar on the left to see my new app.

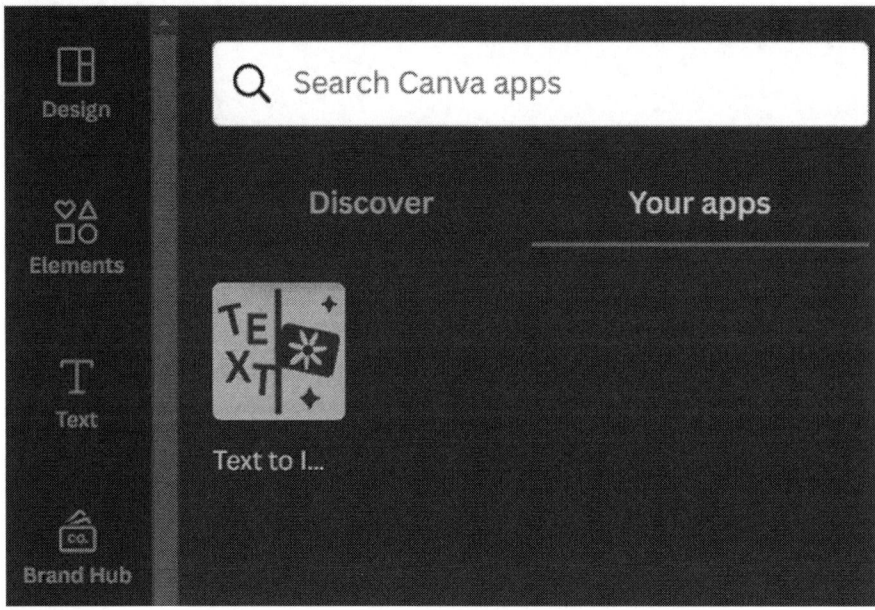

Figure 6.29

When I click on the app, I will then have the opportunity to start using it. Since this app creates an image out of the text that you type, I can type in some text to see how it works. I will use the phrase *dog on a bike wearing a top hat* and then I can choose a style if I like, or I can just click on the *Create your image* button.

If you take a closer look at Figure 6.30, you can see that I can only use this app 50 times since I am not using a Pro account. You will most likely run into situations like this yourself when using Canva apps.

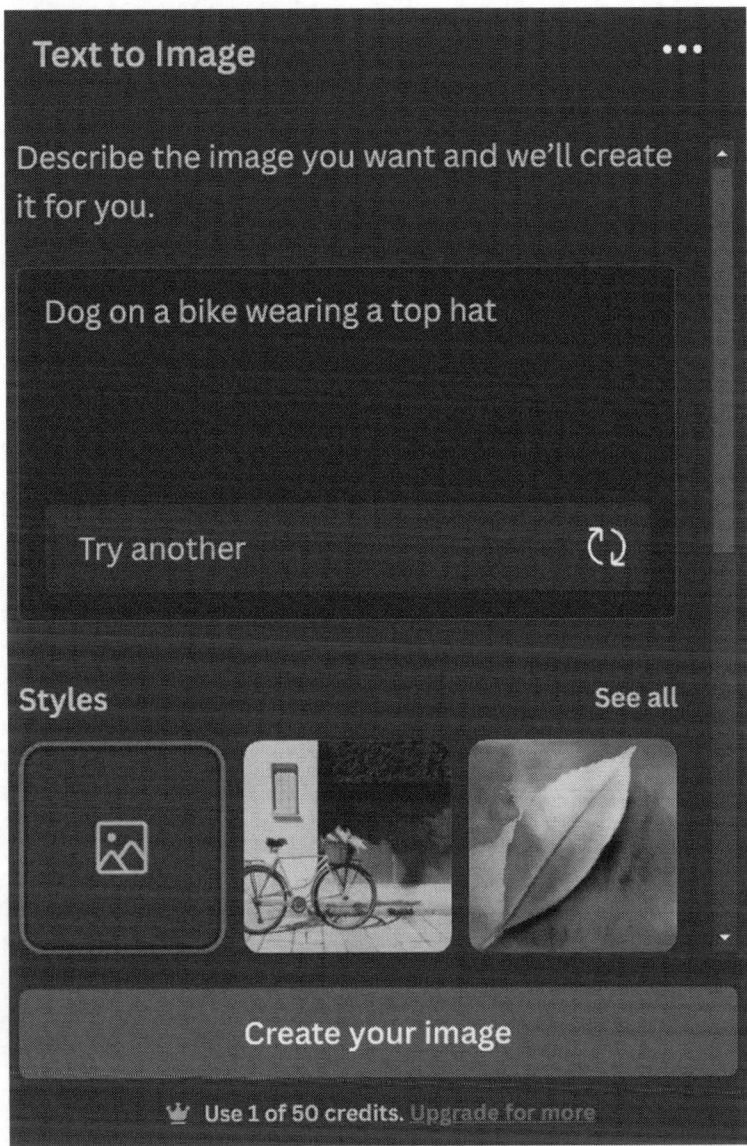

Figure 6.30

Figure 6.31 shows the results that I get after typing in my text to image phrase. I can either use one of the results or click on the *Create again* button to have some new examples created.

Figure 6.31

Once I choose an image, it will be added to my design and then I can start working on it just like any other project. If I do not want to have this app in my Canva account any longer, I can click on the ellipses next to the app itself and then choose the *Remove from your apps* option.

Figure 6.32

Photos

Canva has a built in photo library that you can access to find high quality photos that you can use in your projects. Canva doesn't make it super obvious as to where to find these photos but if you go to the Templates section, you should then see it over at the left side of the screen.

At the top of the page, you will have some categories and you can also choose to have Free, Pro or Free and Pro photos shown. There is also a search box at the top of the page that can be used to help you find what you are looking for.

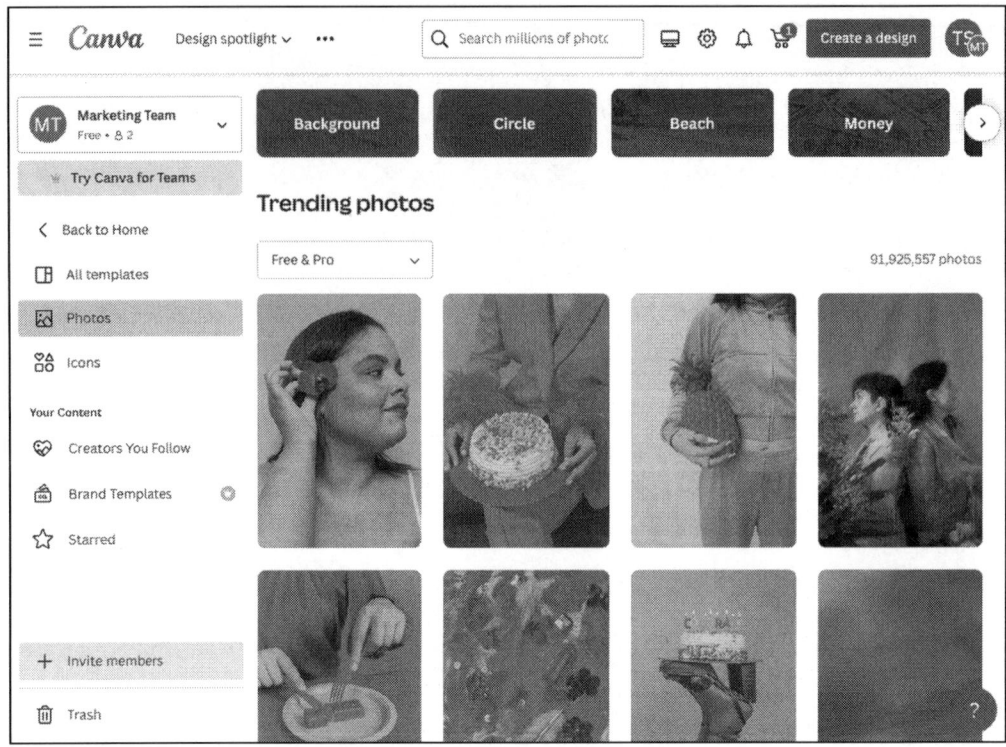

Figure 6.33

Figure 6.34 shows the results when I search for Australian Shepherd, I get over 107,000 results but as you can see, most of the designs are for the Pro version since they have the $ sign in the lower right corner so you will not be able to use these with the free account.

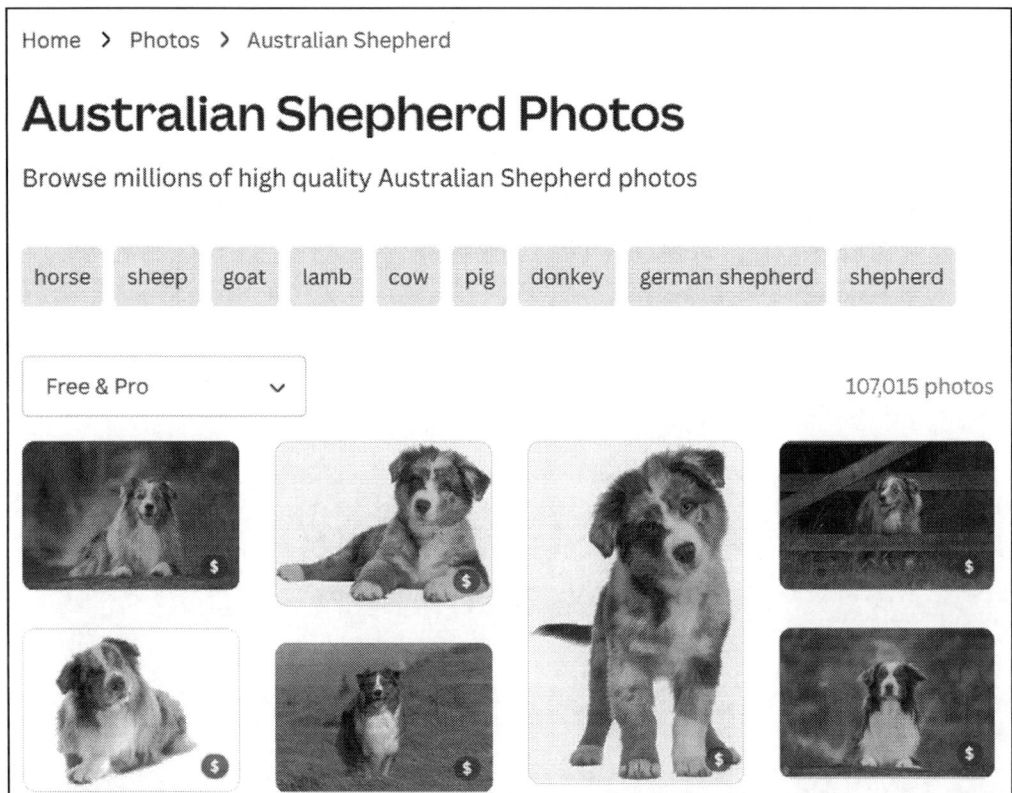

Figure 6.34

If I change the results to only show free photos, I still get over 2,400 that I can choose from.

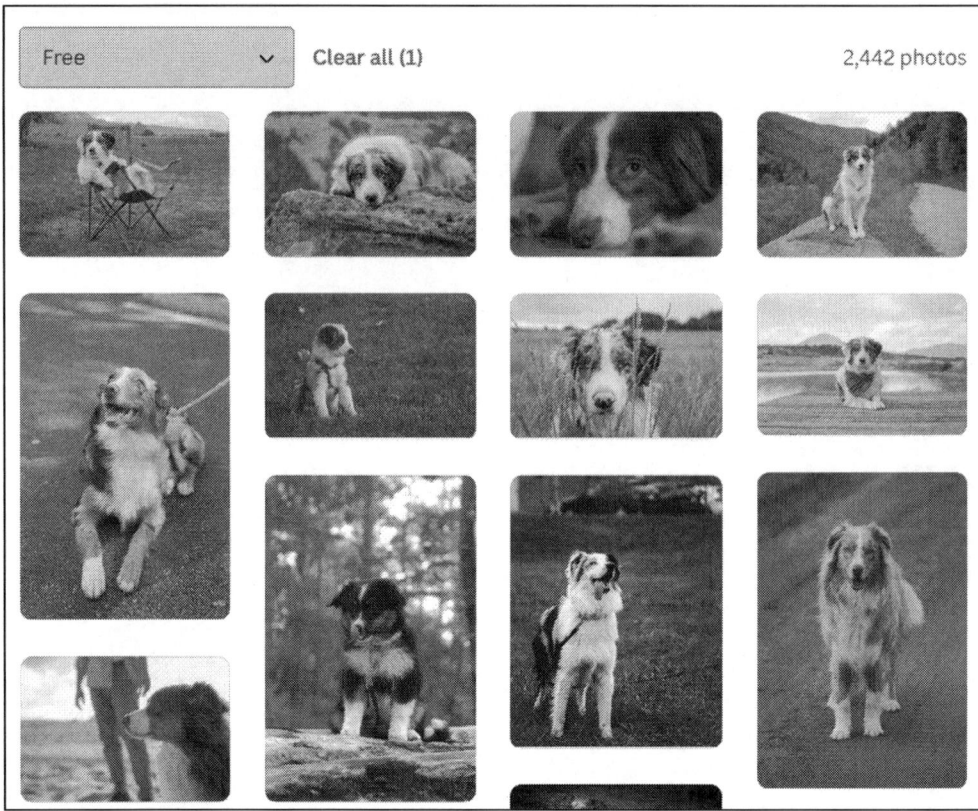

Figure 6.35

When you hover over a photo, you have the option to Star it which will add it to your favorites, or you can report it if there is something offensive with the photo and you think it shouldn't belong on Canva.

Figure 6.36

To use a photo in a project, simply click on it and you will have the option to use it in a design or save it to one of your folders. You will also get some color suggestions that match the photo, and when you click on one of them, you can copy the color hex code to use in your design.

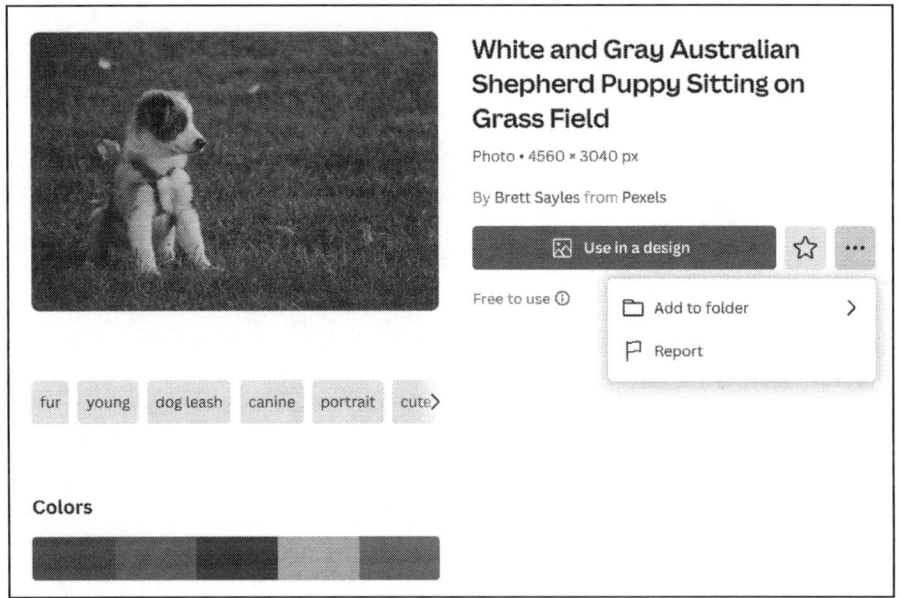

Figure 6.37

Icons

By now you are most likely used to working with the various elements that come included with Canva. When you go to the elements section while working on a project, you will have a variety of graphics including frames, stickers, cartoons, photos, clipart and so on.

Canva has some other clipart type graphics you can use called icons that are available in the same area of the app where you can find the photos discussed in the last section. There are some available categories to choose from that can be found at the top of the page and you can also search for what you are looking for.

And just like with the photos, you can sort them by Free, Pro or both to make sure you only see the results that apply to you.

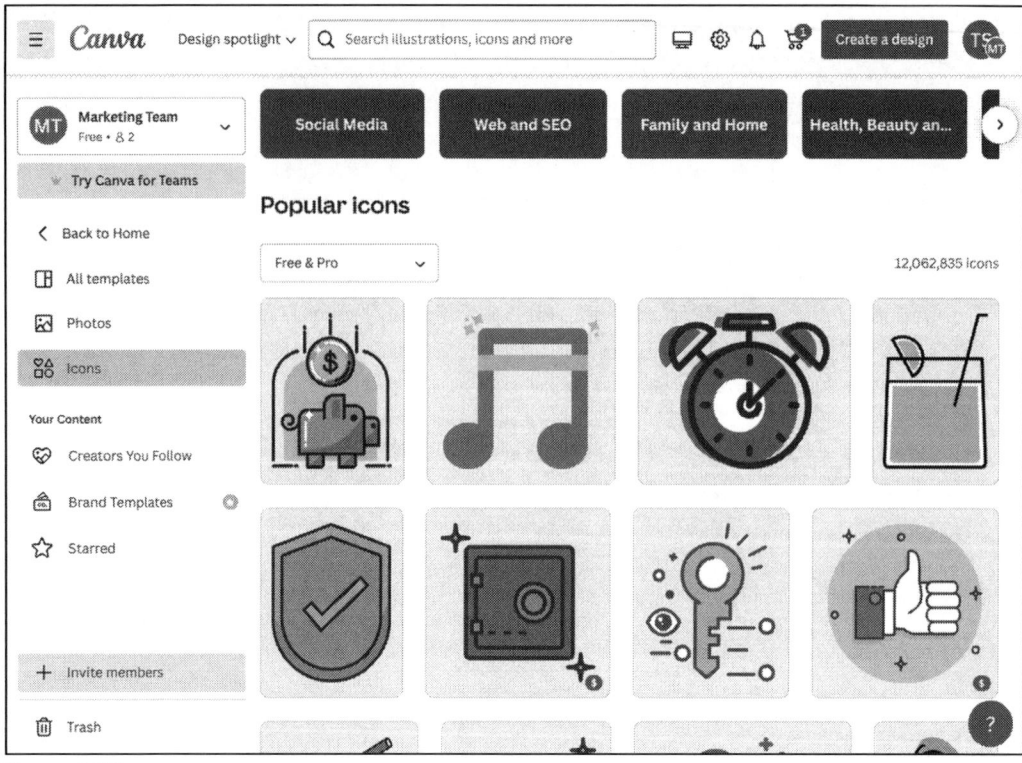

Figure 6.38

If I were to search for the word guitar, I would get almost 18,000 results when I view the Free and Pro versions.

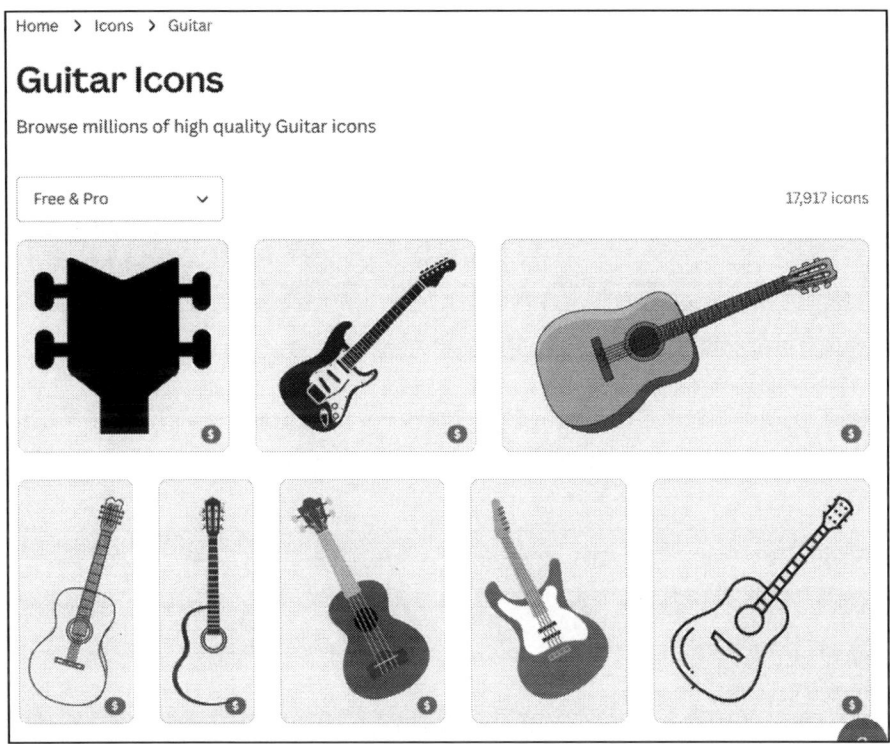

Figure 6.39

If I narrow down the results to only show the Free icons, I only get 85 results but the difference between the results will vary based on what you are searching for.

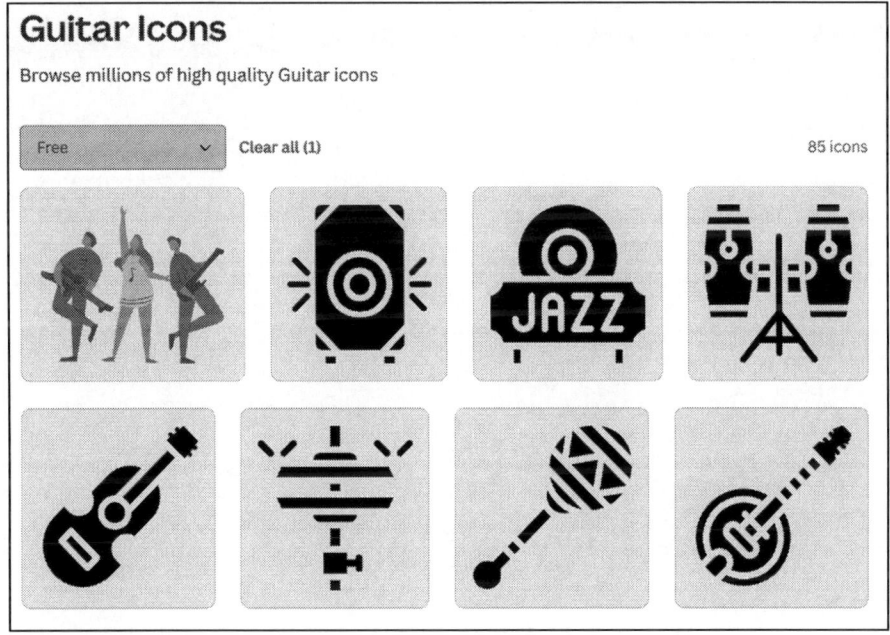

Figure 6.40

Just like with the photos, you can click on an icon you want to use and either star it, copy it to a folder or use it in a project.

Mockups

Having the ability to create mockups of your designs can come in really handy if you plan on selling them or using them for marketing purposes. Canva has a mockup app that makes it easy to see how your designs will look on things such as t-shirts, posters, frames, computer screens and so on.

The easiest way to get to the mockup app is to go to your apps and then do a search for *mockups* and look for the icon shown in figure 6.1.

Figure 6.41

You will then need to decide if you want to add your mockup to an existing design or use it in a new one.

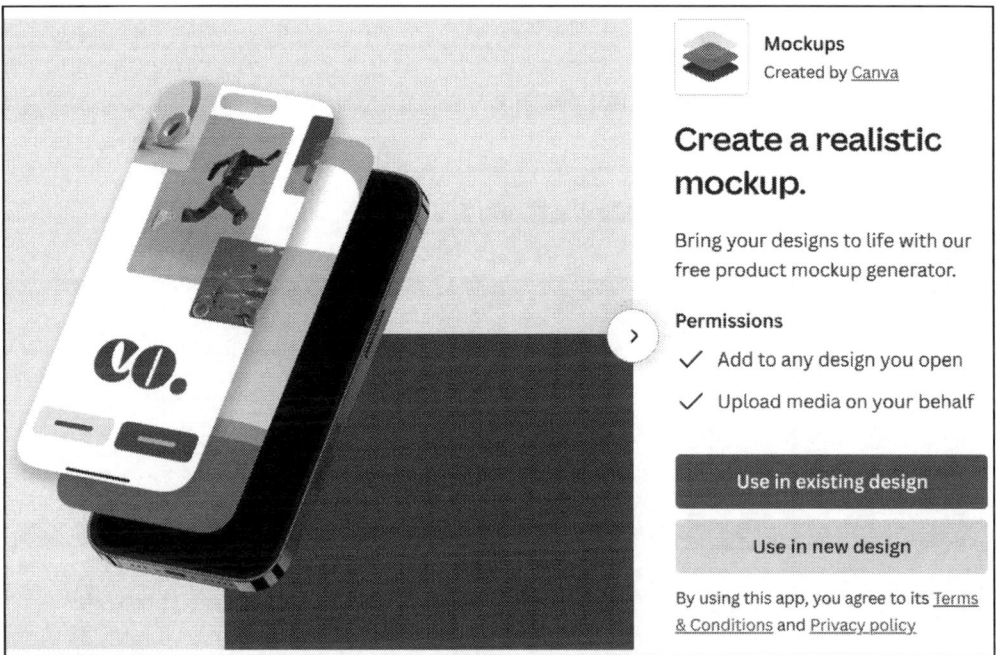

Figure 6.42

You will then be presented with a variety of categories for mockup styles.

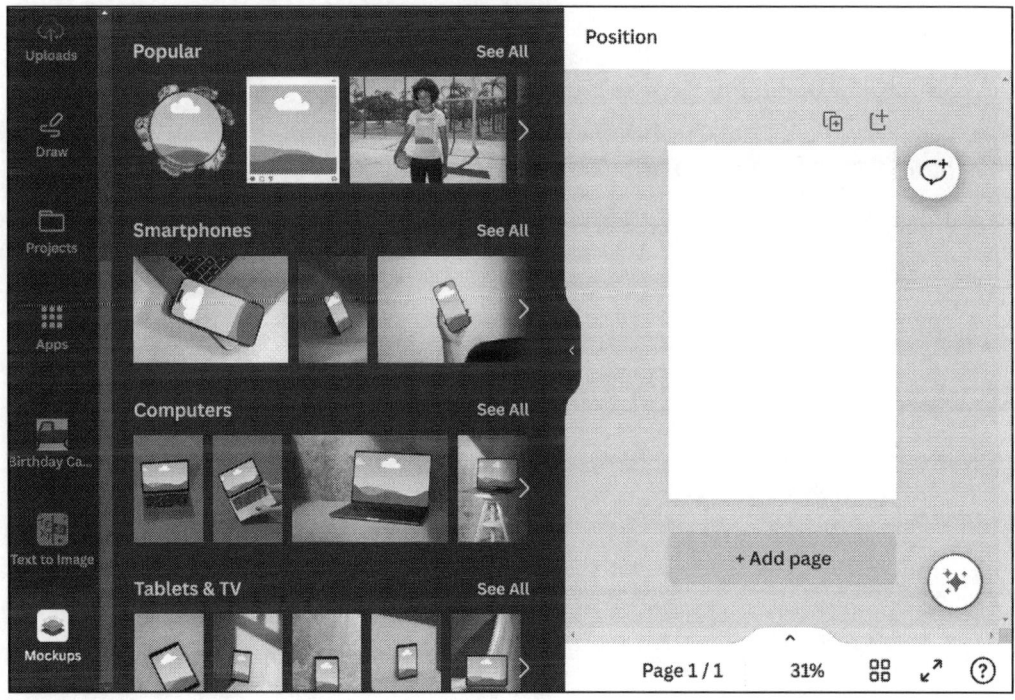

Figure 6.43

Once you choose a mockup, it will be added to your project, and you can then resize it as needed. Then all you need to do is drag an image from your uploads over to the mockup in the project window and Canva will add it and resize it for you.

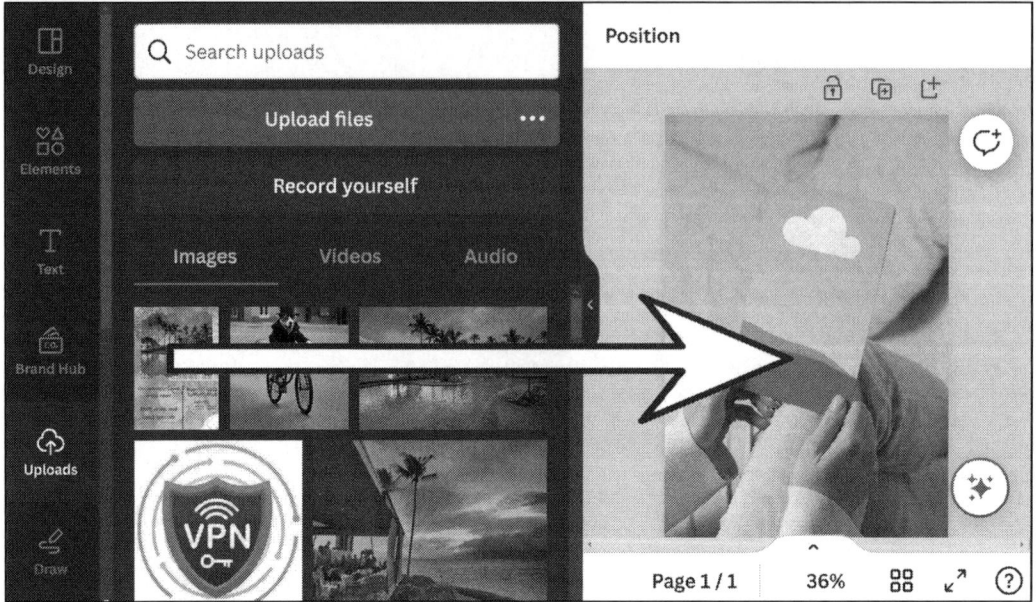

Figure 6.44

You can then download your mockup and use it wherever you need it. If you want to use a previously created project or design in a mockup, you can save it as an image and then add it to the mockup using the same process.

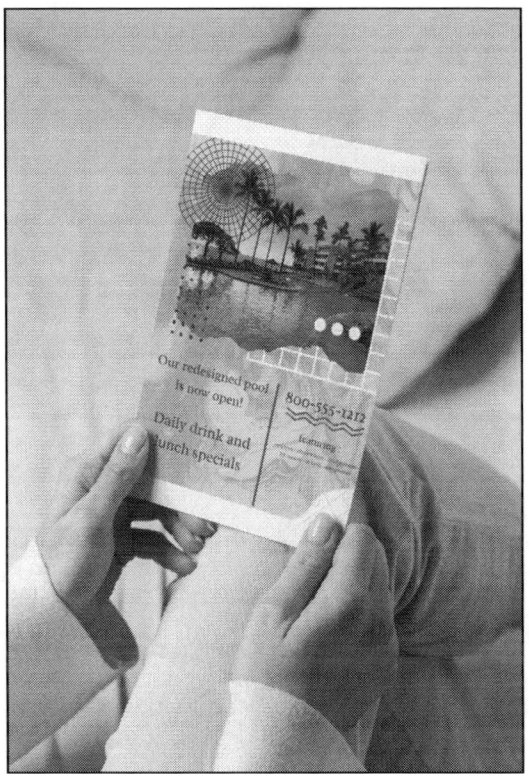

Figure 6.45

Docs

You might not think of Canva when it comes to creating documents but might rather consider using something like Microsoft Word or Google Docs for this kind of task. Canva does have a nice document creator and editor that you can use to create things such as letters, resumes, reports, proposals and so on if you would rather do all your work in one place.

Canva Docs does not have all the advanced features that the big name word processing apps do, but if you want to create basic documents with professional looking graphics, then it just might do the trick.

Once you go to the Docs section in Canva, you will see many different templates just like you do for all the other design types. So if you see something you like, you can simply open that template in a new project or start from a blank document.

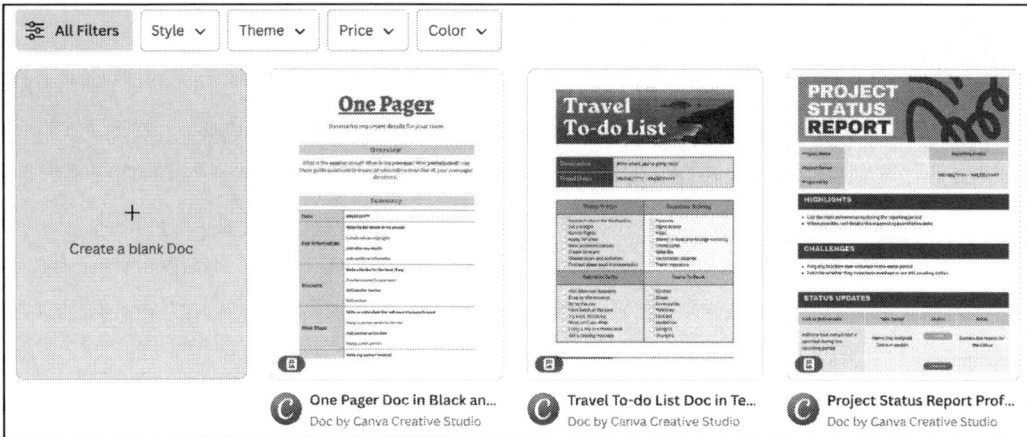

Figure 6.46

If you start from a blank document, you will then be able to add your own text and elements as needed. You will have a basic toolbar at the top of the page with font and paragraph tools.

To add a text or other element to the page, you can click on a blank area, and you will then get a plus (+) sign that you can click on for more options as seen in figure 6.48.

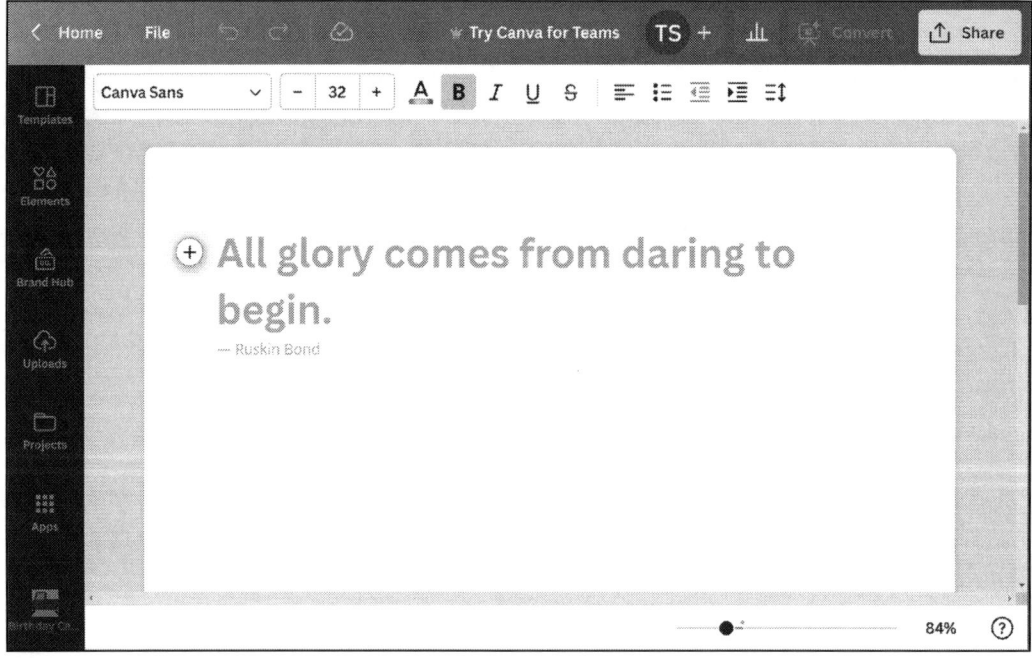

Figure 6.47

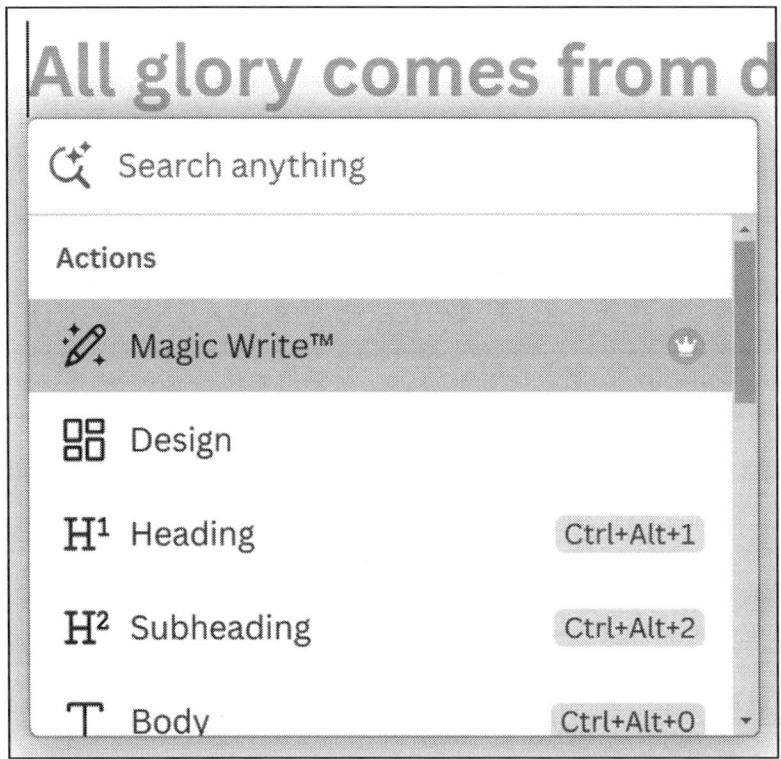

Figure 6.48

For example, if you choose the *Design* option, you will be able to add a custom header graphic to your document or choose a style\theme to have applied to it.

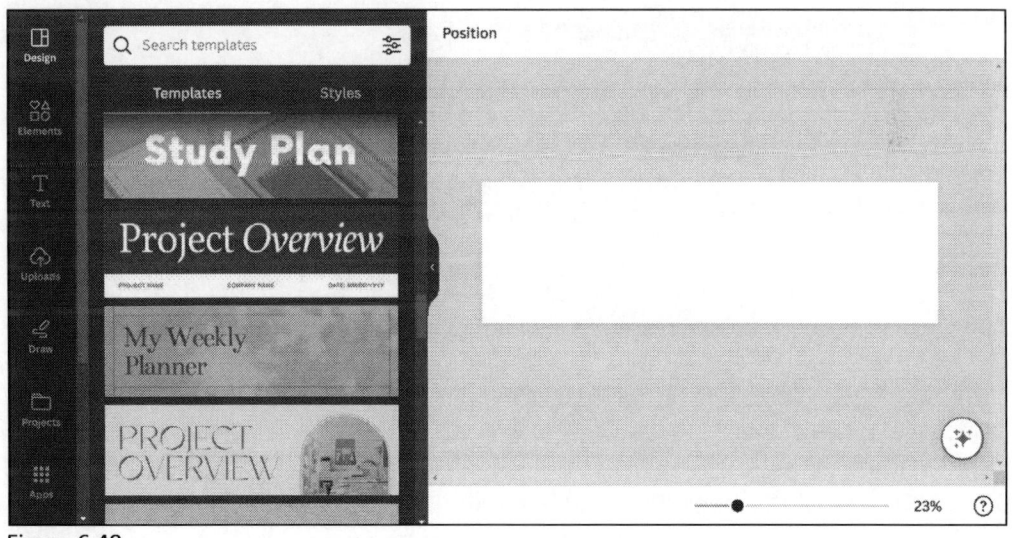

Figure 6.49

I will add a design from the templates and then add some additional elements such as a bulleted list and a chart. For the chart, you can choose from a variety of configurations and then customize it as needed. Figure 6.50 shows the results after taking only a few minutes to create my document.

Figure 6.50

At the top right of the page, you will have an option that says *Convert*. When you use this option, it will convert your document into a presentation with each page of the document as a separate slide.

Figure 6.51

If you want to download your document, you can click the *Share* button and then choose the *Download* option. You will then be able to save your document as a PDF file.

Chapter 7 – Canva Settings and Getting Help

Just like with most other software you have installed on your computer or applications you use online, Canva has a variety of settings you can configure to help the app work the way you want it to. And if you can't get things working the way you want them to, the help section might be the answer to your problems.

Canva Settings

I recommend checking out the Canva settings to ensure that the app is set to work the way you want it to. You might find that everything works great right out of the box but that doesn't mean it can't work even better! To get to the Canva settings, you will need to be on the Home screen and then you will see a gear shaped icon that you can click on to access the settings.

Figure 7.1

The Canva settings are broken down into several categories as seen in figure 7.2. I will now go over what I feel are the more important settings in each category. You may have additional settings if you are using the Teams feature.

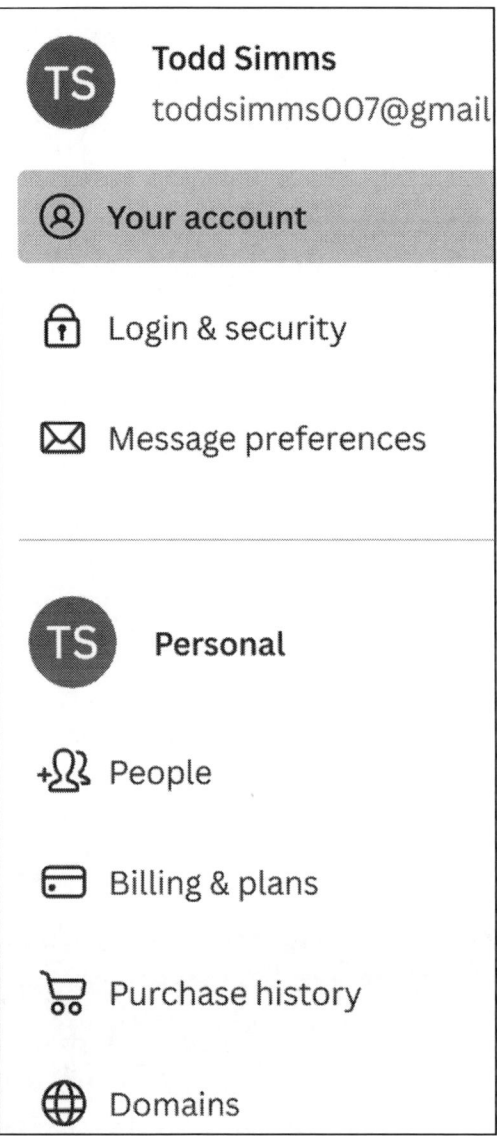

Figure 7.2

Your Account

Here is where you will come to make changes related to your Canva account and you will also find general settings as to how the Canva app itself functions and looks.

If you plan on collaborating or sharing your work with others, you might want to add a profile picture so people will be able to put a face to the design. When you don't have a profile picture associated with your account, Canva will simply use your initials instead as seen in Figure 7.3.

Figure 7.3

Once you do add a profile picture, it will appear in shared projects and when others are working on a project at the same time you are, they will be able to see your profile picture.

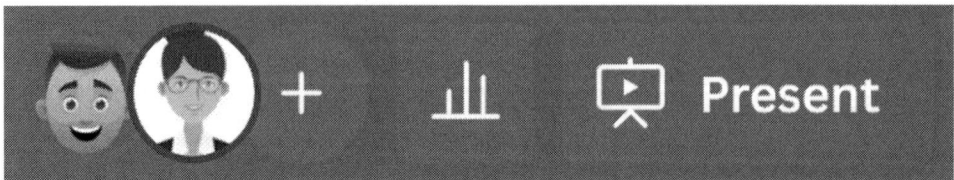

Figure 7.4

Another setting you should know about is the connected apps section. Here you will find which apps you have connected to your Canva account. For example, I have connected a Facebook account for direct posting and also a Google Drive account to import files into Canva. If you want to remove any linked accounts, you can do so by clicking on the Disconnect button.

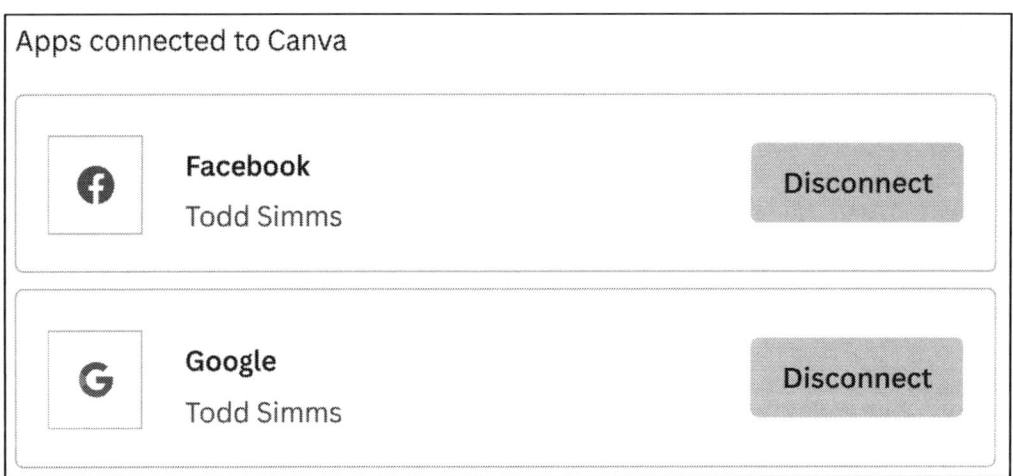

Figure 7.5

The account settings section also has some options that control the color theme of Canva itself as well as other settings that can be used to make Canva more user friendly for those with vision impairments.

Login and Security
There aren't too many settings here but if you need to do things such as change your password, this is where you can do so. And if you have decided you do not want to use Canva ever again, you can delete your account from here as well.

If you have your Canva account logged in on other devices and you want to disconnect those devices, you can click the *Sign out from all devices* button. Just be aware that you might lose some unsaved work when doing so.

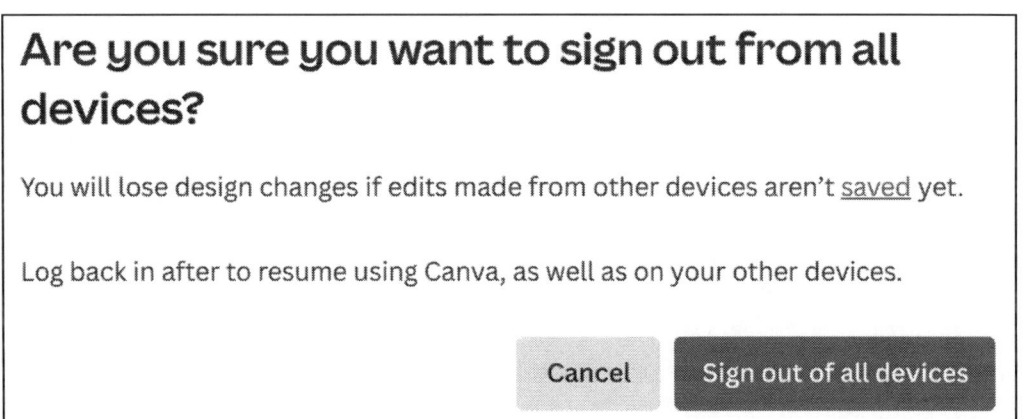

Figure 7.6

If you are using Canva Teams for collaboration purposes, you can request a copy of all your uploads and designs in case you leave the team or are removed from the team. The process can take between a couple of hours and a few days depending on how many uploads and designs you have saved.

Message Preferences
You may have noticed that you get random emails from Canva notifying you about things such as new features or challenges that you could take part in if you wanted to.

If you would rather not get these types of emails, then you can come to this section to disable or opt-out of some or all of the special event type emails that Canva sends out.

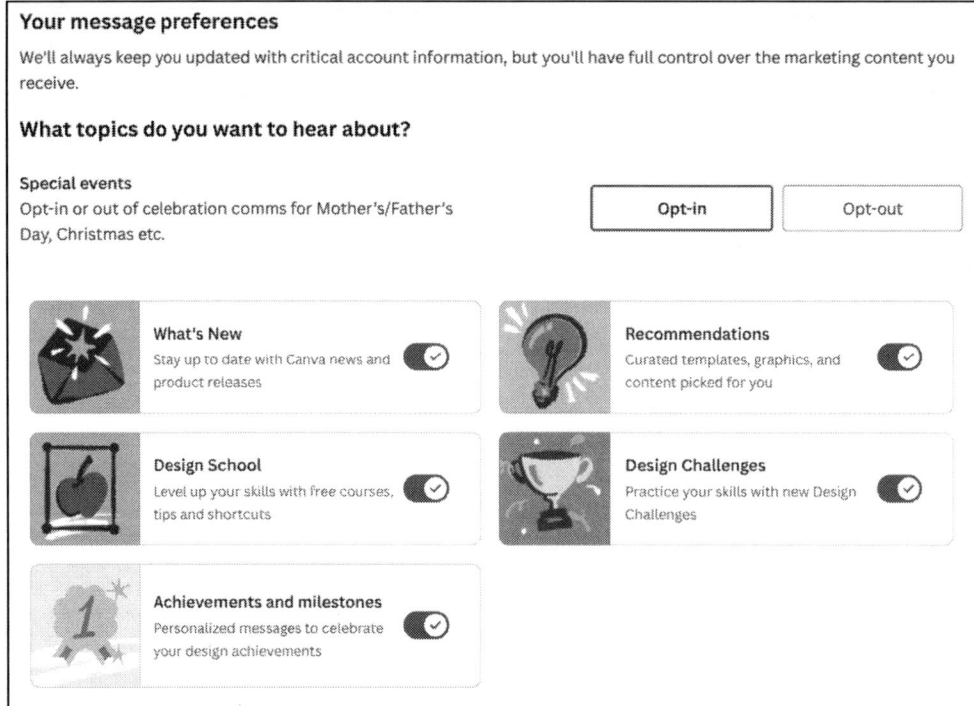

Figure 7.7

You can also change the frequency of these messages and decide if you would rather receive emails, notifications or both. You might also want to disable the data collection setting under privacy.

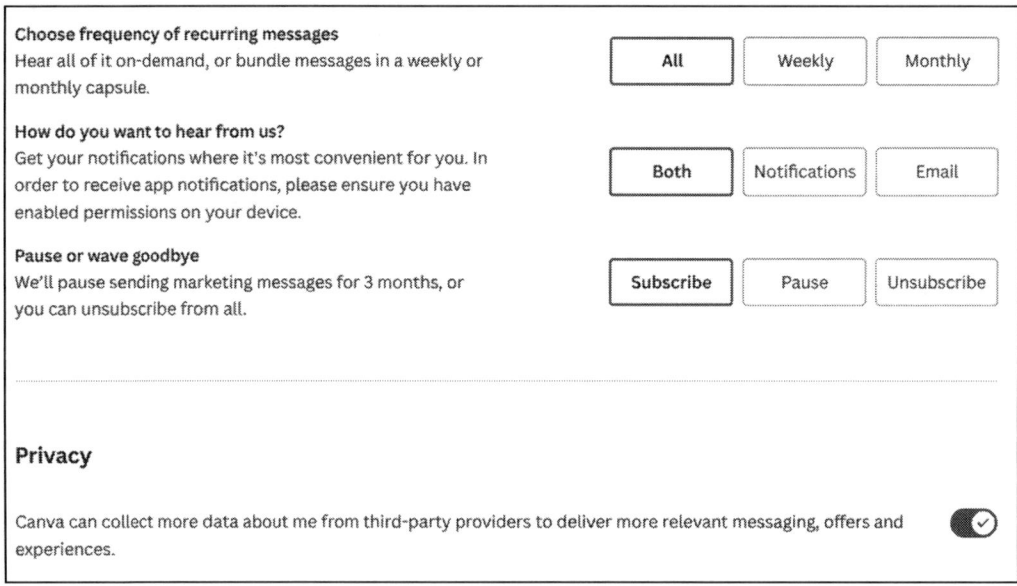

Figure 7.8

People

The People section is where you can come to see who you have invited to collaborate with, and you can even invite people from here by clicking on the Invite button. Then you just need to type in their email address, and they will be invited to your team, and you can then view and work on projects that are shared with this team. You can also come here to change permission levels for your team members or remove them if needed.

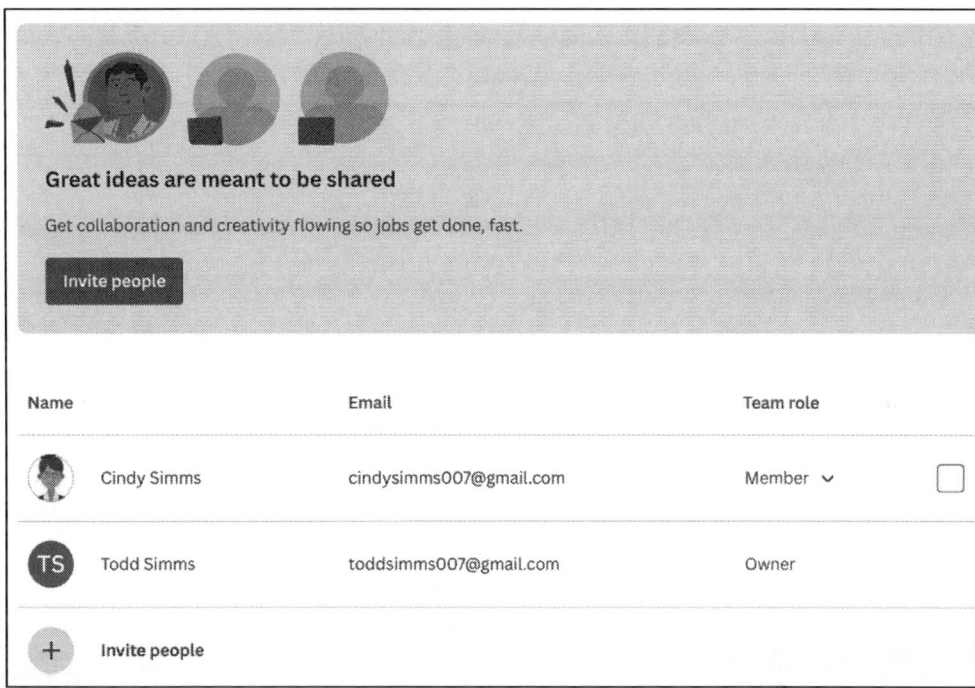

Figure 7.9

I am not a fan of the free Teams feature that Canva offers because it's too easy to get your designs mixed up between your team and your personal account. You may also find that your designs get placed into your team and then if you delete a team, it removes your designs as well!

Groups (Optional)

If you do decide to use Canva Teams, you can then create groups within your teams to help keep things more organized and also assign projects to groups rather than multiple individual team members.

Billing and Plans

As you probably know, there are different versions of Canva that you can use such as the free version as well as the professional version and Canva for Teams. If you decide that you want to upgrade your account, you can come to the Billing and Plans section to do so.

Canva gives you the opportunity to buy premium features such as a photo or other element if you want to make a one time purchase and stay on the free plan. If you add a payment method here, you will be able to buy premium features as needed. Just make sure you don't spend more than it costs to have the Pro account where you get all the features!

If you are a tax-exempt organization, you can come here to enter your tax ID to avoid paying taxes on your subscription.

Permissions (Optional)
You might recall when sharing projects or designs with other people that you can assign various permissions such as edit, comment and view.

If you would like to change the default permissions for members of your team regarding inviting new members, allowing people to leave the team and copying team content between teams, you can do so from here.

Permissions

Team access

Who can invite new members?

All members ⌄

Who can leave this team?

Everyone ⌄

Design management

Who can copy content from Marketing Team into another team?

Everyone ⌄

Figure 7.10

Purchase History

Here you can find any purchases such as artwork or print jobs that you have made. It will show you the description, status, total amount and so on. You can also filter by invoice ID, purchase type and date.

Domains

If you use Canva to create a website and use a domain that you already own, you can find that information here. When I say domain, I mean something like MyDesigns.com or CustomShop.com for example.

Insights

If you plan on sharing your projects with others or maybe even posting a link to a project on your website, you might want to check out the Insights feature to see what kind of traffic or hits your work is getting. To access the insights for your project, you can click on the Insights button while that project is open.

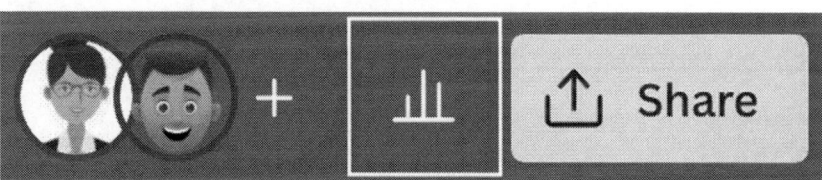

Figure 7.11

If you are using the free Canva account, you will only see basic information such as total views and current viewers as seen in Figure 7.12.

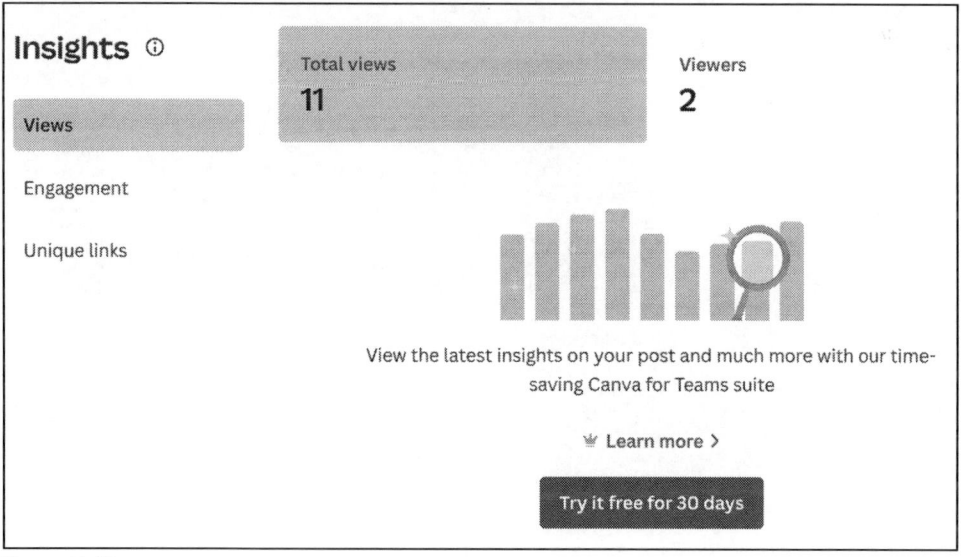

Figure 7.12

Figures 7.13 and 7.14 show the same section using the Pro account. The categories on the left will vary based on the type of project you have open.

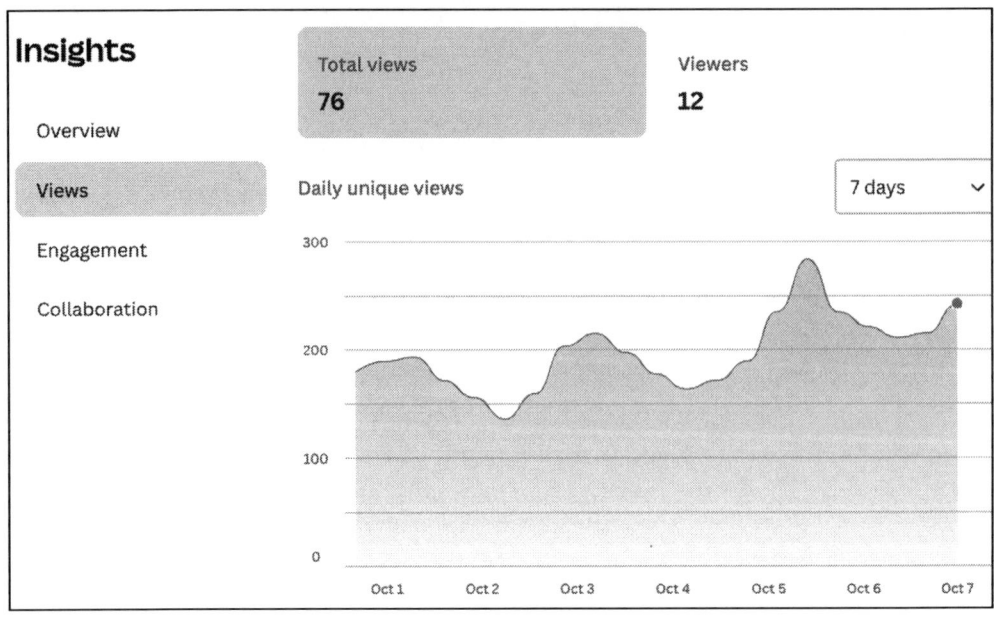

Figure 7.13

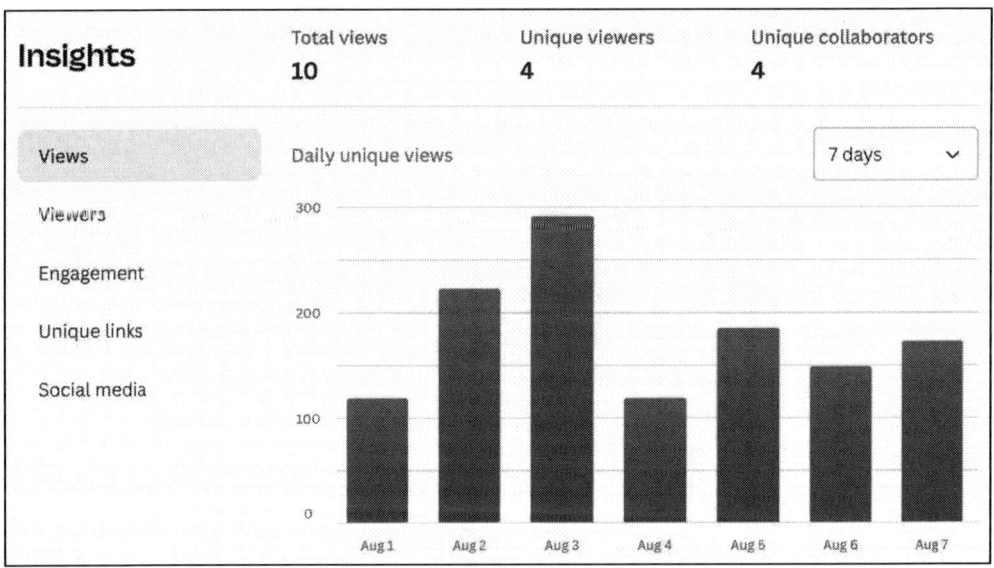

Figure 7.14

Education Resources

If you are a teacher or student, Canva offers some helpful resources and even free accounts to those who qualify. The *Canva for Education* program offers things such as teaching related templates and other elements as well as the ability to integrate your Canva account into online classroom apps such as Canvas and Google Classroom.

Here are the requirements for Canva for Education taken from the Canva website.

To access Canva for Education, you must be currently active in one of the following roles:

- A certified K-12 (primary or secondary) teacher from a formally accredited school, who is currently in a teaching position.
- A certified K-12 (primary or secondary) school librarian.
- A certified K-12 (primary or secondary) learning support assistant or teacher.
- A certified K-12 (primary or secondary) curriculum specialist.
- A certified teacher at a technical or vocational school, serving primary and/or secondary students (or any equivalent).
- Google Certified Educators (GCEs), Google Certified Trainers (GCTs), and Microsoft Innovative Educators (MIEs) who are teaching at a K-12 (primary or secondary) level.

The following government recognized, and formally accredited organizations can also access Canva for Education:

- K-12 (primary, secondary, or pre-college) schools.
- School districts.
- Departments of education.
- Other global school systems.

If you click on the Education dropdown at the top of the Canva website, you will be able to find out more about the various teacher and student options that are available.

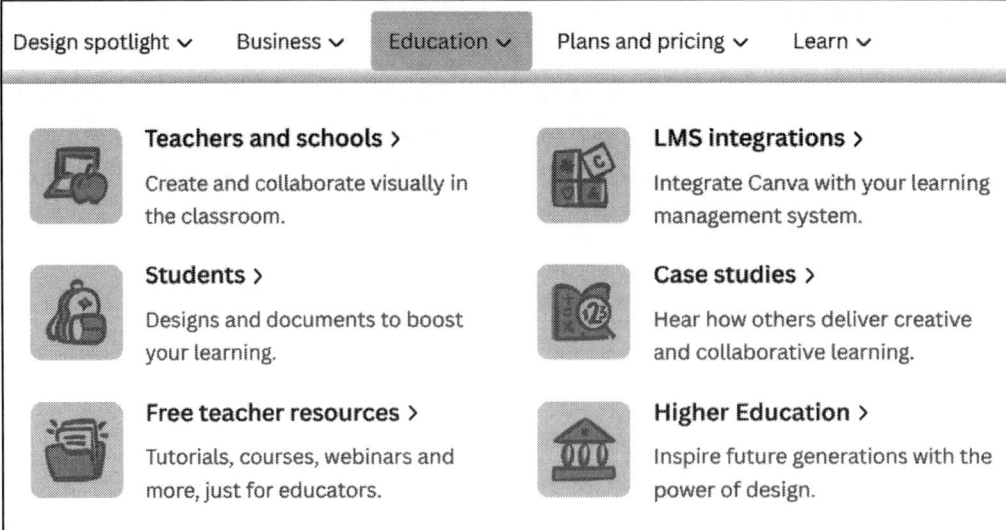

Figure 7.15

Help and Training

While working in Canva, you will most likely come across a situation where you need some help figuring out how to do something or where to find a certain tool etc.

Fortunately, Canva has a detailed help and training system that you can use to find the answers to your questions and even learn something new at the same time. To use the Canva help feature, click on the question mark at the lower right corner of the page to begin the process.

Figure 7.16

Canva will then recommend some help topics for you that may or may not be helpful to you. You can click the *See more* link to get additional recommended topics.

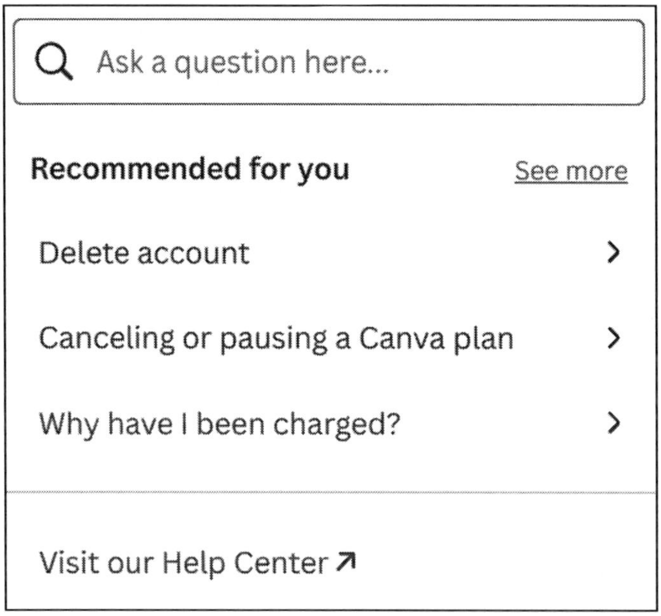

Q   Ask a question here...

Recommended for you   See more

Delete account   >

Canceling or pausing a Canva plan   >

Why have I been charged?   >

Visit our Help Center ↗

Figure 7.17

You will most likely want to type your question into the search box to narrow things down. You will then be shown some suggested topics based on your search query.

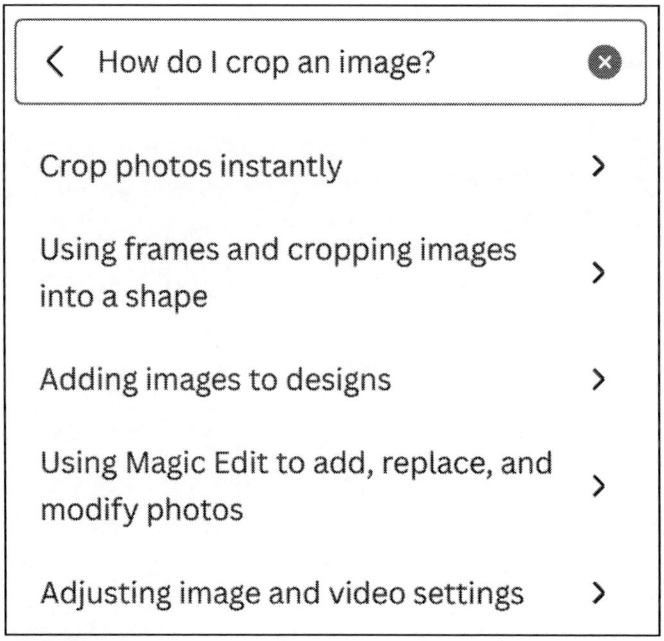

<   How do I crop an image?   ⊗

Crop photos instantly   >

Using frames and cropping images
into a shape   >

Adding images to designs   >

Using Magic Edit to add, replace, and
modify photos   >

Adjusting image and video settings   >

Figure 7.18

When you click on one of the results, you will be shown the answer in the same help section (Figure 7.19). At the bottom of the answer section, you may be shown a link for a related topic that might help you out further.

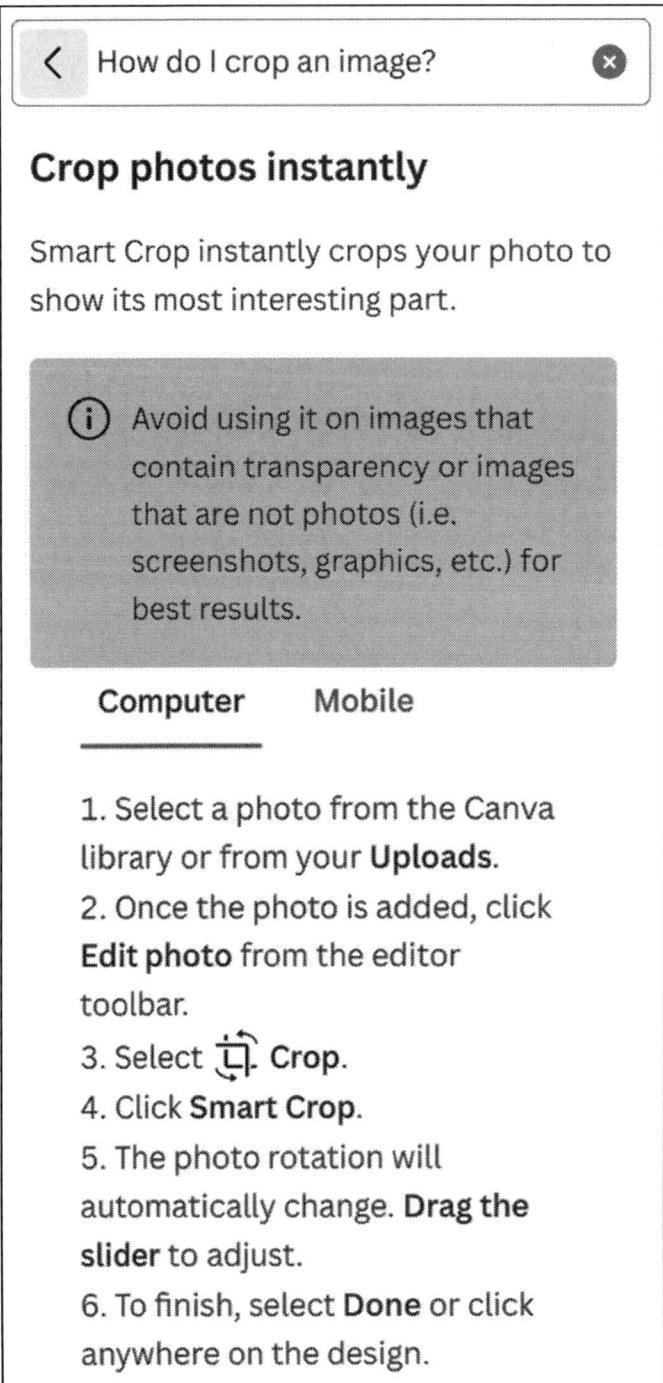

Figure 7.19

If you were to click on *Visit our Help Center* at the bottom of the search box, you will be taken to the main Canva help website where you can browse various articles or type in a new search to see additional results (Figure 7.21).

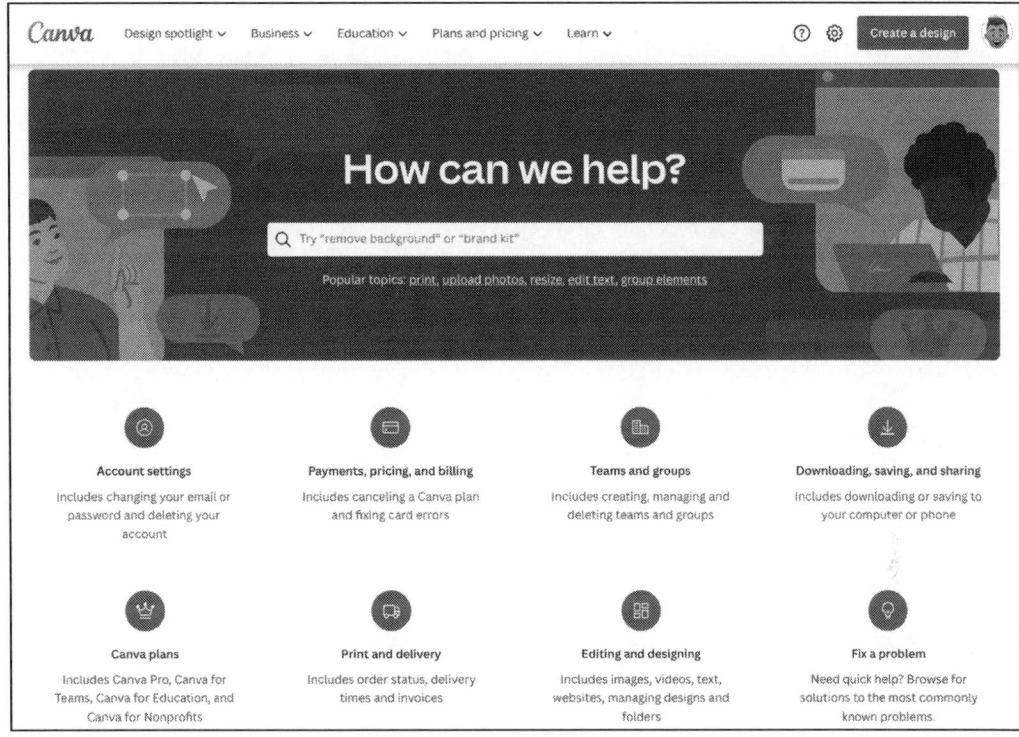

Figure 7.20

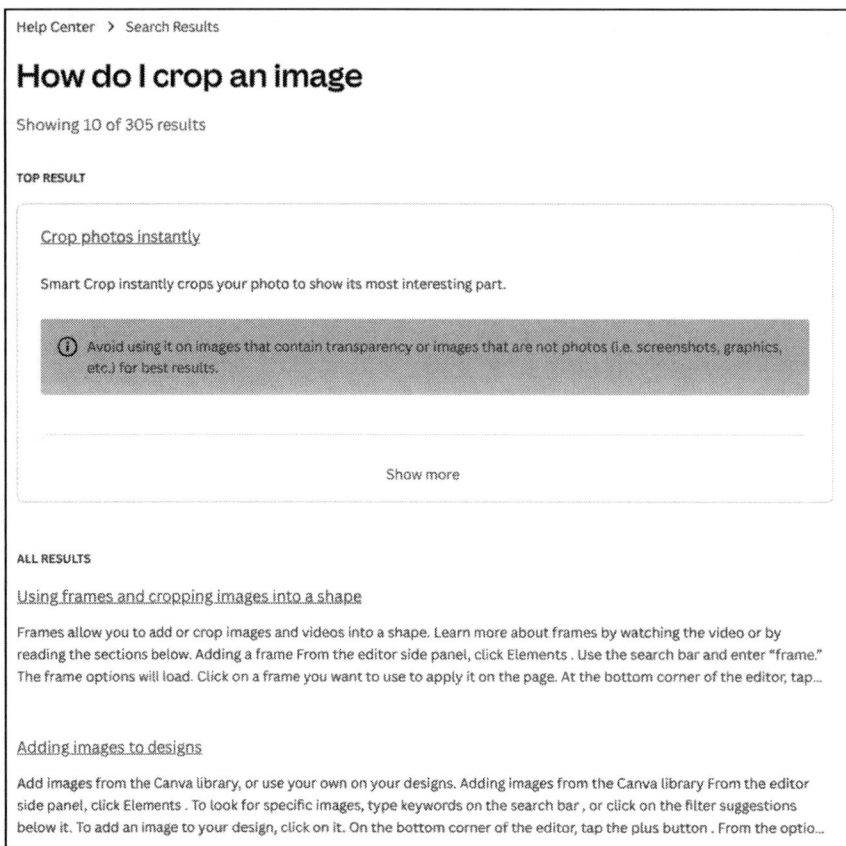

Figure 7.21

If you are looking for additional training resources, you can click the *Learn* dropdown menu item and choose from one of the training resources that are offered (Figure 7.22).

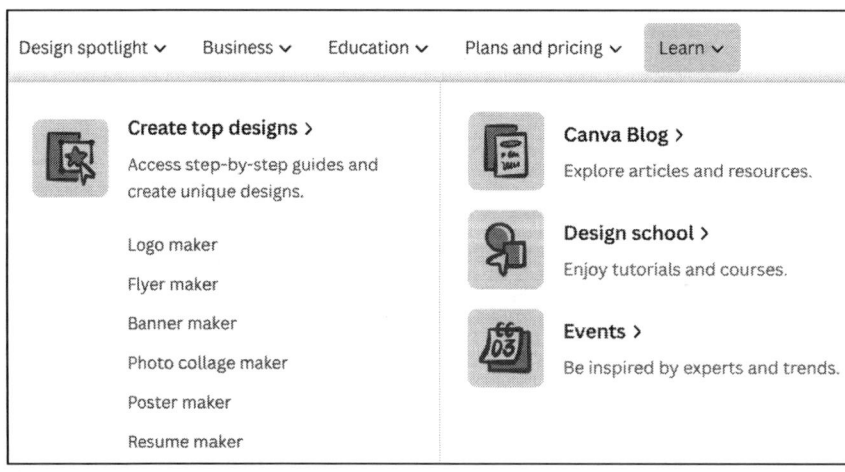

Figure 7.22

The *Design School* has a variety of courses that you can take to improve your Canva skills if you are motivated enough to take the time to go through them.

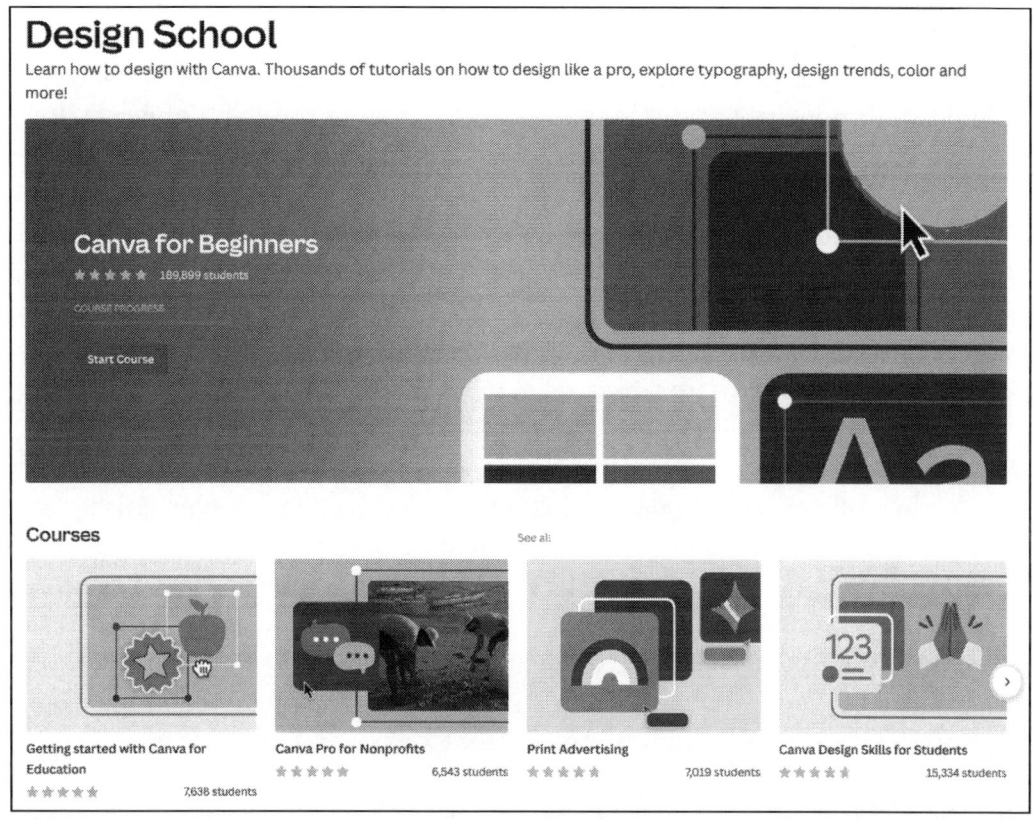

Figure 7.23

You can also click on one of the guides to help you create a specific design.

What's Next?

Now that you have read through this book and learned how Canva works and what you can do with the application, you might be wondering what you should do next. Well, that depends on where you want to go. Are you happy with what you have learned, or do you want to further your knowledge of the available Canva features and become a Canva expert?

If you do want to expand your knowledge and computers in general, then you can look for some more advanced books on basic computers or focus on a specific technology such as Windows, Google Apps, or Photoshop, if that's the path you choose to follow. Focus on mastering the basics, and then apply what you have learned when going to more advanced material.

There are many great video resources as well, such as Pluralsight or CBT Nuggets, which offer online subscriptions to training videos of every type imaginable. YouTube is also a great source for instructional videos if you know what to search for.

If you are content with being a proficient Canva user that knows more than your coworkers and friends, then just keep on practicing what you have learned. Don't be afraid to poke around with some of the settings and tools that you normally don't use and see if you can figure out what they do without having to research it since learning by doing is the most effective method to gain new skills.

Thanks for reading **Canva Made Easy**. You can also check out the other books in the Made Easy series for additional computer related information and training. You can get more information on my other books on my Computers Made Easy Book Series website.

https://www.madeeasybookseries.com/

What's Next?

COMPUTERS MADE EASY — JAMES BERNSTEIN
WINDOWS 10 MADE EASY — JAMES BERNSTEIN
NETWORKING MADE EASY — JAMES BERNSTEIN
CLOUD STORAGE MADE EASY — JAMES BERNSTEIN
GOOGLE APPS MADE EASY — JAMES BERNSTEIN

OFFICE MADE EASY — JAMES BERNSTEIN
ANDROID SMARTPHONES MADE EASY — JAMES BERNSTEIN
THE INTERNET MADE EASY — JAMES BERNSTEIN
WINDOWS HOME NETWORKING MADE EASY — JAMES BERNSTEIN
BUILDING YOUR OWN COMPUTER MADE EASY — JAMES BERNSTEIN

PHOTOSHOP ELEMENTS MADE EASY — JAMES BERNSTEIN
POWERPOINT MADE EASY — JAMES BERNSTEIN
PUBLISHER MADE EASY — JAMES BERNSTEIN
PREMIERE ELEMENTS MADE EASY — JAMES BERNSTEIN
VIRTUALBOX MADE EASY — JAMES BERNSTEIN

ZOOM MADE EASY — JAMES BERNSTEIN
GOOGLE MEET MADE EASY — JAMES BERNSTEIN
SLACK MADE EASY — JAMES BERNSTEIN
GOOGLE CLASSROOM MADE EASY — JAMES BERNSTEIN
GOOGLE DOCS MADE EASY — JAMES BERNSTEIN

GOOGLE SITES MADE EASY — JAMES BERNSTEIN
MICROSOFT OFFICE FOR THE WEB MADE EASY — JAMES BERNSTEIN
WIX MADE EASY — JAMES BERNSTEIN
WINDOWS VIDEO EDITOR MADE EASY — JAMES BERNSTEIN
COMPUTERS FOR SENIORS MADE EASY — JAMES BERNSTEIN

GMAIL MADE EASY — JAMES BERNSTEIN
WINDOWS FILE MANAGEMENT MADE EASY — JAMES BERNSTEIN
WINDOWS 11 MADE EASY — JAMES BERNSTEIN
SOCIAL MEDIA FOR SENIORS MADE EASY — JAMES BERNSTEIN
EMAIL FOR SENIORS MADE EASY — JAMES BERNSTEIN

DROPBOX MADE EASY — JAMES BERNSTEIN
WINDOWS 11 FOR SENIORS MADE EASY — JAMES BERNSTEIN
ONENOTE MADE EASY — JAMES BERNSTEIN
ANDROID SMARTPHONES FOR SENIORS MADE EASY — JAMES BERNSTEIN
WINDOWS MAIL AND CALENDAR MADE EASY — JAMES BERNSTEIN

GOOGLE DRIVE MADE EASY — JAMES BERNSTEIN
THE INTERNET FOR SENIORS MADE EASY — JAMES BERNSTEIN
GOOGLE PHOTOS MADE EASY — JAMES BERNSTEIN
VMWARE WORKSTATION MADE EASY — JAMES BERNSTEIN
CLIPCHAMP VIDEO EDITOR MADE EASY — JAMES BERNSTEIN

MICROSOFT SWAY MADE EASY — JAMES BERNSTEIN
BOX MADE EASY — JAMES BERNSTEIN
MICROSOFT WORD FOR SENIORS MADE EASY — JAMES BERNSTEIN
GOOGLE FORMS MADE EASY — JAMES BERNSTEIN
CANVA MADE EASY — JAMES BERNSTEIN

What's Next?

You should also check out my computer tips website, as well as follow it on Facebook to find more information on all kinds of computer topics.

www.onlinecomputertips.com
https://www.facebook.com/OnlineComputerTips/

About the Author

James Bernstein has been working with various companies in the IT field for over 20 years, managing technologies such as SAN and NAS storage, VMware, backups, Windows Servers, Active Directory, DNS, DHCP, Networking, Microsoft Office, Photoshop, Premiere, Exchange, and more.

He has obtained certifications from Microsoft, VMware, CompTIA, ShoreTel, and SNIA, and continues to strive to learn new technologies to further his knowledge on a variety of subjects.

He is also the founder of the website onlinecomputertips.com, which offers its readers valuable information on topics such as Windows, networking, hardware, software, and troubleshooting. James writes much of the content himself and adds new content on a regular basis. The site was started over 15 years ago and is still going strong today.

Printed in Poland
by Amazon Fulfillment
Poland Sp. z o.o., Wrocław
25 October 2023

b66cdb77-a3b1-4efc-83ac-1dcd9a19c4b8R01